CONTENTS

Foreword 2

Title Page 3

Background to the Life of the Commander of the Faithful 5

Vitrues, Qualities and Achievements of the Commander of the Faithful 29

The Military Exploits of the Commander of the Faithful 64

The Role of the Commander of the Faithful in the Last Year of the Prophet's Life 166

Legal Decisions of the Commander of the Faithful 197

Memorable Words and Speeches of the Commander of the Faithful 236

Some of the Miracles of the Commander of the Faithful 317

The Children of the Commander of the Faithful 371

FOREWORD

Historical figures and events create a mystical perception and imagination in the mind of the reader. The absence of the past fascinates the thinker on how things were done back then.

This book takes an in-depth look into the life of Imam Ali, peace be upon him, the first divinely appointed leader of the Muslim nation after the death of the Prophet Muhammad, peace be upon him.

The content in this book have been compiled by the author from the public domain and do not in any way represent his opinion. Please refer to the book "KITÃB AL-IRSHÃD" by Shaykh al-Mufīd, translated by I. K. A. Howard B.a., M.a., PH.D.

- SARFARAZ KARMALI

IMAM ALI

An Extensive Biography

Sarfaraz Karmali

BACKGROUND TO THE LIFE OF THE COMMANDER OF THE FAITHFUL

Introduction

(This part gives) an account of the Commander of the Faithful, peace be on him, the first of the Imams of the believers, of the rulers (wulāt) of the Muslims and of Allāh's (appointed) successors in religion after the Apostle of Allāh, the truthful one and the trusted one, Muhammad b. 'Abd Allāh, the seal of the Prophets, blessings be on Him and His Pure Family. (He was) the brother of the Apostle of Allāh and his paternal cousin, and his helper (wazīr) in his affair, his son-in-law (being married) to his daughter, Fāṭima the chaste, mistress of the women of the universe. (The full name of) the Commander of the Faithful is 'Alī b. Abī Ṭālib b. 'Abd al-Muṭṭalib b. Hāshim b. 'Abd Manāf. (He was) the Lord of the testamentary trustees of authority (waṣiyyīn), the best of blessing and peace be on him. His kunya was Abū al-Ḥasan.

He was born in the Sacred House (i.e. the Ka'ba) in Mecca on Friday, the thirteenth day of the month of Rajab, thirty years after the Year of the Elephant (c.570). Nobody before or after him has ever been born in the House of Allāh, the Most High. (It was a mark) of him being honoured by Allāh, the Most High, may His name be exalted, and of his position being dignified in its greatness.

His mother was Fāṭima, daughter of Asad b. Hāshim b. 'Abd Manāf, may Allāh be pleased with her. She was like a mother to the Apostle of Allāh, may Allāh bless Him and His Family, and he (the Apostle) was brought up under her care.

He was grateful for her kindness and she was among the first to believe in him and she emigrated with him in the group of the emigrants. When she died, the Prophet shrouded her with his own shirt in order to protect her from the insects of the earth, and he laid her to rest in her grave in order that, through that, she might be protected from (the crushing pressure of) the narrow space within the grave. He dictated to her her last words (which were) the statement of the authority (wilāya) of her son, the Commander of the Faithful, peace be on him, so that at the examination after burial, she would be able to reply with those words. He singled her out with this great favour because of her position with Allāh, may He be magnified and exalted, and with him, peace be on him. The report of that is well known.

The Commander of the Faithful, 'Alī b. Abī Ṭālib, peace be on him, and his brothers were among the leading members of the second generation of descendants of Hāshim. In this way he gained two marks of nobility, through his growing up under the care and education of the Apostle of Allāh, may Allāh bless Him and His Family. He was the first of the family of the House and of the Companions to believe in Allāh and His Apostle. He was the first male whom the Prophet, may Allāh bless Him and His Family, summoned to Islam and who answered. He never ceased to support the religion and to strive against the polytheists. He constantly defended the faith and fought against those who supported deviation (from the truth) and despotism. He spread the teachings of the sunna (the practice of the Prophet) and the Qur'ān, judged with justice and enjoined (people) to do good.

He was with the Apostle of Allāh, may Allāh bless Him and His Family, twenty-three years after the (coming) of the (prophetic) mission. Of these, thirteen years were in Mecca before the emigration when he shared with him all the persecutions and bore most of his hardships. Then there were ten years in Medina after the emigration when he defended him against the polytheists and strove with him against the unbelievers. He protected him with his own life from the enemies of religion until the time Allāh, the Exalted, took (the Prophet) to His heaven, raised him to the highest place in heaven and bestowed His blessings and peace on Him and His Family. On that day the Commander of the Faithful, peace be on him, was thirty-three years of age.

On the day of the death of the Prophet, may Allāh bless Him and His Pure Family, the community differed over his Imamate. His Shī'a who were all the Banū Hāshim, Salmān, 'Ammār, Abū Dharr, al-Miqdād, Khuzayma b. Thābit - the man who is known as the possessor of two testimonies - Abū Ayyūb al-Anṣārī, Jabīr b. 'Abd Allāh al- Anṣārī, Abū Sa'īd al-Khudrī and people like them among the important emigrants and Anṣār, (all these) maintained that he was the successor (khalīfa) after the Apostle of Allāh, may Allāh bless Him and His Family, and the Imam. (They did this) because of his outstanding merit (faḍl) above all mankind, through the fact that there were gathered in him the qualities of outstanding merit, judgement and perfection, such as him being the first of the community to enter the faith, his superiority over them in knowledge of the laws, his precedence over them in fighting (jihād) and the distinction which set him apart from them in the extent of his piety, asceticism and righteousness.

Furthermore he had been specially singled out by the Prophet from among (all) his relations because of (the qualities) which no other relation, apart from him, shared with the Prophet and because of the nomination (naṣṣ) of his authority (wilāya) by Allāh, may Allāh be magnified and exalted, in the Qur'ān where He, may His name be exalted, says: Your authority (walī) is Allāh and His Apostle and those believers who perform the prayer and pay alms (zakāt) while they are bowing (in prayer). (V 55) It is known that no one except him paid alms while bowing (in prayer).

It has been established in language that walī means "the most appropriate for authority" (awlā), without there being any opposition (to this definition). If the Commander of the Faithful, peace be on him, was, by the stipulation of the Qur'ān, more appropriate for authority among the people than themselves because of his being their walī according to the textual nomination (naṣṣ) in the Clear Explanation (i.e. the Qur'ān, tibyān), it was obviously necessary for all of them to obey him, just as obedience to Allāh, the Most High, and obedience to His Apostle, peace be on Him and His Family, was required because of the information about their authority (wilāya) over creatures which is given in this verse with clear proof.

(Another reason for their support for the Commander of the Faithful was) because of what the Prophet, may Allāh bless Him and His Family, said on the day (of the assembly) at his house. He had especially gathered the Banū 'Abd al-Muṭṭalib there in order to make the (following) solemn pledge: "Whoever helps me in this matter will be my brother, my testamentary trustee (waṣī), my helper (wazīr), my heir and my successor after me." Then the Commander of the Faithful, peace be on him, stood up before him among all the gathering of them, and on that day he was the youngest of them, and he said: "O Apostle of Allāh, I will help you."

Then the Prophet, may Allāh bless Him and His Family, said: "Sit down, you are my brother, my trustee, my helper, my inheritor and successor after me."

This is a clear statement about the succession (after the Prophet).

In addition, there is also what (the Prophet), peace be on Him and His Family, said on the day of Ghadīr Khumm. The community had gathered to listen to the sermon (in which he asked): "Am I not more appropriate for authority (awlā) over you than yourselves?"

"Yes," they answered.

Then he spoke to them in an ordered manner without any interruption in his speech: "Whomsoever I am the authority over (mawlā), 'Alī is also the authority over."

Thus he (the Prophet) required for him ('Alī), through laying down obedience to him and his authority (over them), the same authority as he had over them, and which he made them acknowledge and which they did not deny. This is clear (evidence) of the nomination (naṣṣ) of him for the Imamate and for succession to his position.

Furthermore there is (the Prophet's), peace be on Him and His Family, statement to him at the time of setting out to Tabūk: "You are in the same position with respect to me as Aaron (Hārūn) was to Moses (Mūsā) except that there is no prophet after me." Thus he required him (to have) the office of helping (i.e. administering) and to be characterised by love and outstanding merit over everyone. (He also required) his deputising for him both during his life and after his death. The

Qur'ān gives evidence for all that coming to Aaron (Hārūn) from Moses (Mūsā), peace be on them, when Allāh, may He be magnified and exalted, said in giving a report of what Moses, peace be on him, said: "Make Aaron, my brother, a helper for me from my family. Give me support through him and make him participate in my affair so that we may glorify You much and we may remember You frequently in that You have been a watcher over us." (XX 29-35). Allāh, the Most Exalted said: "Your request is granted, Moses." (XX 36). This (verse) confirmed that Aaron had a share with Moses in prophecy, and in helping in delivering the message and his support was strengthened through him by his aid. (Moses) also told him of deputising for him (when he said): "....Deputise for me among my people. Act for (their) benefit and do not follow the path of the corrupters." (VII 142) This confirms his succession by the precise statement of revelation. Therefore when the Apostle of Allāh, may Allāh bless Him and His Family, gave all the ranks which Aaron had from Moses to the Commander of the Faithful, peace be on him, in the same extent, except for prophecy, (all such things) were required of him as helping the Apostle, giving him support, outstanding merit and love, because these qualities were definitely required by that. Then by the clear statement there is his deputising for him during his life and "after the prophethood" which (gives evidence of his succession) by specification of the exception, (of Prophethood) when he excludes him from it by mentioning "after".

Proofs similar to these are so numerous that it would make the book unduly long to mention them all, (especially) as we have examined thoroughly the statement of the evidence for them in other places in our books. Praise be to Allāh.

The Imamate of the Commander of the Faithful, peace be on him, was for thirty years after the Prophet, may Allāh bless Him and His Family. For twenty-four years and six months of these he was prevented from administering the laws (of the office) (and had to) exercise precautionary dissimulation (taqiyya) and withdrawal. For five years and six months of these, he was troubled by wars against the hypocrites, those who broke their pledges, the unjust and those who deviated (from the religion) and he was plagued by the seditions of those who had gone astray. In the same way the Apostle of Allāh, may Allāh bless Him and His Family, had been prevented from (administering) the laws (of his office) through fear and through being spied upon, and through being a fugitive and through being exiled, so that he had no power to fight the unbelievers and no means of defending the believers. Then he emigrated and for ten years after the emigration he remained making war on the unbelievers and being troubled by the hypocrites until the time that Allāh, may His name be exalted, took him unto Himself and made him dwell in the gardens of Paradise.

The death of the Commander of the Faithful, peace be on him occurred before dawn of Friday, the twenty-first of the month of Ramaḍān, in the year 40 A.H. He was a victim of the sword. Ibn Muljam al-Murādī, may Allāh curse him, killed him at the mosque of Kūfā, which he had come out to in order to wake the people for the dawn prayer on the night of the nineteenth of the month of Ramaḍān. He had been lying in wait for him from the beginning of the night. When he (the Commander of the Faithful) passed by him while the latter was hiding his design by feigning sleep amid a group of people who were asleep, he (Ibn Muljam) sprang out and struck him on the top of his head with his sword which was poisoned. He lingered through the day of the nineteenth and the night and day of the twentieth and the first third of the night of the twenty-first. Then he, peace be on him, died a martyr and met his Lord, Most High, as one who has been wronged. He, peace be on him, knew of that before its time and he told the people of it before its time. His two sons, al-Ḥasan and al-Ḥusayn, peace be on them, performed (the tasks) of washing him and shrouding him according to his bequest. Then they carried him to al-Gharī at Najaf in Kūfa and they buried him there. They removed the traces of the place of his burial according to his bequest which was made about that to both of them by him, because of what he, peace be on him, knew about the regime of the 'Umayyads (which would come) after him, and their hostile attitude towards him. (For he knew) the evil action and abuse to which they would be led by their wicked intentions if they had been able to know that (place). His grave, peace be on him, remained hidden until al-Ṣāḍiq Ja'far b. Muḥammad, peace be on them, pointed it out during the 'Abbāsid regime. For he visited it when he came to visit Abū Ja'far (al-Manṣūr) while the latter was in al-Ḥīra. Then the Shī'a knew of it and they began from that time to make visitation to his (grave), peace be on him and on his pure offspring.

On the day of his death he was 63 years of age.

Reports of him, Peace be on him, Mentioning and Knowing about the Event (of his Death) before its Occurrence

[It is reported on the authority of 'Alī b. al-Mundhir al-Ṭarīqī, on the authority of Abū al-Faḍl al-'Abdī, on the authority of Fiṭr, on the authority of Abū Tufayl 'Āmir b. Wāthila, may Allāh be pleased with him, who said:]

The Commander of the Faithful, peace be on him, gathered the people for the pledge of allegiance. 'Abd al-Raḥmān b. Muljam al-Murādī, may Allāh curse him, came but he (i.e. 'Alī) refused to accept his (pledge of allegiance) twice or three times. Then he (let him) make his pledge of allegiance to him. When he did so, he (i.e. 'Alī) said to him: "What prevents the most wretched person of the community (from doing his wicked deed now)?

For I swear by Him in Whose hand is my life, you will colour this (with blood) from this." And he put his hand on his beard and his head.

When Ibn Muljam withdrew and left him, he, peace be on him, recited the following:

Stiffen your breast for death. Indeed death will meet you.

Do not show grief at death, when it arrives in your valley.

[It is related from al-Ḥasan b. Maḥbūb, on the authority of Abū Ḥamza al-Thumālī, on the authority of Abū Isḥāq al-Sabī'ī, on the authority of al-Aṣbagh b. Nubāta, who said:]

Ibn Muljam came to the Commander of the Faithful, peace be on him, and pledged allegiance to him with the (others) who pledged their allegiance, and withdrew from him. Then the Commander of the Faithful, peace be on him, called him back and warned him to be trustworthy and to be sure that he was not treacherous and did not break his oath. He did that (i.e. promised to keep his word). Then he withdrew. A second time the Commander of the Faithful called him (back) and warned him to be trustworthy and to be sure that he was not treacherous and did not break his oath. Ibn Muljam, may Allāh curse him, said: "By Allāh, O Commander of the Faithful, I have not seen you do this with anyone else except me."

Then the Commander of the Faithful said:

I want his friendship and he wants my death. The one who makes excuses to you is one of your bosom friends from (the tribe of) Murād.

(Then the Commander of the Faithful continued): "Go, Ibn Muljam, I do not think that you will keep your word."

[It is related from Ja'far b. Sulaymān al-Dab'ī, on the authority of al-Mu'āllā b. Ziyād, who said:]

'Abd al-Raḥmāan b. Muljam, may Allāh curse him, came to the Commander of the Faithful, peace be on him, to ask to be provided with a horse. "O Commander of the Faithful," he said, "provide me with a horse."

The Commander of the Faithful, peace be on him, turned toward him and then said to him, "You are 'Abd al-Raḥmān b. Muljam al-Murādī?" "Yes," he replied.

"Ghazwan," called (the Commander of the Faithful), "provide him with the roan."

That man came with a roan horse and Ibn Muljam, may Allāh curse him, mounted it and took its reins. When he had gone away, the Commander of the Faithful, peace be on him said:

I want his friendship and he wants my death. The one who makes excuses to you is one of your bosom friends from (the tribe of) Murād.

When he did what he did and struck the Commander of the Faithful, peace be on him, he was captured after he came out of the mosque and then brought to the Commander of the Faithful. The latter said to him: "I have treated you as I have done, even though I knew that you would be my murderer. Yet, I treated you that way in order to seek Allāh's support against you."

There are other reports in which he, peace be on him, announces his own death to his family and companions before his murder.

[Abū Zayd al-Aḥwal reported on the authority of al-Ajlaḥ, on the authority of the shaykhs of Kinda whom al-Ajlaḥ said he heard say more than twenty times:] 'Alī said on the pulpit: "What prevents the most wretched person of the community dyeing this red with blood from above it?" And he, peace be on him, put his hand on his beard.

['Alī b. al-Ḥazawwar on the authority of al-Aṣbagh b. Nubāta, who said:]

'Alī preached in the month in which he was killed and he said: "The month of Ramaḍān has come to you. It is the lord of the months, and foremost of the year. In it the mill of authority makes a (new) turn and you will make the pilgrimage of the (new) year in one rank (i.e. without an Imam to lead you). The sign of that will be that I will no longer be among you."

[Al-Aṣbagh added:] He was announcing his own death but we did not understand.

[It is related from al-Faḍl b. Dukayn, on the authority of Ḥayyān b. al-'Abbās, on the authority of 'Uthmān b. al-Mughīra who said:]

When the month of Ramaḍān began, the Commander of the Faithful, peace be on him, had supper one evening with al-Ḥasan, one evening with al-Ḥusayn, peace be on them, and one evening with 'Abd Allāh b. al-'Abbās. He never had more than three mouthfuls (of food). One of those nights he was asked about that, he replied: "(I would rather) the decision of Allāh come to me while I was hungry." It was only a night of two nights later when he, peace be on him, was struck towards the end of the night.

[Ismā'īl b. Ziyād reported, on the authority of Umm Mūsā, a woman servant of 'Alī, peace be on him, and the wet-nurse of his daughter, peace be on her, who told me:]

‘Alī, peace be on him, said to his daughter, Umm Kulthūm,: “O my little daughter, little time is left for me to be with you.” “Why is that, father?” she asked.

“I have seen the Apostle of Allāh, may Allāh bless Him and His Family, in my sleep,” he replied. “He was rubbing the dust from my face and saying: ‘O ‘Alī, do not be concerned, you have accomplished what you had to.’”

Only three days later he was struck by that blow. Umm Kulthūm cried aloud (with sorrow).

“Don’t do that, my daughter,” he said. “For I see the Apostle of Allāh, may Allāh bless Him and His Family, pointing to me with his hand and saying: ‘O ‘Alī, come to us, for what we have is better for you.’”

[‘Ammār al-Duhnī reported on the authority of Abū Sāliḥ al-Ḥanafī, who said:] I heard ‘Alī, peace be on him, saying: “I saw the Prophet, may Allāh bless Him and His Family, in my sleep and I complained to him about the trouble and quarrelling which I had met from his community. Then I wept. He said: ‘Don’t weep, ‘Alī, but turn around.’ I turned around. Behold, there were two fettered men, and then their heads were crushed by stones (Reference to the punishment Ibn Muljam and Shabīb b. Bajura will receive from Allāh).”

[Abū Sāliḥ added:] I went to him in the morning as I had done every morning, and when I got to the (area of) the butchers I met the people who were saying: “The Commander of the Faithful, peace be on him, has been killed.”

[‘Abd Allāh b. Mūsā related, on the authority of al-Ḥasan b. Dīnār, on the authority of al-Ḥasan al-Baṣrī, who said:]

The Commander of the Faithful, peace be on him, stayed up awake during the night on the morning of which he was killed and he did not go out to the mosque for the night prayer as was his custom. His daughter, Umm Kulthūm, the mercy of Allāh be on her, asked him: "What has kept you awake?" "I will be killed, if I go out in the morning," he replied.

Then Ibn al-Nabbāḥ came to him and summoned him to the prayer. He walked out a little way then returned. Umm Kulthūm said to him: "Tell Ja'da to pray with the people."

"Yes, tell Ja'da to perform the prayer with the people," he answered. But then he said: "There is no escape from the appointed time."

He went out to the mosque and there was the man who had spent the whole night lying in wait for him. However, when it had become cold in the early morning before dawn, he had fallen asleep. Now, the Commander of the Faithful, peace be on him, moved him with his foot and said to him: "The prayer." The man got up and struck him.

[In another account:]

The Commander of the Faithful, peace be on him, spent that night awake and he frequently went out and looked up to the sky, saying: "By Allāh, I have not lied nor have I been lied to. It is the night which I was promised."

Then he went back to his bed. When dawn rose, he put on his waist-cloth (izār) and went out saying:

Stiffen your breast for death. Indeed death will meet you.

Do not show grief at death, when it arrives in your valley.

When he reached the courtyard of his house, the geese met him and hooted in his face. (The people) began to drive them away but he said: "Leave them, they are those who wail (for my death)."

He, peace be on him, went out and was struck down.

Reports which have come down of the Motive for his Murder and how the Event occurred

[What is reported by a group of historians (ahl al-siyar), including Abū Mikhnaf, Ismā'īl b. Rashīd, Abū Hāshim al-Rifā'ī, Abū 'Amr al-Thaqafī and others who relate:]

A group of the Khārijites gathered at Mecca and they mentioned the leaders (of the people) and blamed them and their actions. They mentioned the people of al-Nahrawān and they asked Allāh's mercy for them. Then they said to each other: "If (only) we devoted ourselves to Allāh, and went to the leaders (Imams) of error (ḍalāl) and sought a moment when they were inattentive and then rid the country and men of them for the sake of Allāh, and also avenged our brothers, the martyrs of al-Nahrawān."

They made a compact to do that after performing the pilgrimage. 'Abd al-Raḥmān b. Muljam, may Allāh curse him, said: "I'll take care of (killing) 'Alī for you." Al-Burak b. 'Abd Allāh al-Tamīmī said: "I will take care of (killing) Mu'āwiya for you."

'Amr b. Bakr al-Tamīmī said: "I will take care of (killing) 'Amr b. al-'Aṣ for you."

They made a compact to do that and bound themselves to its

told me: Hishām b. Yūnis al-Nahshalī told us: 'Ā'idh b. Ḥabīb told us on the authority of Abū al-Sabbāḥ al-Kinanī, on the authority of Muḥammad b. 'Abd al-Rahmān al-Sulamī, on the authority of his father, on the authority of 'Ikrima, on the authority of Ibn 'Abbās, who said:]

The Apostle of Allāh, may Allāh bless Him and His Family, said: "'Alī b. Abī Ṭālib is the most learned of my community and the most capable of giving legal decisions after me in (matters upon) which (men) differ."

[Abū Bakr Muḥammad b. 'Umar al-Ji'ābī informed me: Aḥmad b. 'Īsā Abū Ja'far al-'Ijlī told us: Ismā'īl b.'Abd Allāh b. Khālid told us: 'Ubayd Allāh b. 'Umar told us: 'Abd Allāh b. Muḥammad b.'Aqīl told us on the authority of Ḥamza b. Abī Sa'īd al-Khudrī, on the authority of his father (Abū Sa'īd al-Khudrī), who said:]

I heard the Apostle of Allāh, may Allāh bless Him and His Family, say: "I am the city of knowledge and 'Alī is its gate. Therefore whoever wants knowledge should learn it from 'Alī, peace be on him."

[Abū Bakr Muḥammad b. 'Umar al-Ji'ābī informed me: Yūsuf b. al-Ḥakam al-Ḥannāt told us: Dāwud b. Rashīd told us: Salama b. Ṣāliḥ al-Aḥmar told us on the authority of 'Abd al-Malik b. 'Abd al Raḥmān, on the authority of al-Ash'ath b. Ṭalīq who said: I heard al-Ḥasan al-'Aranī relating on the authority of Murra, on the authority of 'Abd Allāh b. Mas'ūd, who said:]

The Apostle of Allāh, may Allāh bless Him and His Family, summoned 'Alī and went apart with him. When he returned to us, we asked him: "What covenant ('Ahd) did he make with you?" He replied: "He taught me a thousand doors of knowledge and he opened from each (of these) doors a thousand (more) doors."

[Abū al-Ḥasan Muḥammad b. al-Muẓaffar al-Bazzāz informed me: Abū Mālik Kuthayyir b. Yaḥyā told us: Abū Ja'far Muḥammad b. Abī al-Sirrī told us: Aḥmad b. 'Abd Allāh b. Yūnis told us on the authority of Sa'd al-Kinānī, on the authority of al-Aṣbagh b. Nubāta who said:]

When the pledge of allegiance was made to the Commander of the Faithful, peace be on him, for the caliphate, he went out to the mosque wearing the turban and cloak of the Apostle of Allāh, peace be on Him and His Family. He went up on the pulpit. After praising and glorifying Allāh, and giving admonition and warning, he sat down confidently, knitted his fingers together and placed them on his stomach. Then he said: "Question me before you lose me. Question me, for I have the knowledge of those who came earlier and those who will come later. If the cushion (on which a judge sits) was folded for me (to sit on), I could give judgements to the people of the Torah by their Torah, to the people of the Gospels by their Gospels, to the people of Psalms by their Psalms and to the people of the Furqān (i.e. Qur'ān) by their Furqān, so that each one of these books will be fulfilled and will declare, 'O Lord, indeed 'Alī has given judgement according to Your decree.' By Allāh, I know the Qur'ān and its interpretation (better) than anyone who claims knowledge of it. If it were not for one verse in the Book of Allāh, most High, I would be able to inform you of what will be until the Day of Resurrection." Then he said: "Question me before you lose me, for by Him Who split the seed and brought the soul into being, if you questioned me about (it) verse by verse, I would tell you of the time of its revelation and why it was revealed, I would inform of the abrogating (verse) and the abrogated, of the specific and general, the clearly defined and the ambiguous, of the Meccan and the Medinan. By Allāh, there is not a party who can lead astray or guide until the Day of Resurrection, without me knowing its leader, the one who drives it forward and the one who urges it on."

Examples of such reports are (so many) that the book would become (unduly) long in (reporting) them.

Reports of his Outstanding Merit, the Blessing of Allāh be on him

[Abū al-Ḥasan Muḥammad b. al-Muẓaffar al-Bazzāz informed me: 'Umar b. 'Abd Allāh b. 'Imrān told us: Aḥmad b. Bashīr told us: 'Abd Allāh b. Mūsā told us on the authority of Qays b. Abī Hārūn who said: I went to Abū Sa'īd al-Khudrī and asked him whether he had witnessed (the battle of) Badr. He said:]

On that day (the Battle of Badr), I heard the Apostle of Allāh, may Allāh bless Him and His Family, speak to Fāṭima, peace be on her, when she came to him weeping and saying: "O Apostle of Allāh, the women of Quraysh are reviling me because of the poverty of 'Alī peace be on him."

"Aren't you satisfied that I have married you to the first Muslim and the most knowledgeable of them?" the Prophet, may Allāh bless Him and His Family, asked her. "Indeed, Allāh, the Most High, looked thoroughly over the people of the earth and chose your father from them and made him a Prophet. Then He looked over them a second time and chose your (present) husband (ba'l) and made him a trustee of authority (waṣī). Allāh inspired me to marry you to him. Didn't you know, Fāṭima, that through Allāh's kindness to you, your husband is the greatest of men in clemency, the most knowledgeable of men and the first of them in Islam."

Fāṭima laughed and rejoiced. Then the Prophet, may Allāh bless Him and His Family, continued: "Fāṭima, 'Alī has eight molar teeth. No one before and after him will have the like. He is my brother in the world and the hereafter. No one else of the people has that (rank). Fāṭima, the mistress of the women of heaven, is his wife. The grandsons of mercy, my grandsons, will be his sons. His brother, who will be adorned by two wings in heaven, will fly with the angels wherever he wishes. He has the knowledge of those who came before and those who will come after. He is the first who believed in me and he will be the last of the people to see me. He is my trustee of authority (waṣī) and the inheritor (wārith) of (all) the trustees of authority (waṣiyyīn)."

[Al-Shaykh al-Mufīd, may Allāh be pleased with him, said: I have found (the following report) in the book of Abū Ja'far Muḥammad b. al-'Abbās al-Rāzī who said: Muḥammad b. Khālid told us: Ibrāhīm b. 'Abd Allāh told us: Muḥammad b. Sulaymān al-Daylamī told us on the authority of Jābir b. Yazīd al-Ju'fī, on the authority of 'Adī b. Ḥakīm, on the authority of 'Abd Allāh b. al-'Abbās, who said:]

We, (the members) of the house (Ahl al-bayt) have seven qualities none of which the (rest of the) people have:

From us (came) the Prophet may Allāh bless Him and His Family;

From us came the trustee of authority (waṣī), the best of this community after him (i.e. Prophet), 'Alī b. Abī Ṭālib, peace be on him

From us came Ḥamza, the lion of Allāh and of His Apostle, and the lord of martyrs;

From us came Ja'far b. Abī Ṭālib who is adorned by two wings with which he flies in heaven wherever he wishes;

From us (came) the two grandsons of this community, the two lords of the youth of paradise, al-Ḥasan and al-Ḥusayn;

From us (came) the (one who will undertake the Imamate for the rest of time) Qā'im of the family of Muḥammad, by which Allāh graced His Prophet; From us (came) the one who was given (final) victory (al-manṣūr).

[Muḥammad b. Ayman related on the authority of Abū Ḥāzim, retainer of Ibn 'Abbās, who said:]

The Apostle of Allāh, may Allāh bless Him and His Family, spoke to 'Alī b. Abī Ṭālib, peace be on him:

"'Ali, you will be engaged in disputes but you will overcome any dispute by seven qualities, the like of which no one else has: you are the first of those who believed with me, the greatest of them in war, the most knowledgeable of them in the battles (ayyām) on behalf of Allāh, the one of them who is most loyal in keeping the covenant ('Ahd) of Allāh, the most compassionate of them towards subjects, the most capable of giving equal treatment and the greatest of them in distinction before Allāh."

Reports like this and in the same sense as this, which are better known by both the general populace and the Shī'a (khāṣṣa) are (so clear) that there is no need to lengthen (matters) with an explanation. Yet if there was only the tradition whose story is well known, whose narration has been spread abroad, of the bird and the words of the Prophet, may Allāh bless Him and His Family: "O Allāh, bring the creature most lovable to you to eat (some) of this bird with me," and then the Commander of the Faithful, peace be on him, came, it would be sufficient (to show that) he was the most lovable creature to Allāh, the greatest in reward from Him, the nearest to Him, and the most outstanding in his action. (Similar) is the case of the words of Jābir b. 'Abd Allāh al-Anṣārī when he was asked about the Commander of the Faithful, peace be on him, and he said, "He is the best of men. Only an unbeliever could doubt clear proof." Jābir had supported that in a narrative which has come through an uninterrupted chain of transmitters, and is well known to the traditionists (ahl al-naql). The evidences for the fact that the Commander of the Faithful, peace be on him, is the most outstanding person after the Apostle of Allāh, may Allāh bless Him and His Family, are mutually verifiable. If our purpose was to establish it (by reporting and analysing all the reports) we would have to set aside a book for it. The reports of what we have outlined are sufficient in so far as our intention is to give a summary, and put that in its (appropriate) place in this book.

Reports of Love for him, Peace be on him, Being a Sign of Faith (in a Person) and Hatred of him Being a Sign of Hypocrisy (in a Person)

[Abū Bakr Muḥammad b. 'Umar - known as Ibn al-Ji'ābī al-Ḥāfiẓ - told us: Muḥammad b. Sahl b. al-Ḥasan told us: Aḥmad b. 'Umar al-Dihqān told us: Muḥammad b. Kathīr told us: Ismā'īl b. Muslim told us: al-A'mash told us on the authority of 'Adī b. Thābit, on the authority of Zirr b. Ḥubaysh, who said:] I saw the Commander of the Faithful, 'Alī b. Abī Ṭālib, on the pulpit and I heard him say: "By Him Who split the seed and brought the soul into being, the Prophet made a promise ('ahd) to me: 'Only believers will love you and only hypocrites will hate you!'"

[Abū 'Abd Allāh Muḥammad b. 'Imrān al-Marzubānī informed me: 'Abd Allāh b. Muḥammad b. 'Abd al-'Azīz al-Baghawī told us: 'Ubayd Allāh b. 'Umar al-Qawārīrī told us: Ja'far b. Sulaymān told us: al-Naḍr b. Hamīd told us on the authority of Abū al-Jārūd, on the authority of al-Ḥārith al-Hamdānī who said:] I saw ʻAlī, peace be on him. One day he came and went up on the pulpit. He praised and glorified Allāh. Then he said: "A decree which Allāh, the Most High, decreed by the tongue of the Prophet, may Allāh bless Him and His Family, was that only believers will love me and only hypocrites will hate me. Whoever forges a lie is lost."

[Abū al-Ḥasan Muḥammad b. al-Muẓaffar al-Bazzāz informed me: Muḥammad b. Yaḥyā told us: Muḥammad b. Mūsā al-Barbarī told us: Khalaf b. Sālim told us: Wakīʻ told us: al-Aʻmash told us on the authority of ʻAdī b. Thābit, on the authority of Zirr b. Ḥubaysh, on the authority of the Commander of the Faithful, peace be on him, who said:]

The Prophet, may Allāh bless Him and His Family, made a promise (ʻahd) to me:

"Only believers will love you and only hypocrites will hate you."

Reports of him, Peace be on him, and his Shīʻa Being the Successful Ones

[Abū ʻAbd Allāh Muḥammad b. ʻImrān al-Marzubānī informed me: ʻAlī b. Muḥammad b. ʻAbd Allāh al-Ḥāfiẓ told me: ʻAlī b. al-Ḥusayn b. ʻUbayd al-Kūfī told us: Ismāʻīl b. Abān told us on the authority of Saʻd b. Ṭālib, on the authority of Jābir b. Yazīd, on the authority of Muḥammad b. ʻAlī al-Bāqir, peace be on them both, who said:]

Umm Salama, the wife of the Prophet, may Allāh bless Him and His Family, was asked about ʻAlī b. Abī Ṭālib, peace be on him, she said: "I heard the Apostle of Allāh say: "ʻAlī and his

Shī'a are the successful ones'"

[Abū 'Abd Allāh Muḥammad b. 'Imrān informed me: Aḥmad b. Muḥammad al-Jawharī told me: Muḥammad b. Hārūn b. 'Īsā al-Hāshimī told me: Tamīm b. Muḥammad b. al-'Alā told us: 'Abd al-Razzāq told us: Yaḥyā b. al-'Alā told us on the authority of Sa'd b. Tarīf, on the authority of al-Aṣbagh b. Nubāta, on the authority of 'Alī, peace be on him, who said:]

The Apostle of Allāh, may Allāh bless Him and His Family said: "Allāh, the Most High, has a cane of ruby which none will obtain except us and our Shī'a. The rest of the people are excluded from it."

[Abū 'Abd Allāh informed me: 'Alī b. Muḥammad b. 'Abd Allāh al-Ḥāfiz told me: 'Alī b. al-Ḥusayn b. 'Ubayd al-Kūfī told us: Ismā'īl b. Abān told us on the authority of 'Amr b. Ḥurayth, on the authority of Dāwūd b. al-Salīl, on the authority of Anas b. Mālik, who said:]

The Apostle of Allāh, may Allāh bless Him and His Family said: "Seventy thousand of my community will enter Heaven without any reckoning and punishment against them." Then he turned to 'Alī, peace be on him and said: "They are your Shī'a and you are their Imam."

[Abū 'Abd Allāh informed me: Aḥmad b. 'Īsā al- Karkhī told me Abū al-'Aynā Muḥammad b. al-Qāsim told us: Muḥammad b. 'Ā'isha told us on the authority of Ismā'īl b. 'Amr al-Bajalī, who told us: 'Umar b. Mūsā told me on the authority of Zayd b. 'Alī b. al-Ḥusayn, on the authority of his father, on the authority of his (Zayd's) grandfather, on the authority of 'Alī, peace be on them, who said:] I complained to the Apostle of Allāh, may Allāh bless Him and His Family, about the people's envy of me. He said: "'Alī, the first four to enter heaven are myself, you, al-Ḥasan and al-Ḥusayn. Our progeny (will come) behind us and our loved ones will be behind our progeny. To our right and left will be our Shīʻa."

Reports of Friendship to him, Peace be on him, Being a Sign of Good Birth and Enmity to him, Being a Sign of Disgraceful Birth

[Abū al-Jaysh al-Muẓaffar b. Muḥammad al-Balkhī informed me: Abū Bakr Muḥammad b. Aḥmad b. Abī al-Thalj told us: Jaʻfar b. Muḥammad al-ʻAlawī told us: Aḥmad b. ʻAbd al-Munʻim told us: ʻAbd Allāh b. Muḥammad al-Fazārī told us on the authority of Jaʻfar b. Muḥammad, on the authority of his father, peace be on them, on the authority of Jābir, b. ʻAbd Allāh al-Anṣārī, who said:] I heard the Apostle of Allāh, may Allāh bless Him and His Family, say to ʻAlī b. Abī Ṭālib, peace be on him: "Shall I not make you happy, give you a gift, tell you good news?"

"Please do, Apostle of Allāh," he replied.

"Both I, myself, and you have been created from one (piece of) clay. Part of it was left over and from that Allāh created our Shīʻa. On the Day of Resurrection (all) the people will be summoned by the names of their mothers except our Shīʻa. They will be summoned by the names of their fathers because of their good birth."

[Abū al-Jaysh al-Muẓaffar b. Muḥammad informed me on the authority of Muḥammad b. Aḥmad b. Abī al-Thalj who said: Muḥammad b. Muslim al-Kūfī told us: ʻUbayd Allāh b. Kathīr told us: Jaʻfar b. Muḥammad b. al-Ḥusayn al-Zuhrī told us: ʻUbayd Allāh b. Mūsā told us on the authority of Isrāʼīl, on the authority of Abū Ḥusayn, on the authority of ʻIkrima, on the authority of Ibn ʻAbbās:]

The Apostle of Allāh, may Allāh bless Him and His Family, said: "On the Day of Resurrection all the people will be summoned by the names of their mothers except our Shī'a. They will be summoned by the names of their fathers because of their good birth."

[Abū al-Qāsim Ja'far b. Muḥammad al-Qummī told us: Abū 'Alī Muḥammad b. Hammām b. Suhayl al-Iskāfī told us: Ja'far b. Muḥammad b. Mālik told me:

Muḥammad b. Ni'ma al-Salūlī told us: 'Abd Allāh b. al-Qāsim, told us on the authority of 'Abd Allāh b. Jabala, on the authority of his father, who said: I heard Jābir b. 'Abd Allāh b. Ḥizān al-Anṣārī say:]

One day a group of us Anṣār were with the Apostle of Allāh, may Allāh bless Him and His Family. He said to us: "O people of the Anṣār, instill in your children a love for 'Alī b. Abī Ṭālib, peace be on him. Whoever loves him should know that he is rightly guided and whoever hates him should know that he is in error."

Reports of the Apostle of Allāh, may Allāh bless Him and His Family Naming him, Peace be on him, Commander of the Faithful during (the Prophet's) Lifetime.

[Abū al-Jaysh al-Muẓaffar b. Muḥammad al-Balkhī informed me: Abū Bakr Muḥammad b. Aḥmad b. Abī al-Thalj informed me: al-Ḥusayn b. Ayyūb informed me on the authority of Muḥammad b. Ghālib, on the authority of 'Alī b. al-Ḥusayn, on the authority of al-Ḥasan b. Maḥbūb, on the authority of Abū Ḥamza al-Thumālī, on the authority of Abū Isḥāq al-Sabī'ī, on the authority of Bashīr al-Ghiffārī, on the authority of Anas b. Mālik, who said:]

I was a servant of the Apostle of Allāh, may Allāh bless Him and His Family. One night Umm Ḥabība, daughter of Abū Sufyān, brought water for ablutions to the Apostle of Allāh, may Allāh bless Him and His Family. He said to me: "Anas, at this moment there will come to you through this door the Commander of the Faithful, the best of testamentary trustees of authority (waṣiyyīn), the foremost of the people in Islam, and the most knowledgeable and most mindful of them." "O Allāh, make him one of my tribe," I said.

However, almost immediately 'Alī b. Abī Ṭālib, peace be on him, came through the door. The Apostle of Allāh, may Allāh bless Him and His Family, performed his ablutions. Then the Apostle of Allāh threw the water into, the face of the Commander of the Faithful, peace be on them both, so that both his eyes were filled with water.

"Apostle of Allāh, has any impurity occurred in me?" asked 'Alī.

"Only good has been occasioned in you," replied the Prophet, may Allāh bless Him and His Family. "You belong to me and I belong to you. You will act on my behalf, fulfill my duties, wash my (corpse) and bury me in my grave. You will listen to the people's (questions) about me and you will explain to them after me."

"Apostle of Allāh," 'Alī said, "haven't you told them?" "Yes, but you will explain the things they differ on after me."

[Abū al-Jaysh al-Muẓaffar b. Muḥammad informed me on the authority of Muḥammad b. Aḥmad b. Abī al-Thalj who said: My grandfather told me: 'Abd Allāh b. Dāhir told us: My father,

Dāhir b. Yaḥyā al-Aḥmarī al-Muqrī told me on the authority of al-A'mash, on the authority of 'Abāya al-Asadī, on the authority of Ibn 'Abbās:]

The Prophet, may Allāh bless Him and His Family, said to Umm Salama, may Allāh be pleased with her: "Listen and bear witness that this 'Alī is the Commander of the Faithful and the master of the testamentary trustees."

[With the same isnād on the authority of Muḥammad (b. Aḥmad) b. Abī al-Thalj who said: my grandfather told me: 'Abd al-Salām b. Ṣāliḥ told us: Yaḥyā b. al-Yamān told us: Sufyān al-Thawrī told us on the authority of Abū al-Jaḥḥāf, on the authority of Mu'āwiya b. Tha'laba who said:]

Abu Dharr, may Allāh be pleased with him, was told: "Make a will." "I have made my will," he answered. "To whom?" he was asked.

"To the Commander of the Faithful," he replied.

"To 'Uthmān?"

"No," he said. "To the Commander of the Faithful, 'Alī b. Abī Ṭālib, peace be on him. Indeed he is the pivot of the earth and the master of this community. If you lost him, you would not know the earth and those who were on it."

The report of Burayda b. Ḥuṣayb al-Aslamī is famous and well known among the religious scholars with (so many) isnāds that their full elucidation would be very long. He reported:

The Apostle of Allāh, may Allāh bless Him and His Family, ordered me while I was the seventh of a group of seven which included Abū Bakr, 'Umar, Ṭalḥa and al-Zubayr: "Greet 'Alī with the title of Commander of the Faithful."

We greeted him with that title while the Apostle of Allāh, may Allāh bless Him and His Family, lived among us.

There are many reports like these which would make the book too long (to report them all). Allāh is the bringer of truth.

His Qualities

As for his many qualities, the fact that they are so famous, so well authenticated and reported by tradition and by the consensus of the religious scholars (means) that they do not need their chains of authority to be put forward; for since they are (also) so numerous their full explanation would make the book too long. In our outline, an extract from them will do instead of reporting them all, in accordance with the purpose which we set down for this book, Allāh willing.

1. The Meeting of the Banu 'Abd al-Muṭṭalib

Among these is the account that the Prophet, may Allāh bless Him and His Family, gathered his own family and tribal kin together at the beginning of his mission for Islam. He showed them the faith and sought their help against the people of unbelief and enmity, and guaranteed for them, if they did that, favour and honour in this world and a reward in heaven. None of them answered him except the Commander of the Faithful, 'Alī b. Abī Ṭālib, peace be on him. Because of that he granted him the achievement of brotherhood (with himself), the office of helping him, of being his nominated trustee, his inheritor and his successor, and announced that his going to heaven was inevitable.

This is reported in the account of the (meeting in the) house, whose authenticity the reporters of tradition are agreed upon:

When the Apostle of Allāh, may Allāh bless Him and His Family, gathered members of the clan of 'Abd al-Muṭṭalib in the house of Abū Ṭālib, they were more or less forty men on that day as the reporters mention. He ordered food to be set for them, a leg of an ewe with a measure of wheat. He measured a ṣā'a of milk. Each man of them was known to be able to eat a lamb in one sitting and to drink a farq (A ṣā'a and farq are measures of cubic capacity) of drink in the same sitting. He, peace be on Him and His Family, intended by preparing little food and drink for their gathering, to reveal a clear sign to them through satisfying them and quenching their thirst with what would not normally satisfy and quench the thirst of one of them. He ordered the food and drink to be offered to them. From that little amount the whole group ate (and drank) until they were full and what they had eaten and drunk was not clear. He dazzled them by that and showed them the clear sign of his prophetic mission and the evidence for his truthfulness, through the proof of Allāh, the Exalted, with regard to it. After they had eaten and drunk their fill, he said to them: "Banū 'Abd al-Muṭṭalib, Allāh has sent me to all creation and He has especially sent me to you. He has said: Warn your clan (who are your) kin (XXVI 214). I call you to make two statements light to the tongue but heavy in the scales (of Allāh). By them you will be master of Arab and foreigner, by them nations shall submit to you, by them you will enter heaven and by them you will escape from hell. They are the (two fold) testimony that there is no God but Allāh and that I am the Apostle of Allāh. Whoever answers me in this matter, helps me in it and in carrying it out, will be my brother, my trustee, my helper, my inheritor and my successor after me."

None of them answered.

The Commander of the Faithful reported: I stood up before him amid them. At that time I was the youngest of them, still with very thin legs and with dirt still in the corners of my eyes. I said: "Apostle of Allāh, I will help you."

"Sit down," he told me. Then he repeated his words to the people again. They were silent and I arose and said the same as I had said the first time. Again he told me to sit down and he repeated his words to the people a third time. None of them spoke a word. I arose and said:

"I will help you, Apostle of Allāh, in this matter."

"Sit down," he said and then he went on, "You are my brother, my trustee, my helper, my inheritor, and my successor after me."

The people got up and they were saying to Abū Ṭālib: "Abū Ṭālib, you should be congratulated today that you have entered the religion of your nephew and he has made your son a commander over you."

This outstanding quality is exclusive to the Commander of the Faithful, peace be on him. None of the first emigrants or the Anṣār share in it, nor does anyone else of the people of Islam. No one else has the equal of it in merit, nor even an approximate in (the) circumstance (of it). What is shown by the report of it is that through him, peace be on him, the Prophet, may Allāh bless Him and His Family, was able to communicate his message, to make public his mission and declare the truth of Islam. If it had not been for him, the religion would not have been established, the law of Islam (sharī'a) would not have been set down and the mission would not have been made public. He, peace be on him, is the support of Islam, the helper of the one who undertook its mission on behalf of Allāh, the Mighty and High. Through his guaranteeing support to the Prophet of guidance, peace be on Him and His Family, he brought about for (the Prophet) what he wanted with regard to the prophetic mission. In that there is such merit that not even the weight of mountains could outweigh it, nor do all other virtues go beyond it in position and rank.

2. *The Circumstances of the Prophet's Emigration from Mecca*

Another example of his qualities occurs when the Prophet, may Allāh bless Him and His Family, ordered the emigration after the council of Quraysh had decided to kill him and he, peace be on him, would not have been able to defeat their plans by leaving Mecca. For He, peace be on him, wanted to keep his departure secret and keep the reports about him hidden from them so that he could carry out his departure in safety from them. He told his news to the Commander of the Faithful and made him keep it secret. He gave him the responsibility of protecting him by spending the night on his (i.e. the Prophet's) bed so that they would not know that it was 'Alī who was sleeping on the bed and they would think that the Prophet, may Allāh bless Him and His Family, was sleeping there as he had normally done on previous nights. The Commander of the Faithful, peace be on him dedicated his life to Allāh, the Exalted, devoted it to Allāh, the Exalted, in obedience and exchanged it for His Prophet, the blessings and peace of Allāh be on Him and His Family, in order that he might save him from the plots of his enemies and thus make sure of his safety and survival and also arrange properly his purpose in summoning (the people) to the faith, establishing the religion and making public Allāh's law (sharī'a). He, peace be on him, spent the night on the bed of the Apostle of Allāh, may Allāh bless Him and His Family, hidden by his waist-cover (izār). The people who had plotted to kill the Prophet, may Allāh bless Him and His Family, came to him and surrounded him. They were carrying weapons. They waited until the dawn rose so that they could kill him openly and thus his blood would be shed in such a way that Banū Hāshim would see that his murderers were from all the clans (of Quraysh). Then it would not be possible for them to take vengeance (on them) for him because everyone had shared in taking his blood and every tribe would be spared from fighting his group and being separate from his family.

That (i.e. 'Alī's action) was the reason for the Prophet, may Allāh bless Him and His Family, being saved, his blood being kept safe and his survival until he died at (the time of) his Lord's command. If it had not been for the Commander of the Faithful, peace be on him, and his action, it would not have been possible for the Apostle of Allāh, may Allāh bless Him and His Family, to propagate and carry out (his mission), nor would he have remained alive and continued to survive. Thus through him he overcame the envy (of the people) and his enemies. In the morning when the people were intending to rush upon him, he, peace be on him, rushed towards them. They scattered from him when they recognized him and departed. Their plot against the Prophet, peace be on Him and His Family, had gone wrong. The preparations they had made to kill him had been destroyed. Their plans had been betrayed and their hopes brought to nought. In this way was the faith properly set up, Satan humiliated and the people of unbelief and enmity betrayed. None of the people of Islam share this achievement with the Commander of the Faithful, peace be on him, nor is any equal to it in any circumstance known, nor is there anything approaching it in merit according to any correct consideration. Concerning the Commander of the Faithful, peace be on him, and the night he spent on the (Prophet's) bed, Allāh, glory be to Him, revealed: Whoever among the people sells his life out of a desire to please Allāh, Allāh is kind to (such) servants (II 207).

3. *The Commander of the Faithful fulfils the Prophet's Obligations in Mecca*

(Another example) of that is that the Prophet, may Allāh bless Him and His Family, was the one trusted by the Quraysh with the things which they wished to deposit. When the situation occurred which required his sudden flight from Mecca, he could not find anyone among his people and his family to entrust (the things) which he had been entrusted with except the Commander of the Faithful, peace be on him. He appointed him (i.e. the Commander of the Faithful) as his deputy to return the things deposited with him to their owners and to pay the debts which he owed. Then he gathered his daughters, the womenfolk of his family and his wives and their emigration was entrusted to him for he did not consider that anyone could take his (i.e. the Commander of the Faithful's) place among all the people. Thus he set his trust on his faithfulness, depended upon his courage and bravery, and in the defence of his family and his close associates he relied upon his fearlessness and his ability. He rested upon his reliability to look after his family and his womenfolk. He recognized in his piety and protection from error that by which the soul could feel sure of his reliability in those matters.

'Alī, peace be on him, carried out (these tasks) very well: he returned every deposit to its owner; he paid every debt to the person to whom it was owed; he looked after the daughters and womenfolk of the Prophet, may Allāh bless Him and His Family; and he emigrated with them, he himself going on foot to protect them from the enemies and guard them against adversaries; he took them gently on the journey until he brought them to him at Medina, (having provided them) with complete protection and guarding, good companionship and excellent organization. The Prophet gave him accommodation in his house when he arrived in Medina and allowed him to stay with him and mix with his womenfolk and children. He did not exclude him from anything which was special to himself, nor did he withhold from him the inner meaning and the secrets of his affair. This is a quality which is uniquely held by (the Commander of the Faithful) peace be on him, from among all his house and Companions. None of his followers or supporters shared in it and there occurred in no other creature any merit like it, which equalled it in appearance and came near to it in its testing quality. It was in addition to his outstanding achievements which we have mentioned and their overwhelming merit and their nobility in the hearts of those who think.

4. The Commander of the Faithful puts right Crimes committed by Khālid b. al-Walīd

(Another example) of that is that Allāh, the Exalted specified him for the task of putting right what had been done wrong by those who opposed the orders of His Prophet, may Allāh bless Him and His Family, and of reforming what had been corrupted so that through him the causes of righteousness were established. It (i.e. righteousness) was brought about by his hand, by the happiness of his endeavour, his good organization, and the necessary success (he brought) to the affairs of the Muslims. Through him, the pillars of religion were held firm.

The Prophet, may Allāh bless Him and His Family, sent Khālid b. Walīd to the Banū Jadhīma to summon them to Islam and he did not send him to make war (on them). He disobeyed his order, renounced his treaty, rebelled against his religion and killed people who had embraced Islam. He betrayed their protected status when they were people who had accepted the faith. In that he had been acting according to the wild ways of the Jāhiliyya and the methods of people of unbelief and enmity.

The result of his evil action (would have affected) Islam and through it those whom its Prophet, peace be on Him and His Family, had called to the faith, would have broken away and it is likely that the system of organization in religion would have been brought to nothing as a result of his action. Therefore the Apostle of Allāh, may Allāh bless Him and His Family, sought to repair the wrong that had been done and to reform what had been corrupted. He gave the blood-wit according to the law from Allāh for that to the Commander of the Faithful, peace be on him, and sent him to conciliate the people, to draw out their hatred and to show gentleness to them in making firm their faith. He told him to pay the blood-wit for the dead and in that way satisfy the next of kin responsible for keeping their blood alive (by vengeance).

The Commander of the Faithful, peace be on him, achieved complete satisfaction in that, for he gave more than was necessary by making a personal contribution to them from money which he had. He said to them: "I have paid the blood-wit for your dead and in addition to that I have given you money which you can hand down to your successors so that Allāh may be pleased with His Apostle and you may be pleased with his kindness to you." The Apostle of Allāh, may Allāh bless Him and His Family, made a public renunciation in Medina of Khālid's action against them, which he, then, had communicated to them. By the Apostle of Allāh's, may Allāh bless Him and His Family, renunciation of Khālid's crime, and by the conciliation of the Commander of the Faithful, peace be on him, the people agreed (to be reconciled) despite what had been done to them. In that way righteousness was achieved and those who carried out corrupt acts were foiled. No one was entrusted with that task except the Commander of the Faithful, peace be on him, nor did anyone else from the community (jamā'a) except him undertake such actions, nor was the Apostle of Allāh, may Allāh bless Him and His Family, satisfied to entrust anyone else with such a task. This is an achievement which is greater in merit than any claimed by men other than the Commander of the Faithful, peace be on him. No one else among them shared in it, nor was an action equal to it carried out by anyone else.

5. *Keeping the Conquest of Mecca Secret*

Another example of that is that when the Prophet, may Allāh bless Him and His Family, wanted to conquer Mecca, he asked Allāh, may His name be exalted, to keep the reports of it hidden from Quraysh so that he could enter it unexpectedly. He, peace be on him, had based the plan for his going there on the secrecy of that. However, Ḥāṭib b. Abī Balta'a wrote to the Meccans to inform them of the decision of the Apostle of Allāh, may Allāh bless Him and His Family, to conquer it. He gave the letter to a black woman who had come to Medina to seek intercession there for the people and to ask for them to be forgiven. He instructed her to take it to some Meccans whose names he gave her and he ordered her not to take the (main) road. Revelation about that came down on the Apostle of Allāh, may Allāh bless Him and His Family. He summoned the Commander of the Faithful, peace be on him, and told him: "One of my companions has written to the Meccans to inform them about us. I had asked Allāh, the Mighty and High, to keep the reports about us hidden from them. The letter is with a black woman who has not taken the (main) road. Take your sword, follow her and take the letter from her. Let her go and bring it to me."

Then he summoned al-Zubayr b. al-'Awwām and told him: "Go

with ʻAlī b. Abī Ṭālib on this mission."

The two departed and did not take the (main) road. They caught up with the woman. Al-Zubayr got to her first and he asked her about the letter which was with her. She denied it and swore that she had nothing with her and wept.

"I can't see a letter with her, Abū al-Ḥasan," said al-Zubayr. "Let us go to the Apostle of Allāh, may Allāh bless Him and His Family, and tell him that her journey is innocent."

"The Apostle of Allāh, may Allāh bless Him and His Family, told me that she had a letter," replied the Commander of the Faithful, peace be on him, "and he ordered me to take it from her. You say that she has no letter."

Then he drew his sword and advanced towards her and said to her: "By Allāh, if you don't produce the letter, I will compel you to show it. Then I'll cut off your head."

"Since there is no escape from doing that," she answered, "turn your face away from me, Ibn Abī Ṭālib."

He, peace be on him, turned his face away from her. She took off her veil and took the letter from her hair. The Commander of the Faithful, peace be on him, caught hold of it and took it to the Prophet, may Allāh bless Him and His Family. He ordered that the call should be given: "The prayer is general" (al-ṣalāt jāmiʻa) (i.e. everybody should attend). The call was made among the people and they gathered at the mosque until it was crowded with them. Then the Prophet, may Allāh bless Him and His Family, went up on the pulpit and he took the letter in his hand. He said: "People, I had asked Allāh, the Mighty and High, to keep reports about us hidden from Quraysh. However, one of you wrote to the Meccans to inform them about us. Let the writer of the letter stand up. If he does not, then revelation will make him known."

No one stood up. The Prophet repeated his words a second time. He said: "Let the writer of the letter stand up. If he does not, then revelation will make him known:"

(At this) Ḥāṭib b. Abī Balta'a stood up. He was shaking like a palm-bough on the day of a violent storm. He said: "Apostle of Allāh, I am the writer of the letter. I have committed no (other) act of hypocrisy after becoming a Muslim, nor have I had any (other) doubt after my firm conviction (in Islam)."

"What made you write this letter?" the Prophet, may Allāh bless Him and His Family, asked him.

"Apostle of Allāh, I have a family in Mecca," he said, "and I have no other tribal connections ('ashīra) there. I was afraid that they would be overcome on account of us. So this letter of mine was (an attempt) to offer a helping hand to my family, (to give) support to them. I did not do it because of any doubt on my part in the religion."

"Apostle of Allāh," said 'Umar b. al-Khaṭṭāb, "command me to kill him. He has committed an act of hypocrisy."

"He is one of the men (who fought) at Badr," said the Apostle of Allāh, may Allāh bless Him and His Family. "Perhaps Allāh will look down on them and forgive them. Take him out of the mosque."

[He reported:]

Then people began to push him in the back until they had taken him out, while he had been turning towards the Prophet, may Allāh bless Him and His Family, begging him for mercy. The Apostle of Allāh ordered him to be brought back and he said to him: "I have forgiven you and your crime, so seek the forgiveness of your Lord and never do such a crime as you committed again."

The achievement belongs with his other achievements, peace be on him, which have been mentioned earlier. As a result of it, it was possible for the Apostle of Allāh, may Allāh bless Him and His Family, to organise the entry into Mecca, to protect against trouble from the people and to avoid their knowledge of his intention towards them until he had come upon them unawares. In the matter of extracting the letter from the woman, he could only trust the Commander of the Faithful, peace be on him. In that he did not regard anyone else as a faithful adviser except him, nor did he rely on anyone else. Through him, peace be on him, the task was carried out and his purpose attained; his organization was properly established as was the advantage of the Muslims in the matter, and the religion was able to be spread. No merit can be attributed to al-Zubayr in terms of him being sent with the Commander of the Faithful, peace be on him, because he did not fulfil his task and he was useless in carrying it out. The Apostle of Allāh, may Allāh bless Him and His Family, only sent him because he was included in the number of Banū Hāshim through his mother, Ṣafiyya, daughter of 'Abd al-Muṭṭalib, and he wanted to entrust the task, in the execution of which there was need for secrecy, to those specially belonging to his family. Al-Zubayr had courage and boldness in addition to the relationship which there was between him and the Commander of the Faithful, peace be on him. He (the Prophet) knew that he (al-Zubayr) would help him (the Commander of the Faithful) in his mission since they both had (an interest) in the fulfilment of the task and since it referred to them both it so far as what was general to Banū Hāshim was specific to them both. Al-Zubayr was a follower of the Commander of the Faithful, peace be on him. There occurred from him during his mission (actions) which did not conform to correct reasoning and the

Commander of the Faithful, peace be on him, prevented him (from following these actions).

In what we have explained in this story, there is clear evidence for the special achievement and virtue of the Commander of the Faithful, peace be on him, which is shared by no one else. No one else approached him with any merit without him having more than it. Allāh be He Who is praised.

6. The Carrying of the Standard at the Conquest of Mecca.

(Yet another example) is the fact that the Prophet, may Allāh bless Him and His Family, gave the standard to Sa'd b. 'Ubada on the day of the conquest of Mecca and ordered him to carry it in front of him into Mecca. Sa'd took it and began to declare: "Today is the day of slaughter, the day of capturing (any) daughter."

"Haven't you heard what Sa'd b. 'Ubada is saying?" some of the people asked the Prophet, may Allāh bless Him and His Family. "We are afraid that today will (simply mean) to him, attacking Quraysh."

"'Alī, go to Sa'd," he, peace be on him, told the Commander of the Faithful, peace be on him, "and take the standard from him. You be the one to enter with it."

Thus the Apostle of Allāh, may Allāh bless Him and His Family, set right through the Commander of the Faithful, peace be on him, what was about to go astray in the organization through Sa'd rushing forward and attacking the Meccans. He knew that the Anṣār would not be pleased if any (other) person had taken the standard from their leader Sa'd and taken that position from him except one who was similar in circumstance to the Prophet, may Allāh bless Him and His Family, through the exaltedness of his rank, his high position, and the duty of obeying him, and someone who would not make Sa'd delay in giving up that command to him. If there had been with the Prophet, may Allāh bless Him and His Family, someone suitable for that other than the Commander of the Faithful, peace be on him, he would have set the affair right through him, or he would have mentioned there his suitability for what the Commander of the Faithful, peace be on him, undertook. Since decisions are only required by virtue of the actions which actually happened and what the Prophet, may Allāh bless Him and His Family, did to the Commander of the Faithful was to magnify and exalt him, to consider him worthy of what he did consider him worthy in terms of putting right affairs and attaining what would not have been possible through the action of any one else as we have mentioned, it is necessary to judge him in this achievement as someone set apart from others who were not equal to him, and (someone) preferred through the honour of it over all others.

7. *The Conversion of Yemen*

(Another example) of that which is agreed upon by all the historians (biographers ahl al-sīra) is that the Prophet, may Allāh bless Him and His Family, sent, Khālid b. Walīd to the people of Yemen to call them to Islam. With him, he sent a group of Muslims, among whom was al-Barā' b. 'Āzib, may Allāh have mercy on him. Khālid stayed with the people for six months calling them (to Islam) but no one of them responded. That depressed the Apostle of Allāh, may Allāh bless Him and His Family. He summoned the Commander of the Faithful, peace be on him, and ordered him to send back Khālid and those who were with him. However, he told him that if anyone of those who had been with Khālid wanted to stay, he should let him.

[al-Barā' reported:]

I was one of those who followed him. When we came to the first people among the Yemenīs and the news reached the people (generally), they gathered before him. 'Alī b. Abī Ṭālib, peace be on him, prayed the dawn prayer with us, then he advanced in front of us. He praised and glorified Allāh. Then he read the letter of the Apostle of Allāh. The whole of Hamdān became Muslim in one day. The Commander of the Faithful, peace be on him, wrote about that to the Apostle of Allāh, may Allāh bless Him and His Family. When he read his letter, he was pleased and delighted. He prostrated in thanks to Allāh, the Exalted. He raised his head and sat. He said: "Greetings to Hamdān. After the submission to Islam of Hamdān, (the rest of) the people of Yemen will follow (them) into Islam."

This is another achievement of the Commander of the Faithful, peace be on him, which no other of the Companions had done anything like or similar to. For (the Prophet), when he wanted to stop Khālid from carrying on with the mission on which he had sent him and he was afraid that corruption would be caused by him, could not find anyone to succeed him except the Commander of the Faithful, peace be on him. So he asked him (i.e. 'Alī) and the latter undertook it in the best possible manner. And as was Allāh's custom with him, he performed it with success since it conformed to the preference of the Prophet, may Allāh bless him and grant him peace. He was a man of righteousness, gentleness, good administrative ability and sincere intentions in obedience to Allāh, the Mighty and High, (a man) with the ability to guide those of the people who would be guided, and to respond to those of them who responded to (the call of) Islam. He was (an important element) in the building of the religion, the strength of the faith in (explaining) the message of the Prophet, may Allāh bless Him and His Family, according to the meaning he (the Prophet) had traced for him. (Indeed he was capable) of organising matters in a way which delighted him (i.e. the Prophet). The promise of heaven was revealed about him (as was) his delight in his perfection among all the people of Islam. It has been confirmed that obedience is of great importance by virtue of the great importance of the benefit gained by it, just as sin is of great consequence by virtue of the great harm which comes through it. Thus prophets, peace be on them, are the creatures with the greatest rewards by virtue of the greatness of their benefit through their call to the rest of the beneficial things (which can be gained) by acts (performed) by the rest of the people.

8. *Taking up the Standard at Khaybar*

(The two defeated men are identified as Abū Bakr and 'Umar)

Similar to that was the putting to flight of those who were put to flight at Khaybar. The exalted rank of carrying the standard is considered highly. By the (standard-bearer's) being put to flight, there occurred such disarray as could not be hidden from those with discernment. Then the standard was given to another man after that. However, he was put to flight in the same way as the first man had been before. In that there was fear for Islam and its position after two men (carrying its standard) had been put to flight. That troubled the Apostle of Allāh, may Allāh bless Him and His Family, and made public the disobedience to him and the bad attitude towards him. So he said in a (public) announcement: "Tomorrow, I will give the standard to one whom Allāh and His Apostle love. Allāh and His Apostle love him as one who returns to the battle without fleeing: he will not come back until Allāh has brought victory at his hands."

Then he gave (the standard) to the Commander of the Faithful, peace be on him, and victory came at his hands. His words, peace be on him, guided and prevented those who wanted to flee from leaving the rank which had been assigned to the Commander of the Faithful, peace be on him. Thus by the Commander of the Faithful, peace be on him, coming out to attack, giving support to the battle and restoring the situation at Khaybar, which had been beyond everyone else, there is evidence of his unequalled merit which no one else shared. Concerning that al-Ḥassān b. Thābit al-Anṣāri said:

'Alī was ashen-eyed needing medicine, even then he did not find (the help of anyone) to nurse him.

The Apostle of Allāh healed him with saliva. He blessed the healer (raqī) and He blessed the healed.

He said: I will give the standard today to a dauntless man, brave, one who loves Allāh as a follower.

He loves my Allāh and Allāh loves him. Through him Allāh will overcome the fortress returning it to Allāh.

He distinguished 'Alī by that apart from all other creatures and he named him his helper (wazīr) and brother.

9. Delivery of the Verses of Renunciation in Mecca

Similar to that is the story of (the document of renunciation (barā'a)) which the Prophet, may Allāh bless Him and His Family, gave to Abū Bakr so that he could abrogate the alliance with the polytheists through it. When he had travelled far away, Gabriel, peace be on him, descended to the Prophet, may Allāh bless Him and His Family. He told him: "Allāh recites His greeting to you and says to you that the act of renunciation should not be performed for you except by yourself or a man (related) to you."

The Apostle of Allāh, may Allāh bless Him and His Family, summoned 'Alī, peace be on him, and told him: "Ride my camel, al-'Aḍbā', and go after Abū Bakr. Take (the document of) renunciation from him and go with it to Mecca. You abrogate the alliance with the polytheists through it. Give Abū Bakr the choice of continuing to ride with you or of returning to me."

The Commander of the Faithful, peace be on him, rode al-'Aḍbā', the camel of the Apostle of Allāh, may Allāh bless Him and His Family and caught up with Abū Bakr. The latter was disturbed at being caught up with by him.

"Why have you come, Abū al-Ḥasan?" he asked as he greeted him. "Are you going to travel with me? Or is it for some other reason?"

"The Apostle of Allāh, may Allāh bless Him and His Family, ordered me to come after you," the Commander of the Faithful, peace be on him, said, "to take the verses of renunciation (barā'a) from you and to abrogate the treaty with the polytheists through them. He ordered me to let you choose between going with me or returning to him."

"Indeed, I will return to him," he said.

He went back to the Prophet, may Allāh bless Him and His Family. When he came to him, he said: "Apostle of Allāh, you regarded me as worthy to undertake a mission on account of which men craned their necks towards me. When I had set out on it, you dismissed me from it. What has come down in revealed message (Qur'ān) concerning me?"

"The trusty one, Gabriel, peace be on him, came down to me from Allāh, the Mighty and Exalted," the Prophet, may Allāh bless Him and His Family, answered, "with (the command) that: 'The act of renunciation should not be performed for you except by yourself or a man (related) to you.' 'Alī is related to me and it should only be performed for me by 'Alī."

(This account occurs) in a famous tradition. The abrogation of a treaty was limited to the one who made it or to one who could take his place in terms of the necessary obedience, dignified regard, high rank, noble position, and one who was above suspicion in his actions and whose words could not be (legitimately) opposed - one who was the same as the maker of the treaty and whose affair was his affair. Since it was judged by what he had done in the past it was established and was secure from opposition and (since) the strength of Islam, the completion (of the laws) of religion, the well-being of the Muslims, the conquest of Mecca, and the good organization of well-being was involved in the abrogation of the treaty, Allāh, the Exalted, preferred that that should be entrusted to one who was illustrious in name, exalted in fame. This indicates the outstanding merit of such a man; it gives evidence of his high rank and distinguishes him from others. Those (things) belonged to the Commander of the Faithful, peace be on him. None of the other people had merit which came near to the merit which we have described nor did any of them share with him (any) of what we have explained.

Examples of what we have mentioned are so numerous that our work in presenting them would lengthen this book, and the speeches would encompass it. It is sufficient for those of intelligence to include what we have set out in the aims which we have outlined.

THE MILITARY EXPLOITS OF THE COMMANDER OF THE FAITHFUL

As for armed struggle (jihād) by which the rules of Islam were established and by the establishment of which the religious stipulations and laws of the community (milla) were settled, the Commander of the Faithful, peace be on him, was so outstanding that his fame is spread among men and reports about him are abundant both among his special followers and the general populace. The learned do not differ on that nor do the specialists in law dispute its truth. The only doubt (which could be raised) about that would be (as a result of) the deliberate neglect of one who did not consider the historical reports. None of those who reflect on the account can reject it except an obstinate liar who has no shame.

The Battle of Badr

An example of that is what he did at the Battle of Badr, which is mentioned in the Qur'ān. It was the first battle in which there was a test (of the Muslims') faith. Fear filled the hearts of a number of Muslims and they wanted to hold back from it out of that fear and dislike, as is shown absolutely in the Explanation (tibyān i.e. Qur'ān) where He, may His name be exalted, speaks of them in what He reports of them with full explanation and clarity: Similarly your Lord brought you out of your house according to the truth while a group of believers were unwilling to (follow you) and were disputing with you about the right course after it had been explained as though they were being driven to death while they were watching. (VIII 5-6). Concerning the verses connecting that to Allāh's words: Do not be like those who came out of their houses in insolence and as hypocritical people to stop (them) from the path of Allāh. And Allāh encompasses what they do (VIII 47) to the end of the sūra.

Most accounts of their circumstances in that follow each other; even though the expressions may be different yet their import agrees. The brief outline of the account of this attack is that the polytheists came to Badr intent on battle and determined to gain victory in it because of their vast equipment, their number, supplies and men. At that time the Muslims were a group, few in number. Some of them came (to the battle) unwillingly and showed their reluctance and compulsion. Quraysh challenged them to single combat and called on them to draw up in battle line and to take the field. They suggested that equals (in rank) among them should meet (in battle). The Anṣār delayed coming forward. Indeed, the Prophet, may Allāh bless Him and His Family, stopped them from doing that.

"The people have asked for equals to them," he told them. Then he ordered 'Alī to go out against them. He summoned Ḥamza b. 'Abd al-Muṭṭalib and 'Ubayda b. al-Ḥārith, the pleasure of Allāh be with them, to go forward with him.

When they had drawn up before them, the people did not accept them at first because they were wearing helmets.

"Who are you?" they asked.

They told them their ancestry.

"Noble equals," they replied. Then the battle began between them.

Al-Walīd came out against the Commander of the Faithful, peace be on him. Soon he (i.e. the Commander of the Faithful) killed him. 'Utba came out against Ḥamza, may Allāh be pleased with him, and Ḥamza killed him. Shayba came out against 'Ubayda, may Allāh have mercy on him. Blows were exchanged between them. One of them cut the thigh of 'Ubayda. The Commander of the Faithful, peace be on him, rescued him by striking Shayba with a blow which surprised him and killing him. Ḥamza, may Allāh be pleased with him, participated in that.

The killing of those three was the first (sign) of weakening within (the ranks of) the polytheists. Weakness came upon them and terror by which they were overcome with fear of the Muslims. In that way indications of a Muslim victory were (already) apparent. Then the Commander of the Faithful, peace be on him, came forward (to fight) al-'Āṣ b. Sa'īd b. al-'Āṣ after all (the Muslims) except him had drawn away from him. Soon he had slain him. Ḥanẓala b. Abī Sufyān came against him and he killed him. Ṭu'ayma b. 'Adī came against him and he killed him. After him, he killed Nawfal b. Khuwaylid - he was one of the devils (shayāṭīn) of Quraysh. He, peace be on him, continued to slay one of them after another until he had managed (to kill) half of those of them who were killed. There were seventy men (killed) in all, of whom all the Muslims who were present at al-Badr together with three thousand angels who had been sent undertook the killing of half of them while the Commander of the Faithful, peace be on him, undertook the killing of the other half alone with Allāh's help for him, His support, success and victory. Thus victory was brought about at his hands. The matter was finally sealed by the Prophet, may Allāh bless Him and His Family, taking a handful of pebbles and throwing it into their faces while he said, "May their faces be deformed in ugliness (through the evil eye)." None of them remained without turning their backs in flight. Allāh had been sufficient in battle for the believers through the Commander of the Faithful and his partners in support of religion, who were from the special group of family of the Apostle, peace be on Him and His Family, and those who supported him among the noble angels. As Allāh the Most High said: Allāh was sufficient in the battle for the believers. Allāh was Strong and Mighty. (XXXIII 25)

The narrators, both non-Shī'a ('āmma) and Shī'a (khāṣṣa), confirmed the names of those of the polytheists whom the Commander of the Faithful killed at Badr; (this has been established) with agreement and accord about what they have reported. Among those whom they named were:

1.\ Al-Walīd b. 'Utba: he, as we have mentioned before, was brave, daring, brazen and murderous; a man whom men were terrified of;

2.\ Al-'Āṣ b. Sa'īd: he was a very awesome man whom (even) heroes feared and he was the man from whom 'Umar b. al-Khaṭṭab fled - the story of him concerning what we have just mentioned is well known and we will present it later, Allāh willing;

3.\ Ṭu'ayma b. 'Adī b. Nawfal: he was one of the leaders of the misguided people;

4.\ Nawfal b. Khuwaylid: he was one of the fiercest in opposition to the Apostle of Allāh, may Allāh bless Him and His Family, and Quraysh used to give him precedence and great position and obey him. He was the one who bound Abū Bakr and Ṭalḥa together in Mecca before the emigration (hijra) and tied them with a rope and tortured them night and day so that he might interrogate them about their involvement (amr). When the Apostle of Allāh, may Allāh bless Him and His Family, knew of his presence at Badr, he beseeched Allāh that his affair would be sufficient (to destroy) him. He said: "O Allāh, be sufficient on my behalf (to destroy) Nawfal b. Khuwaylid." Thus, the Commander of the Faithful, peace be on him, killed him.

5.\ Zam'a b. al-Aswad;

6.\ 'Aqīl b. al-Aswad;

7.\ Al-Ḥārith b. Zam'a;

8.\ Al-Naḍr b. al-Ḥārith b. 'Abd al-Dār;

9.\ 'Umayr b. 'Uthman b. Ka'b b. Taym, the paternal uncle of Ṭalḥa b. 'Ubayd Allāh;

10.\ 'Uthmān

11.\ and Mālik, the two sons of 'Ubayd Allāh and brothers of Ṭalḥa b. 'Ubayd Allāh;

12.\ Mas'ūd b. Abī Umayya b. al-Mughīra;

13.\ Qays b. al-Fākih b. al-Mughīra;

14.\ Ḥudhayfa b. Abī Ḥudhayfa b. al-Mughīra;

15.\ Abū Qays b. al-Walīd b. al-Mughīra;

16.\ Ḥanẓala b. Abī Sufyān;

17.\ ‘Amr b. Makhzūm;

18.\ Abū al-Mundhir b. Abī Rifā‘a;

19.\ Munabbih b. al-Ḥajjāj al-Sahmī;

20.\ Al-‘Āṣ b. Munabbih;

21.\ ‘Alqama b. Kalda;

22.\ Abū al-‘Āṣ b. Qays b. ‘Adī;

23.\ Mu‘āwiya b. al-Mughīra b. Abī al-‘Āṣ;

24.\ Lawdhān b. Rabī‘a;

25.\ ‘Abd Allāh b. al-Mundhir b. Abī Rifā‘a;

26.\ Mas‘ūd b. Umayya b. al-Mughīra;

27.\ Ḥājib b. Sā’ib b. ‘Uwaymir;

28.\ Aws b. al-Mughīra b. Lawdhān;

29.\ Zayd b. Mulīs;

30.\ ‘Āsim b. Abī ‘Awf;

31.\ Sā‘id b. Wahb, ally of the Banū ‘Āmir;

32.\ Mu‘āwiya b. ‘Abd al-Qays;

33.\ ‘Abd Allāh b. Jamīl b. Zuhayr b. al-Ḥārith b. al-Asad;

34.\ Al- Sā’ib b. Mālik;

35.\ Abū al-Ḥakam b. al-Akhnas;

36.\ Hishām b. Abī Umayya b. al-Mughīra.

That is thirty-six men, excluding those with regard to whose (death) there is some dispute or in which the Commander of the Faithful, peace be on him, participated with others. They are more than half those killed at Badr as we have mentioned.

(Here is) a brief survey of the reports which have come down in explanation of what we have put forward.

[The report which Shu'ba related on the authority of Abū Isḥāq, on the authority of al-Ḥārith b. Muḍarrib, who said:]

I heard 'Alī b. Abī Ṭālib, peace be on him, say:

We came to Badr without there being a horseman among us except al-Miqdād b. al-Aswad. We spent the night before Badr and there was not a man among us who did not sleep except the Apostle of Allāh, may Allāh bless Him and His Family. He was standing upright at the trunk of a tree where he performed the ritual prayer and called to Allāh until morning.

['Alī b.Hāshim reported on the authority of Muḥammad b. 'Ubayd Allāh b. Abī Rafī', on the authority of his father, on the authority of his grandfather, Abū Rafī', the retainer of the Apostle of Allāh, may Allāh bless Him and His Family, who said:]

When the people awoke on the morning of the day of the battle of Badr, Quraysh drew up their ranks. At their front was 'Utba b. Rabī'a and his brother, Shayba, and his son, al-Walīd. 'Utba called out to the Apostle of Allāh, may Allāh bless Him and His Family, saying: "Muḥammad, send out against us our equal from Quraysh."

Three young men of the Anṣār went forward against them. 'Utba said to them:

"Who are you?" They gave their lineage to him.

"There is no need for us to take part in single combat with you," he replied. "We only seek (to fight) our kinsmen."

"Withdraw to your positions," the Apostle of Allāh, may Allāh bless Him and His Family, ordered the Anṣār. Then he said: "Arise, 'Alī. Arise, Ḥamza. Arise, 'Ubayda. Fight for your truth with which Allāh sent your Prophet, since they have brought their falsehood to extinguish the light of Allāh."

They arose and arrayed themselves before the people. They were wearing helmets so that they were not recognized.

'Utba said to them, "Speak. If you are our equals then we will fight you."

"I am Ḥamza b. 'Abd al-Muṭṭalib, the lion of Allāh and the lion of His Apostle, may Allāh bless Him and His Family," declared Ḥamza "A noble equal," said 'Utba.

"I am 'Alī b. Abī Ṭālib b. 'Abd al-Muṭṭalib," declared the Commander of the Faithful, peace be on him.

"I am 'Ubayda b. al-Ḥārith b. 'Abd al-Muṭṭalib," declared 'Ubayda. Then 'Utba told his son al-Walīd: "Arise, al-Walīd."

The Commander of the Faithful, peace be on him, came forward against him. At that time they were both the youngest of the assembled company. They exchanged blows. Al-Walīd's blow missed the Commander of the Faithful, peace be on him, and then he warded off the blow of the Commander of the Faithful, peace be on him, with his left hand and (the blow) cut it off.

It is related that he (i.e. the Commander of the Faithful) used to mention Badr and the killing of al-Walīd. He would say in his conversation: "It was just as if I was looking at the flashing of the ring on his left hand. Then I struck him with another blow, brought him down and plundered him. I saw he had a robe of saffron and I realised that he had recently been married."

'Utba advanced against Ḥamza, may Allāh be pleased with him, and Ḥamza killed him. 'Ubayda, who was the oldest of the people, marched against Shayba. They exchanged blows and the sharp edge of Shayba's sword struck 'Ubayda's knee and cut it. However, the Commander of the Faithful and Ḥamza rescued him from Shayba and they killed Shayba and carried 'Ubayda away. He died at al-Safrā'.

Hind, the daughter of 'Utba, recited concerning the killing of 'Utba, Shayba and al-Walīd:

O my eye, profuse with flowing tears, he never withdrew to a better man of Khindif.

His group and the Banū Ḥāshim and Banū al-Muṭṭalib summoned him at morning.

They made him taste the blades of their swords. They stripped him after he had perished.

[Al-Ḥasan b. Ḥumayd reported: Abū Ghāssan told us: Abū Ismā'īl 'Umayr b. Bakkār told us on the authority of Jābir, on the authority of Abū Ja'far, peace be on them, who said:]

The Commander of the Faithful, peace be on him, said: "I was amazed at the bravery of the people at Badr. I had killed al-Walīd. Ḥamza had killed 'Utba and I shared with him in the killing of Shayba. Then Ḥanẓala b. Abī Sufyān advanced towards me. When he was near me, I struck him a blow with my sword and his eyes flowed with tears as he cleaved to the ground, dead."

[Abū Bakr al-Hudhalī reported on the authority of al-Zuhrī, on the authority of Ṣāliḥ b. Kaysān, who said:]

'Uthmān b. 'Affān passed Sā'īd b. al-'Āṣ and said: "Come with us to the Commander of the Faithful, 'Umar b. al-Khaṭṭab so that we may talk with him." They both went.

Sā'īd reported: As for 'Uthmān, he could take whatever place he wished, but as for me, I had to keep to the side of the people. 'Umar looked towards me and said: "What is (the feeling) towards me which I see in you; as if you felt some (animosity) towards me? Do you think that I killed your father? By Allāh, if I had wanted to be his killer and if I had killed him, I would not have made any excuse for killing an unbeliever. However I passed him on the day of Badr and I saw him seeking for battle just as an ox seeks for its mate. His jaws were foaming like a lizard. When I saw that, I became terrified of him and turned aside from him. He said: 'Where are you going, Ibn al-Khaṭṭab?' Then 'Alī directed himself towards him and caught up with him. By Allāh, I remained in my place until he killed him."

'Alī, peace be on him, was present at the assembly (when 'Umar was telling this). He said: "O Allāh, let there be forgiveness; polytheism has gone with what was in it. Islam has wiped out what existed before. Why do you (say that)? You will rouse the people against me."

So 'Umar desisted.

Sā'īd, (later) commented: "Yet it was the only pleasure for me (in the death of my father) that the one who killed him was 'Alī b. Abī Ṭālib."

The people put forward (this story) in another narration.

[Muḥammad b. Isḥāq reported on the authority of Yazīd b. Rūmān on the authority of Urwa b. al-Zubayr:]

At the battle of Badr, 'Alī, peace be on him, advanced toward Tu'ayma b. 'Adī b. Nawfal and thrust his spear at him, saying to him: "By Allāh, you will never oppose us concerning Allāh after today."

['Abd al-Razzāq reported on the authority of Ma'mar on the authority of al-Zuhrī, who said:]

When the Apostle of Allāh, may Allāh bless Him and His Family knew of the presence of Nawfal b. Khuwaylid at Badr, he said: "O Allāh, be sufficient (to destroy) Nawfal on my behalf."

When Quraysh were routed, 'Alī b. Abī Ṭālib, peace be on him, saw him. He was perplexed, not knowing what to do. He directed himself towards him and struck at him with his sword. He took hold of his shield and pulled it away from him. Then he struck his leg as his armour was covering (the top of his body). He cut it and then gave him a final blow and killed him. When he returned to the Prophet, may Allāh bless Him and His Family, he heard him say: "Who has knowledge of Nawfal?"

"I have killed him, O Apostle of Allāh," he, peace be on him, replied.

The Prophet, may Allāh bless Him and His Family, said: "Allāh is greater! Praise be to Allāh who has answered my prayer concerning him."

(The poet) Usayd b. Abī Iyyās said about the exploits of the Commander of the Faithful, peace be on him, at Badr, in order to urge on the polytheists of Quraysh against him:

At every meeting there is a purpose which confounds you, a strong youngster who overcomes experienced full-grown horses.

Your abundance comes from God! Do you not deny (it)? Perhaps the noble free man does deny and feels shame.

This is the son of Fāṭima who has destroyed you in slaughter and death with a single blow not with (wild) striking.

They gave him money to avoid his blows - the action of the servile, a contract which brings no profit.

Where were the mature men? Where were all the chiefs (of the people) amid (these) misfortunes? Where was the best of the valley (al-abṭaḥ)?

He destroyed them with violent death and blows which he struck as he used his sword whose blade did not (cease) striking (down).

The Battle of Uḥud

The battle of Uḥud came after Badr. During it the standard of the Apostle of Allāh, may Allāh bless Him and His Family, was carried by the Commander of the Faithful, peace be on him, as it had been at Badr. On that day he also carried the banner (liwā'): he was noted as the one who carried both the standard and the banner. The same (individual) success was (achieved) by him during this battle as had been (achieved) by him at Badr. However, during it he was outstanding for his noble (suffering) of misfortune, his endurance and his firm footedness when the feet of other men were slipping (backwards). His distress for the Apostle of Allāh, may Allāh bless Him and His Family, was such as no other of the people of Islam had. Allāh killed through his sword (many of) the leaders of the people of polytheism and misguidance. Through him Allāh dispelled the tragedy (of the battle) from His Prophet, peace be on him. Gabriel, peace be on him, spoke to the angels of heaven and earth about his merit in that situation. The Prophet of guidance, peace be on him, set him apart by virtue of his characterising him with what was hidden from ordinary men.

[Of that is what Yaḥyā b. 'Umāra reported: al-Ḥasan b. Mūsā b. Riyāḥ, retainer of the Anṣār, told me: Abū al-Bakhtarī al-Qurashī:]

The standard and banner of Quraysh were both in the hands of Qusayy b. Kilāb. The standard remained in the hand of the sons of 'Abd al-Muṭṭalib, the one of them who was present at war used to carry it until Allāh sent His Apostle, may Allāh bless Him and His Family. The standard and the rest of the things came (under the authority of) the Prophet, may Allāh bless Him and His Family. He settled it on the Banū Hāshim. The Apostle of Allāh, may Allāh bless Him and His Family, gave it to 'Alī b. Abī Ṭālib, at the battle of Waddān; it was the first battle at which the standard was carried in Islam, on behalf of the Prophet, may Allāh bless Him and His Family. It remained with him (i.e. 'Alī) at the events at Badr -- the greatest victory -- and at the battle of Uḥud. At that time the banner was in the hands of the sons of 'Abd al-Dār. However, the Apostle of Allāh, may Allāh bless Him and His Family, gave it to Muṣ'ab b. 'Umayr. He was martyred and the banner fell from his hand. The tribes (men) were looking down at him. The Apostle of

Allāh, may Allāh bless Him and His Family, seized it and thrust it to 'Alī b. Abī Ṭālib, peace be on him. On that day he made him combine the standard and the banner and both of them remain to the present day with the Banū Hāshim.

[Al-Mufaḍḍal b. 'Abd Allāh reported on the authority of Simāk, on the authority of 'Ikrima, on the authority of 'Abd Allāh b. 'Abbās, who said:]

Four things were given to 'Alī b. Abī Ṭālib, peace be on him, which were not given to anyone else: he was the first person, Arab or non-Arab, to pray with the Apostle of Allāh, may Allāh bless Him and His Family; he was the one who carried his banner in every march; he was the one who remained with him at the Battle of Mihrās, that is the Battle of Uḥud; and he was the one who took (his corpse) into his tomb.

[Zayd b. Wahb al Juhnī reported through the following isnād: Aḥmad b. 'Ammār told us: al-Ḥimmānī told us: Sharīk told us on the authority of 'Uthman b. al-Mughīra, on the authority of Zayd b. Wahb,8 who said: One day we found 'Abd Allāh b. Mas'ūd in a good mood. We asked him if he would tell us about the Battle of Uḥud and how it had been. "Yes," he replied and he carried on the account until he came to the mention of the battle itself. He said:]

The Apostle of Allāh, may Allāh bless Him and His Family, ordered (us): "Go out against them with the name of Allāh."

We went out and we arrayed ourselves in a long line against them. He positioned fifty men of the Anṣār over the hill-pass. He put one of their number in charge of them and he told them: "Do not leave this position of yours, for if we are going to be killed right up to the last of us, we will be attacked through your position."

Abū Sufyān Ṣakhr b. Ḥarb positioned Khālid b. al-Walīd opposite them. The banners of Quraysh were in (the possession of) Banū 'Abd al-Dār and the banner of the polytheists was in (the hands of) Ṭalḥa b. Abī Ṭalḥa - he was called the leader of the phalanx. The Apostle of Allāh, may Allāh bless Him and His Family, gave the banner of the emigrants (muhājrīn) to 'Alī b. Abī Ṭālib, peace be on him. He went forward and stood beneath the banner of the Anṣār. Abū Sufyān came up to the banner-carriers and declared: "Banner-carriers, perhaps you know that the people will only come forward for the sake of their banners. At the battle of Badr, you only came forward for the sake of your banners. (Today) if you think that you will be too weak (to defend) them, give them to us to defend them for you."

Ṭalḥa b. Abī Ṭalḥa became angry and said: "Are you saying this to us? By Allāh, I will lead you with them today to the waters of death." Ṭalḥa was called the leader of the phalanx.

He advanced and 'Alī b. Abī Ṭālib, peace be on him, advanced.

"Who are you?" demanded 'Alī.

"I am Ṭalḥa b. Abī Ṭalḥa," he replied. "I am the leader of the phalanx. Who are you?"

"I am 'Alī b. Abī Ṭālib b. 'Abd al-Muṭṭalib," he answered.

They drew together and blows were exchanged between them. 'Alī b. Abī Ṭālib, peace be on him, struck him on the front of the head. His eyes flowed with tears and he let out a scream, the like of which has never been heard (before or since). The banner fell from his hand. His brother called Mūs'āb seized hold of it but 'Āṣim b. Thābit shot an arrow at him and killed him. Then his brother called 'Uthman seized hold of it. Again 'Āṣim b. Thābit shot an arrow and killed him.

Their slave called Ṣawāb, who was one of the fiercest of men, took hold of it. 'Alī, peace be on him, struck his hand and cut it. He took the banner with his left hand and he cut that (too). He took hold of the banner with his chest and both his severed arms. 'Alī, peace be on him, struck him on the crown of his head and he fell prostrate.

The people were put to flight and the Muslims occupied themselves with spoils. When the men at the mountain-pass saw the people plundering, they said: "Those men will take (all) the spoils while we stay (here)."

They asked their leader, 'Abd Allāh b. 'Umar b. Ḥazm: "We want to take part in the plunder like the people are."

"The Apostle of Allāh, may Allāh bless Him and His Family, has ordered me not to leave this position," he replied.

"He ordered you to do that without knowing that the matter would come to what we now see," they told him and went off towards the booty leaving him behind. He remained in his position. Khālid b. al-Walīd attacked and killed him. Then (Khālid) came up behind the Apostle of Allāh, may Allāh bless Him and His Family, making straight for him. He could see the Prophet, may Allāh bless Him and His Family, amid a small troop of his Companions. He said to those with him: "Behold this is the man you want. Your business is with him."

They attacked him as one, striking with swords, thrusting with spears, shooting arrows and hurling stones. The Companions of the Prophet, may Allāh bless Him and His Family, began to fight to (defend) him until seventy of them were killed. The Commander of the Faithful, peace be on him, Abū Dujāna and Sahl b. Ḥunayf supported the people in defending the Prophet, may Allāh bless Him and His Family. The polytheists attacked them. The Apostle of Allāh, may Allāh bless

Him and His Family, had been overcome by faintness from (a wound) which he had received. He opened his eyes and saw the Commander of the Faithful, peace be on him.

"'Alī," he said, "what have the people done?"

"They have broken their pledge and turned their tracks in flight," he answered. "But these who have shown purposefulness will be sufficient for me (to carry out) my purpose."

The Commander of the Faithful, peace be on him, attacked them and routed them. Then he went back (to the Prophet), who had been attacked from another side. He launched himself against them and routed them. Abū Dujāna and Sahl b. Ḥunayf stood beside him, each with a sword in his hand, in order to defend him. Fourteen of his Companions who had fled came back to him. Among them were Ṭalḥa b. 'Ubayd Allāh and 'Āṣim b. Thābit.

The rest had gone up the hill and people began to cry out throughout Medina: "The Prophet has been killed." As a result of that their spirits abandoned them, and defeated and confused they scattered to right and left.

Hind, the daughter of 'Utba, had urged a savage man to kill the Apostle of Allāh, or the Commander of the Faithful or Ḥamza b. 'Abd al-Muṭṭalib, peace be on them. He had told her: "As for Muḥammad, there is no way I can get to him because his Companions always surround him. In the case of 'Alī, when he fights, he is more wary than a wolf. However, I am quite hopeful with regard to Ḥamza, for when he becomes angry, he does not see what is in front of him."

At that time, Ḥamza could be recognized by an ostrich feather (he wore) on his breast. The savage man lay in wait for him. He reported: "My lance quivered (in my hand) until I was in a good position to hurl it at him. Then it struck him just above the thigh and pierced it. I left him until when he was cold (with death), I went back to him and took my spear from him. Meanwhile the Muslims had been distracted by their flight from (what had happened between) him and me."

Hind had come forward and ordered Ḥamza's stomach to be split open, his liver to be cut out and his body to be mutilated. They cut off his nose and ears. The Apostle of Allāh, may Allāh bless Him and His Family, was also too occupied to be aware of what had happened to him.

[The narrator of the account - Zayd b. Wahb - reported:] I asked Ibn Mas'ūd: "Did the people flee from the Apostle of Allāh, may Allāh bless Him and His Family, so that only 'Alī b. Abī Ṭālib, peace be on him, Abū Dujāna and Sahl b. Ḥunayf remained with him?"

"Ṭalḥa b. 'Ubayd Allāh joined them," he answered.

"Where were Abū Bakr and 'Umar?" I asked.

"They were among those who had turned their backs," he answered.

"Where was 'Uthmān?" I asked.

"He only came three hours after the battle," he replied. The Apostle of Allāh, may Allāh bless Him and His Family, said to him: "Have you brought a petition for (your absence from) it?"

"Where were you?" I (i.e. Zayd) asked (Ibn Mas'ūd).

"I was among those who had turned their backs (in flight)," he said.

"Who told you about this, then?" I enquired.

"'Āṣim and Sahl b. Ḥunayf," was his answer.

"The confirmation of 'Alī in that position is a source of wonder," I said.

"You may well be amazed at that," he said, "for the angels themselves were amazed at it. Didn't you know that Gabriel, peace be on him, said, as he was ascending to heaven: "There is no sword except Dhū al-Fiqār; there is no young man except 'Alī?"

"How is that known about Gabriel, peace be on him?" I asked.

"The people heard a voice crying that, in the sky," was his reply. "They asked the Prophet, may Allāh bless Him and His Family, about it. He told them that that was Gabriel."

[In the account of 'Imrān b. Ḥusayn, he reported:]

At the battle of Uḥud when the people scattered from the Apostle of Allāh, may Allāh bless Him and His Family, 'Alī, peace be on him, came, girding his sword. He stood in front of him and the Apostle of Allāh, may Allāh bless Him and His Family, raised his head and asked: "Why haven't you fled with the people?" "Apostle of Allāh, would I return to being an unbeliever after I had submitted to Islam?" he answered.

(The Prophet) pointed out to him some of the enemy who had come down from the hill. ('Alī) attacked them and put them to flight. Then, (the Prophet) pointed out to him some more of the enemy. Again he attacked them and put them to flight. The Prophet then pointed out to him another group of the enemy. Yet again he attacked them and put them to flight.

Gabriel, peace be on him, came and said: "The angels are amazed, and we are amazed with them, at the selflessness of 'Alī."

"What could prevent him from being like this?" replied the Apostle of Allāh, may Allāh bless Him and His Family. "He is from me and I am from him." "And I, Apostle of Allāh, am from you both," said Gabriel.

[Al-Ḥakam b. Ẓuhayr reported on the authority of al-Suddī, on the authority of his father, on the authority of Ibn 'Abbās:]

On that day Ṭalḥa b. Abī Ṭalḥa went forward, stood between the two ranks and called out: "Companions of Muḥammad, you claim that Allāh will hurry us towards hellfire through your sword and that we will hurry you towards heaven with our swords. Which of you will come forward to fight me in single combat?" The Commander of the Faithful, peace be on him, went forward and declared: "By Allāh, today I will not leave you until I have hurried you towards hell-fire with my sword."

The two men exchanged blows. 'Alī b. Abī Ṭālib, peace be on him, struck him on both his legs and cut them. He fell down and was overcome. He said to 'Alī: "I implore you before Allāh and kinship (to leave me), cousin."

Then he withdrew from him to his position. The Muslims said to him: "You have not finished him."

"He implored me by Allāh and kinship (to leave him)," ('Alī) told them, "but he will never survive after that."

Ṭalḥa died where he was. The good news of that was reported to the Prophet, may Allāh bless Him and His Family. He was delighted with that and said: "This is the captain of the phalanx."

[Muḥammad b. Marwān reported on the authority of 'Umāra, on the authority of 'Ikrima, who said: I heard 'Alī, peace be on him, say:]

When the people fled from the Apostle of Allāh, may Allāh bless Him and His Family, at the battle of Uḥud, I became more worried than I have ever been and I was unable to control myself. I had been in front of him fighting with my sword. I went back to look for him. I could not see him. I said to myself: 'The Apostle of Allāh would not flee.' Yet I could not see him among those who had been killed. I thought he had been taken up, amid us, into heaven. I broke the sheath of my sword and said to myself: 'I will fight with my sword without (ever putting it back into a sheath) until I am killed.' I attacked the enemy and they scattered away from me. Then suddenly (I found that) the Apostle of Allāh, may Allāh bless Him and His Family, had fallen to the ground, unconscious. I stood beside his head. He looked towards me and spoke: "'Alī, what have the people done?" "They have lost their faith, Apostle of Allāh," I answered. "They have turned their backs in flight and surrendered you."

The Prophet, may Allāh bless Him and His Family, looked towards a phalanx (of the enemy) which had approached him. He told me: "Drive this phalanx away from me, 'Alī".

I attacked them with my sword and struck out at them to right and left until they turned their backs in flight.

"'Alī, don't you hear the praise for you in the heavens?" the Prophet, may Allāh bless Him and His Family, asked me.

An angel called Raḍwān was calling out: "There is no sword except Dhū al-Fiqār; there is no young man except 'Alī."

I wept with joy and praised Allāh, all praise be to Him and may He be extolled for His favour.

[Al-Ḥasan b. 'Arafa reported on the authority of 'Umāra b. Muḥammad, on the authority of Sa'd b. Ṭarīf, on the authority of Abū Ja'far Muḥammad b. 'Alī, on the authority of his fathers, peace be on them:]

At the battle of Uḥud an angel called out from heaven: "There is no sword except Dhū al-Fiqār; there is no young man except 'Alī."

[Similarly Ibrāhīm b. Muḥammad b. Maymūn has reported on the authority of 'Amr b. Thābit, on the authority of Muḥammad b. 'Ubayd Allāh b. Abī Rafi', on the authority of his father, on the authority of his (i.e. Muḥammad's) grandfather, who said:]

"We still hear the Companions of the Prophet say that at the battle of Uḥud a voice called out from heaven: "There is no sword except Dhū al-Fiqār; there is no young man except 'Alī."

[Sallām b. Miskīn reported on the authority of Qatāda, on the authority of Sa'īd b. al-Musayyib, who said:]

If I had seen the position of 'Alī, peace be on him, at the battle of Uḥud, I would have found him standing at the right of the Apostle of Allāh, may Allāh bless Him and His Family, defending him with his sword when all except him had turned their backs in flight.

[Al-Ḥasan b. Maḥbūb reported: Jamīl b. 'Ṣāliḥ told us on the authority of Abū 'Ubayda, on the authority of Abū 'Abd Allāh Ja'far b. Muḥammad, on the authority of his fathers, peace be on them, who said:]

At the battle of Uḥud, nine persons held the banner (of Quraysh). 'Alī b. Abī Ṭālib, peace be on him, killed them down to the last of them and the enemy were put to flight. On that day (the clan of) Makhzūm tried to escape but 'Alī, peace be on him, destroyed them.

'Alī, peace be on him, went forward to fight al-Ḥakam b. al-Akhnas. He struck his leg off from half way up his thigh and he died from that.

When the Muslims scattered in that way, Umayya b. Abī Ḥudhayfa b. al-Mughīra advanced. He was in armour and he was declaring: "Today is the day (of vengeance) for Badr." One of the Muslims opposed him but Umayya b. Abī Ḥudhayfa killed him. 'Alī b. Abī Ṭālib directed himself towards him and struck him on the head with his sword and it was caught in the middle of his helmet. Umayya struck out with his sword and the Commander of the Faithful, peace be on him, warded off the blow with his leather shield. It (also) got caught there. The Commander of the Faithful, peace be on him, pulled his sword away from his helmet and Umayya also freed his sword from the shield. They both attacked each other again.

'Alī, peace be on him, reported: "I could see a gap (in his armour, below his arm-pit. I struck at it with my sword and killed him. Then I went away from him."

When the people fled from the Prophet, may Allāh bless Him and His Family, at the battle of Uḥud and the Commander of the Faithful, peace be on him, stood firm, the Prophet, may Allāh bless Him and His Family, asked him: "Why don't you go with the people?"

"Go and leave you, Apostle of Allāh!" exclaimed the Commander of the Faithful, peace be on him. "By Allāh, I will not leave you until I am killed or Allāh has fulfilled His promise of help to you."

"Know the good news. 'Alī," the Prophet, may Allāh bless Him and His Family, told him. "Indeed Allāh is one who fulfils his promises, and they will never inflict the like of this on us again."

Then he looked towards a troop which had advanced towards him. He said to him: "Attack them, 'Alī."

The Commander of the Faithful, peace be on him, attacked them. He killed Hishām b. Umayya al-Makhzūmi, who was among them, and the people fled.

Another troop advanced. (Again) the Prophet, may Allāh bless Him and His Family, told him: "Attack them." He attacked them and killed 'Amr b. 'Abd Allāh al-Jumaḥī, who was among them. They also fled. Yet another troop advanced and again the Prophet, may Allāh bless Him and His Family, told him to attack them. He attacked them and killed Bishr b. Mālik al-'Āmirī, who was among them. The troop fled.

After that none of them returned and those of the Muslims who had fled began to come back to the Prophet, may Allāh bless Him and His Family. The polytheists withdrew towards Mecca and the Muslims went back to Medina with the Prophet, may Allāh bless Him and His Family. Fāṭima, peace be on her, met him. She had with her a jar of water. He washed his face with it and then the Commander of the Faithful, peace be on him, followed him. Blood covered him from his arm to his shoulder. He had (his sword) Dhū al-Fiqār with him and he gave it to Fāṭima, peace be on her.

"Take this sword," he told her. "It has been true to me today." He began to recite:

Fāṭima, this sword in not without honour and I am no coward, nor am I blameworthy.

By my life, I have been free from blame in the support (I gave to) Aḥmad (i.e. Muḥammad) and in the obedience (I showed) to a Lord Who knows about (those who perform) the worship (of Him).

Remove the blood of the people from it. Indeed it has offered the cup of death to the family of 'Abd al-Dār for them to drink.

"Take it, Fāṭima," the Apostle of Allāh, may Allāh bless Him and His Family, told her. "For your husband has done his duty and through his sword Allāh has killed the leaders of Quraysh."

The biographers of the Prophet (ahl al-siyar) mention the dead of the polytheists at Uḥud and the majority were slain by the Commander of the Faithful.

['Abd al-Malik b. Hishām reported: Ziyād b. 'Abd Allāh told us on the authority of Muḥammad b. Isḥāq, who said:]

The standard-bearer of Quraysh at the battle of Uḥud was Ṭalḥa b. Abī Ṭalḥa b. 'Abd al-'Uzzā b. 'Uthmān b. 'Abd al-Dār. He was killed by 'Alī b. Abī Ṭālib. The latter killed his son Abū Sa'īd b. Ṭalḥa and his brother Khālid b Abī Ṭalḥa. He also killed 'Abd Allāh b. Ḥumayd b. Zuhra b. al-Ḥārith b. Asad b. 'Abd al-'Uzzā and he killed Abū al-Ḥakam b. al-Akhnas b. Sharīq al-Thaqafi and al-Walīd b. Abī Ḥudhayfa b. al-Mughīra. He killed the latter's brother, Umayya b. Abī Ḥudhayfa b. al-Mughīra. He also killed Arṭa'a b. Sharḥabīl, Hishām b. Umayya, 'Amr b. 'Abd Allāh al-Jumaḥī and Bishr b. Mālik. He killed Sawāb, the retainer of the Banū 'Abd al-Dār.

His was success. The people came back from their rout to the

Prophet, may Allāh bless Him and His Family, (while he was in) the same position in which he had been, defending him apart from them. Allāh, the Most High, sent disgrace down on all of them because of their flight on that day except for him and those of the Anṣār who stood firm with him. They were eight or (as) it has been said four or five. Concerning (the prowess of the Commander of the Faithful in) killing those whom he killed at the battle of Uḥud, his hardship and his noble suffering, al-Ḥajjāj b. 'Alāṭ al-Sulamī recited:
A man who protects Allāh's people (ḥizb) belongs to Allāh -- I mean the son of Fāṭima (i.e. 'Alī), the man with important paternal and maternal uncles.

How two hands acted against him with a speedy thrust when you left Ṭalḥa, lying dead (because of a blow) to his forehead.

You attacked fiercely like a brave man and you scattered them at the foot of the hill when they were descending to the bottom.

You gave your sword a second draught of blood and you did not refuse it while it was thirsty until it had quenched its thirst.

The Campaign against the Banū al-Naḍīr

When the Apostle of Allāh, may Allāh bless Him and His Family, set out against the Banū al-Naḍīr with the intention of besieging them, he set up his tent in the furthest (dry) river bed of the Banū Khaṭma. When it was dark night, a man from the Banū al-Naḍīr shot an arrow at him and hit the tent. The Prophet, may Allāh bless Him and His Family, ordered his tent to be moved to the foot of the mountain, and the Emigrants and Anṣār surrounded him. In the confusion of darkness, they lost the Commander of the Faithful, peace be on him. The people said: "O Apostle of Allāh, we cannot see 'Alī."

He, peace be on him, answered: "I can see him engaged in some enterprise which will bring advantage to your task."

It was not long before ('Alī), peace be on him, came back with the head of the Jew who had shot at the Prophet, may Allāh bless Him and His Family. He was called Gharūr. He threw it down before the Prophet, may Allāh bless Him and His Family. The latter asked him: "How did you do that, Abū al-Ḥasan?"

"I saw this wicked man coming forward bravely," he, peace be on him, answered. "I lay in wait for him. I said to myself: 'What has encouraged him to come out in the middle of the night is that he seeks to catch us unawares.' He advanced with his sword drawn amid a group of nine Jews. I attacked him and killed him. His companions escaped but they are still near. Send me with a group of men and I hope that I will overcome them."

The Apostle of Allāh, may Allāh bless Him and His Family, sent ten men with him. Among them were Abū Dujāna Simāk b. Kharasha and Sahl b. Ḥunayf. They reached them before they could take refuge in the fort and they killed them. They brought back their heads to the Prophet, may Allāh bless Him and His Family. He ordered that they should be thrown in the wells of the Banū Khaṭma. That was the reason for the conquest of the forts of the Banū al-Naḍīr. On that night Ka'b b. al-Ashraf was killed.

The Apostle of Allāh, may Allāh bless Him and His Family, appropriated the property of the Banū al-Naḍīr. It was the first palm grove which the Apostle of Allāh, may Allāh bless Him and His Family, had divided among the earliest Emigrants. He ordered 'Alī, peace be on him, to take possession of that part of it which was (allocated) to the Apostle of Allāh, may Allāh bless Him and His Family. He made it ṣadaqa and it was in (the Prophet's) possession throughout his life. Then it came into the possession of the Commander of the Faithful, peace be on him, after him. It is in the possession of the offspring of Fāṭima to this day.

Concerning the part played by the Commander of the Faithful, peace be on him, in this campaign and his killing of the Jew and bringing the heads of the group of nine to the Prophet, may Allāh bless Him and His Family, Ḥassān b. Thābit recited:

To Allāh belongs any adversity with which you were tested by the Banū Qurayẓa and the men who came in search.

He destroyed their chief and he brought back ten (heads). Time after time he dashed against them and drove them away.

The Campaign against the Allies (Aḥzāb)

The campaign against the allies took place after the campaign against the Banū al-Naḍīr. A group of Jews including Sallām b. Abī al-Ḥuqayq al-Naḍīrī, Ḥuyayy b. Akhṭab, Kināna b. al-Rabī', Hawdha b. Qays al-Wā'ilī and Abū 'Umāra al-Wā'ilī together with a number of the Banū Wā'ilī left for Mecca. They went to Abū Sufyān Ṣakhr b. Ḥarb because they knew of his hostility to the Apostle of Allāh, may Allāh bless Him and His Family, and his (desire) to hasten to fight him. They told him about how he (i.e. the Prophet) had treated them and they asked him to help them to fight against them.

Abū Sufyān told them: "I will support you in whatever you want. Therefore go to Quraysh and urge them to make war on him and give them guarantees of help and support in order to root him out."

They went around the leaders of Quraysh and urged them to make war on the Prophet, may Allāh bless Him and His Family. They said to them: "Our hands will be with your hands and we will be with you until we have rooted him out."

Quraysh answered: "People of the Jews, you are the people of the first Scripture and of former knowledge. You know the religion which Muḥammad has brought and the religion which we believe in. Is our religion better than his religion or is he more endowed with truth than we are?"

"Indeed, your religion is better than his," they answered them.

Quraysh were encouraged because of the war which they had urged them to against the Apostle of Allāh, may Allāh bless Him and His Family. Abū Sufyān came to them and said to them: "God has given you power over your enemy and these Jews will fight alongside you and they will not part from you until all of them are destroyed or until we extirpate him and those who follow him."

At that time their passion to fight against the Prophet, may Allāh bless Him and His Family, became intense. The Jews left and went to the tribes of Ghaṭafān and Qays 'Aylān. They urged them to make war on the Apostle of Allāh, may Allāh bless Him and His Family. They guaranteed them help and aid and informed them of Quraysh's (desire) to pursue that course.

They assembled together. Quraysh came and their leader at that time, Abū Sufyān Ṣakhr b. Ḥarb. Ghaṭafān came with their leader 'Uyayna b. Ḥiṣn, accompanied by the Banū Fazāra. With the Banū Murra was al-Ḥārith b. 'Awf and Mas'ūd b. Rukhayla b. Nuwayra b. Ṭarīf (came) with his people, the clan of Ashja'. Quraysh gathered with them.

When the Apostle of Allāh, may Allāh bless Him and His Family, heard of the gathering of the allies (aḥzāb) against him, and the strength of their desire to fight against him, he consulted his Companions. It was their unanimous view that they should remain in Medina and fight the people if they came against them across the mountain paths. Salmān, may Allāh have mercy on him, suggested to the Apostle of Allāh, may Allāh bless Him and His Family, about a trench. He ordered it to be dug. He himself worked on it as did the Muslims.

The allies advanced against the Apostle of Allāh, may Allāh bless Him and His Family. Their power filled the Muslims with fear and they felt terror at their number and their gathering. They camped near the ditch and remained in their positions for some twenty days without any action taking place between them except for the shooting of arrows and (the throwing of) stones. When the Apostle of Allāh, may Allāh bless Him and His Family, perceived the weakness of spirit of the majority of Muslims as a result of the siege, and their reluctance to fight, he sent to 'Uyayna b. Ḥiṣn and al-Ḥārith b. 'Awf - they were both leaders of Ghaṭafān. He urged to make peace with him, to leave him and to withdraw with their people from the war against him, on the condition that he would give them a third of the produce of Medina. He consulted Sa'd b. Mu'ādh and Sa'd b. 'Ubāda about the terms he sent to 'Uyayna and al-Ḥārith. They said: "Apostle of Allāh, this situation requires us to adopt this plan because Allāh has ordered you to do what you have done with regard to it and inspiration from Allāh has come to you. Therefore do what seems appropriate to you. If you choose to do this on our behalf, then that is our view on the matter." "Inspiration from Allāh has not come to me," he, peace be on him, answered. "However, I saw the Arabs united against you (lit., shooting at you from one bow) and they had come from every side and I wanted to break up their attack against you for a while."

"These people and ourselves used to be polytheists and worship idols," said Sa'd b. Mu'ādh. "We did not know of Allāh and we did not worship him. But then we did not feed them with our produce except by invitation or by selling it. Now when Allāh has honoured us with Islam, has guided us with it and has made us strong through you, shall we give them our property? What need have we to do this? By Allāh, we will give them nothing except the sword until Allāh decides between us and them."

"I realise your attitude," replied the Apostle of Allāh, may Allāh bless Him and His Family. "Therefore remain in your belief. Allāh, the Most High, will never desert his Prophet nor hand him over to (his enemy) until He fulfils His promise."

The Apostle of Allāh, may Allāh bless Him and His Family, stood up before the Muslims and urged them to strive against the enemy. He encouraged them and he told them of Allāh's help.

Leading horsemen of Quraysh volunteered to take part in single combat against (Muslim fighters). (They were) 'Amr b. 'Abd Wudd b. Abī Qays b. 'Āmir b. Lu'ayy b. Ghālib, 'Ikrima b. Abī Jahl, Hubayra b. Abī Wahb - (the last two were both from the clan of) Makhzūm - Ṛirār b. al-Khaṭṭāb and Mirdās al-Fihrī. They dressed for battle and went out until they passed the houses of the Banū Kināna. They called out: "Banū Kināna, get ready for battle."

They went on, with their horses hurrying forward, until they stopped at the trench. After they had pondered it, they said: "This is a cunning trick which the Arabs have never used."

They aimed themselves at a place in the trench which was narrow. They struck their horses and they rushed blindly at it. (Their horses) brought them on to the swampy ground between the ditch and (the hill of) Sulay'.

The Commander of the Faithful, peace be on him, came out with a group of Muslims so that they could hold the gap (in their defences) which these men had charged through. 'Amr b. 'Abd Wudd advanced with the group who had come out with him. He raised his standard so that his position could be seen. When he saw the Muslims, he and the cavalry with him stopped.

"Is there anyone who will engage in single combat?" he called out. The Commander of the Faithful, peace be on him, advanced towards him. "Go back, cousin," 'Amr told him. "I don't want to kill you."

"You have made a promise to God, 'Amr, that no man of Quraysh would give you two courses without you choosing one of them from him," said the Commander of the Faithful, peace be on him.

"Indeed," he replied, "what is that?"

"I summon you to Allāh, His Apostle and to Islam," he said.

"I have no need of that," he answered.

"Then I summon you to fight."

"Go back," he told him, "there was great friendship between me and your father and I don't want to kill you."

"By Allāh, I am willing to kill you as long as you continue to deny the truth," retorted the Commander of the Faithful, peace be on him. At that he became angry and said: "Will you kill me?"

He dismounted from his horse, hocked it and struck its face

until it leapt away. Then he advanced towards ‘Alī, peace be on him, with his sword drawn. He brought his sword quickly against him but he got his sword caught in the shield of ‘Alī, peace be on him. The Commander of the Faithful, peace be on him, struck a (fierce) blow against him and killed him.

When ‘Ikrima b. Abī Jahl, Hubayra b. Abī Wahb and Ḍirār b. al-Khaṭṭāb saw ‘Amr lying prostrate they turned their horses and fled until they rushed across the trench without looking at anything.

The Commander of the Faithful, peace be on him, went back to his former position. The spirits of those who had come out to the trench with (‘Amr) were full of grief while (‘Alī) recited:

He supported stone idols because of his view which lacked judgement while I supported the Lord of Muḥammad because of true guidance.

I struck him and I left him fallen like the stump of a palm tree between sandy ground and hills.

I refrained from taking his clothes even though if I had fallen, he would have robbed me of my clothes.

O people of the alliance (aḥzāb), do not think that Allāh will abandon His religion and His Prophet.

[Muḥammad b. ‘Umar al-Wāqidī reported: ‘Abd Allāh b. Ja‘far told me on the authority of Abū ‘Awn on the authority of al-Zuhrī, who said:]

‘Amr b. ‘Abd Wudd, ‘Ikrima b. Abī- Jahl, Hubayra b. Abī Wahb, Nawfal b. ‘Abd Allāh b. al-Mughīra and Ḍirār b. al-Khaṭṭāb came one day during the campaign of the alliance to the trench. They began to go around it looking for a narrow place along it so that they could cross. They came to an (unguarded) place where they forced their horses to cross. They began to ride their horses in the area between the trench and Sulay'.

The Muslims held back: none of them advanced against them. 'Amr b. 'Abd Wudd began to call for a single-combat while he chided the Muslims saying:

I have become hoarse through calling to all of you, is there anyone who will come forward to fight in single combat?

All that time 'Alī was standing ready to go out and fight against him. The Apostle of Allāh, may Allāh bless Him and His Family, ordered him to sit down and wait so that someone else might take action. However, on that day, the Muslims remained motionless as if birds were resting their heads because of the (great) status of 'Amr b. 'Abd Wudd and their fear of him, and those with him and those behind him.

After 'Amr had been calling for battle for a long time and the Commander of the Faithful, peace be on him, started to stand up again, the Apostle of Allāh, may Allāh bless Him and His Family, said to him: "Come close to me, 'Alī."

He went close to him and (the Prophet) took off his turban from his own head and put it on him and he gave him his sword, saying: "Carry out your task." Then he said: "O Allāh, give him assistance."

He ran out towards 'Amr. With him went Jābir b. 'Abd Allāh al-Anṣāri, may Allāh have mercy on him, so that he might see what happened between the two men. When the Commander of the Faithful, peace be on him, reached 'Amr, he said to him: "'Amr, in the days of ignorance (before the Prophet's mission), you used to say: 'No one will summon me to three - meaning al-Lāt, al-'Uzzā (and Manāt) - without me accepting them or one of them.'" "Indeed," he replied.

"I summon you to the testimony that there is no God but Allāh and that Muḥammad is the Apostle of Allāh, and to submit to Allāh, Lord of the worlds," he said. "Cousin," he answered, "delay this matter from me for a time."

"It would be better for you, if you adopted it," replied the Commander of the Faithful, peace be on him. Then he said, "Here is an alternative." "What is that?"

"That you go back to where you came from," he replied.

"The women of Quraysh would never accept that," he answered. "Then here is yet another alternative." "What is that?"

"That you dismount and fight me," ('Alī) replied.

'Amr laughed and said: "This is not the course that I thought an Arab would desire of me. I am unwilling to kill a noble man like you. Moreover your father was a bosom companion of mine. (Go back, you are only a young man. I only want to fight the two older men (shaykhayn) of Quraysh, Abū Bakr and 'Umar.)"

"But I want to fight you," retorted 'Alī, peace be on him.

'Amr became angry and dismounted. He struck his horse in its face so that it went back.

[Jābir, may Allāh have mercy on him, reported:]

The dust rose up around them so that I could not see them. But I heard the words Allāhu Akbar (Allāh is greater) coming out of it and I knew that 'Alī, peace be on him, had killed him. His companions fled with the horses jumping over the trench. The

Companions of the Prophet, may Allāh bless Him and His Family, hurried forward when they heard the words Allāhu Akbar, searching for what these people had done. They found Nawfal b. 'Abd Allāh in the middle of the trench. His horse could not jump out of it. They began to hurl stones at him.

"Death should be nobler than this," he shouted to them. "Let one of you come down to me and fight against me."

The Commander of the Faithful, peace be on him, went down to him, struck him down and killed him.

He followed Hubayra and hit him from behind. Then the binding of his saddle was struck and the armour on (his horse) fell off. 'Ikrima fled and Ḍirār b. al-Khaṭṭāb made his escape.

Jābir said (of this): I do not know how to describe 'Alī's killing of 'Amr except with the words which Allāh used to tell the story of David and Goliath where He, may His affair be exalted, says: So by the permission of Allāh, they routed them and David killed Goliath (II 251).

[Qays b. Rabī' reported: Abū Hārūn al-'Abdī told us on the authority of Rabī'a al-Sa'dī, who said:]

I went to Ḥudhayfa b. al-Yamān and asked him: "O Abū 'Abd Allāh, let us talk about 'Alī, peace be on him, and his great qualities, for the Baṣrans say to us that we exaggerate (the qualities of) 'Alī. Aren't you someone who reports traditions about him?"

Ḥudhayfa answered: "Rabī'a, do not ask me about 'Alī, peace be on him. For, by Allāh in Whose hand is my soul, if all the actions of the Companions of Muḥammad, may Allāh bless Him and His Family, from the time of Allāh giving Muḥammad his mission until this present day were put in one balance of the scales and the actions of 'Alī, peace be on him, were put in the other, 'Alī's actions, peace be on him, would outweigh all their actions."

"This is something which no one could accept either standing or sitting," retorted Rabī'a.

"O vile fellow," declared Ḥudhayfa, "how do you think (otherwise)? Where were Abū Bakr, 'Umar, Ḥudhayfa and all the Companions of Muḥammad, may Allāh bless Him and His Family, on the day 'Amr b. 'Abd Wudd (called them to fight)? He called on them to fight in single combat and all the people drew back in fear except 'Alī, peace be on him. He went forward to fight him and Allāh killed him acting through his hand. By Allāh in Whose hand is Ḥudhayfa, his action on that day was greater in measure than the action of the Companions of Muḥammad, may Allāh bless Him and His Family, until the Day of Resurrection."

[Hishām b. Muḥammad reported on the authority of Ma'rūf b. Kharrabūdh, who said:]

At the battle of the Trench, 'Alī b. Abī Ṭālib recited:

Was it against me that the horsemen rushed? Tell my companions about me and it.

On that day, my zeal (to defend the Prophet) prevented me from fleeing.

A penetrating sword in the head is not a blunt one.

I destroyed 'Amr because he became tyrannical, with a sword of Indian iron, (a sword) of pure iron, a sharp cutting (sword).

I went away after I had left him fallen like the stump of a palm tree between sandy ground and hills.

I refrained from taking his clothes even though if I had fallen, he would have robbed me of my clothes.

[Yunūs b. Bukayr reported on the authority of Muḥammad b. Isḥāq:]

When ʻAlī b. Abī Ṭālib, peace be on him, had killed ʻAmr, he came towards the Apostle of Allāh, Allāh bless Him and His Family, with a smiling face. ʻUmar asked him: "ʻAlī, have you plundered his armour, for there is not any like it among the Arabs?"

"I was ashamed to uncover the private parts of my cousin," answered the Commander of the Faithful, peace be on him,

[ʻUmar b. Abī al-Azharī reported on the authority of ʻAmr b. ʻUbayd on the authority of al-Ḥasan:]

When ʻAlī, peace be on him, killed ʻAmr b. ʻAbd Wudd, he cut off his head, and took it and threw it before the Prophet, may Allāh bless Him and His Family. Abū Bakr and ʻUmar got up and kissed the head of ʻAlī, peace be on him.

[ʻAlī b. al-Ḥakīm al-Awdī reported: I Heard Abū Bakr. b. ʻAyyāsh say:]

ʻAlī struck a more powerful blow than any other in Islam - that is the blow (which killed) ʻAmr b. ʻAbd Wudd. He, peace be on him, was struck down by a blow more inauspicious than any struck in Islam - that is the blow of Ibn Muljam, may Allāh curse him.

With regard to (the campaign) against the allies, Allāh the Exalted revealed: When they came against you from above you and from below you and when your eyes looked away and your hearts were in your throats and you were entertaining doubts about Allāh, then at that place were the believers tested and violently shaken. The Hypocrites and those with sickness in their hearts were saying: Allāh and His Apostle have promised us nothing except deceit. (XXXIII 10-12) Allāh relieved the believers from fighting. Allāh was powerful and mighty. (XXXIII 25)

Thus he directed against them censure, blame, reproof and a sermon. By (common) consent the only person excluded from the blame was the Commander of the Faithful, peace be on him, since the conquest had been brought about by him and through his hands. His killing of 'Amr and Nawfal b. 'Abd Allāh was the cause of the defeat of the polytheists. The Apostle of Allāh, may Allāh bless Him and His Family, said: "From this moment we will raid them, and they will (no longer) raid us."

[Yūsuf b. Kulayb reported on the authority of Sufyān b. Zayd, on the authority of Qurra and others, on the authority of 'Abd Allāh b. Mas'ūd:]

He ('Abd Allāh b. Mas'ūd) used to recite this verse (XXXIII 25): Did not Allāh relieve you from fighting (through 'Alī?) Allāh was powerful and mighty.

About the killing of 'Amr b.'Abd Wudd, Ḥassān b. Thābit, may Allāh have mercy on him, used to recite:

The young 'Amr b. 'Abd has come close to the flanks of Yathrib.

Repayment (for his death) is not expected.

You found our swords drawn, you found our good horses were not deficient.

On the morning of the battle of Badr you saw a band who struck you with a blow which was not weak.

You have come (to a state), 'Amr, when you will (no longer) be summoned to a great campaign, or to the mighty execution of repugnant deeds.

It is said that when the poetry of Ḥassān b. Thābit reached the Banū 'Amīr, one of their young men. answered him. He recited in reply to Ḥassān's boasting and great praise about the Anṣār:

By the Sacred House of God, you have lied. You did not kill us but it was by the sword of the Hāshimites, so boast on (about nothing to do with yourselves).

By the sword of the son of 'Abd Allāh, Aḥmad (i.e. Muḥammad) and by the arm of 'Alī in the battle, you gained that. So stop.

You did not kill 'Amr b. 'Abd through your courage. But it was a rival like a great old lion.

It was 'Alī, whose standing in pride has lasted long. So do not make so many claims against us and look scornful.

At Badr, you came out for battle and the leaders of Quraysh openly held back from you and delayed.

Then when Ḥamza and 'Ubayda came against them and 'Alī came forward brandishing his Indian sword,

They said: "Yes these are truly our equals." So they came forward against them quickly since they wished (for battle) and showed pride.

'Alī circled the field in Hāshimite style. (It was he who) destroyed them when they showed haughtiness and pride.

There is no case for your pride over us with anyone else. There is no case for your proud boasts to be considered and mentioned.

[Aḥmad b 'Abd al-'Azīz reported: Sulaymān b. Ayyūb told us on the authority of Abū al-Ḥusayn al-Madā'inī, who said:]

When 'Alī b. Abī Ṭālib, peace be on him, killed 'Amr b. 'Abd Wudd and the news of his death was given to his sister, she asked: "Who attacked him?" "'Alī b. Abī Ṭālib," they told her.

She said: "His death can only be considered (as being brought about) at the hand of a noble equal. There is no reason that my tears should cease since I have shed them for him who has killed heroes and has come forward in battle against an equal. His fate was at the hand of a noble equal. I have not heard of a man with more (right to) pride than this man, O Banū 'Amīr."

Then she began to recite:

If the killer of 'Amr had been any other man, I would have wept for ever.

But the killer of 'Amr cannot be charged with any defect. He was a man who was called of old the foremost of the land.

She also recited concerning the killing of her brother and remembrance of 'Alī b. Abī Ṭālib, the blessings and peace of Allāh be on him:

Two lions attacked one another in a narrow field of battle, each of them was a noble and brave equal.

Both of them wanted to tear the souls away from each other in the middle of the battlefield, either by stealth or by fighting.

Both attended the struggle with zeal. No distracting distraction diverted either man from that.

Then 'Alī, go, for you have never gained a victory like this. That is a true statement in which there is no unfairness.

'Alī, vengeance will be mine. Would that I could come upon him, then my blood-vengeance would be complete.

Quraysh have been humiliated after the death of a (noble) horseman. Thus humiliation is what will destroy them and disgrace is all-embracing.

Then she said: "By Allāh, as long as Quraysh do not avenge my brother, the old she-camel will remain unmarried."

The Campaign against the Banū Qurayẓa

When the allies were routed and turned their backs (in flight) from the Muslims, the Apostle of Allāh, may Allāh bless Him and His Family, turned his attention to the Banū Qurayẓa. He sent the Commander of the Faithful, peace be on him, to them with thirty men from (the tribe) of Khazraj. He told him: "See whether Banū Qurayẓa have left their fortresses."

When he looked over their walls, he heard them cursing. He returned to the Prophet, may Allāh bless Him and His Family, and gave him the information. He said: "Leave them. Indeed Allāh will give us power over them, for He who gave you power over 'Amr b. 'Abd Wudd will not desert you. Therefore wait until the people gather before you and tell them of the victory brought through Allāh. Allāh, the Most High, has helped me by (spreading) terror from here to a distance of a month's (travel)."

'Alī, peace be on him, reported: The people gathered before me. I went up close to their walls. One of them shouted out: "The killer of 'Amr has come against you." Another called out: "The killer of 'Amr has come towards you." They began to shout to one another, telling each other about that. Allāh threw terror into their hearts and I heard a reciter say:

'Alī has killed 'Amr.

'Alī has hunted down a hawk.

'Alī has punished a wrongdoer.

'Alī has weakened (their) affair.

'Alī has brought (them) shame.

I said: "Praise be to Allāh Who has given victory to Islam and suppressed polytheism."

The Prophet, may Allāh bless Him and His Family, had said to me when I had set off towards the Banū Qurayẓa: "Go with the blessing, of Allāh, the Most High. Indeed Allāh has promised you their land and their estates."

I went in the certainty of the help of Allāh, the Mighty and High. I planted the standard at the chief fortress. They received me, while remaining in their fortresses, with curses against the Apostle of Allāh, may Allāh bless Him and His Family.

When I heard them cursing him, I so hated to hear that being said against the Apostle of Allāh, may Allāh bless Him and His Family, that I determined to return to him. Yet he, may Allāh bless Him and His Family, had already appeared and had heard them cursing him. He called out to them: "Brothers of apes and pigs, when we arrive at the court of the people, then how evil will be the morning of those who have been warned."

They replied: "Abū al-Qāsim, you did not use to be an ignorant man nor one who cursed much."

The Apostle of Allāh, may Allāh bless Him and His Family, felt ashamed and went back for a little while. Then he ordered his tent to be pitched opposite their fortresses. The Prophet, may Allāh bless Him and His Family, remained besieging the Banū Qurayẓa for twenty-five days. At last they asked him (for surrender terms), agreeing that they should submit to the judgement of Sa'd b. Mu'ādh. Sa'd decreed the sentence that the men should be killed, the women and children enslaved and their property divided out.

"Sa'd, you have given judgement on them according to Allāh's judgement from above the seven firmaments," the Prophet, may Allāh bless Him and His Family, told him. Then the Prophet ordered their men to be brought - they were nine hundred - and they were taken to Medina. The property was divided out and the women and children were enslaved. When the prisoners were brought to Medina, they were detained in the houses of the Banū al-Najjār.

The Apostle of Allāh, may Allāh bless Him and His Family, went out to the place which is now the market. Trenches had been dug there. The Commander of the Faithful, peace be on him, was present and with him were the Muslims. He had ordered them to come out. He had earlier told the Commander of the Faithful, peace be on him, that the heads (of the prisoners) should be struck (so that they fell) into the trench. (The prisoners) were brought out in groups. Among them were Ḥuyayy b. Akhṭab and Ka'b b. Asad. At that time they were the leaders of the people. They had said to Ka'b when they were about to be taken to the Apostle of Allāh: "Ka'b, what do you think he will do with us?"

He answered: "You don't seem to understand anything anywhere. Don't you see that the man who summons you will not desist and that whoever goes will not return? By God, (your future) is to be killed."

Ḥuyayy b. Akhṭab was brought out with his two hands tied around his neck. When he looked towards the Apostle of Allāh, may Allāh bless Him and His Family, he said: "By God, I do not blame myself for my hostility to you. Yet whomsoever God deserts, is deserted."

Then he approached the people and said: "People, there is no escape from the order of God. It is written and ordained. It has been decreed that such slaughter is the lot of the Banū Isrā'īl."

Then he stood before the Commander of the Faithful, peace be on him, while saying: "Noble victims are slain by a noble hand."

"Rather," replied the Commander of the Faithful, peace be on him, "the select of the people will kill the evil ones among them and the evil ones among them will kill the select. There will be woe to those whom the select and noble kill and there will be happiness for those whom the wicked unbelievers kill." "True," he replied, "but do not plunder my robes."

"It would be most despicable of me to do that," he answered.

"You have covered me, may God cover you," he said and stretched out his neck. 'Alī, peace be on him, struck it and he did not plunder him in front of them. Then the Commander of the Faithful, peace be on him, asked those who had brought him: "What was Ḥuyayy saying while he was being led to his death?"

They replied that he was saying:

By your life, Ibn Akhṭab does not blame himself but whomsoever God deserts is deserted.

He strove until his soul attained (the maximum) of its exertion, and he has attempted to search for greatness in every disturbing situation.

The Commander of the Faithful, 'Alī, blessings and peace be on him, said:

He was a man of earnestness, earnestness in his unbelief. He was brought out to us in bonds as he was forcibly pulled along.

I put my sword around his neck with a blow of one who preserves (the truth). He went to the pit of Hell as the captive he was.

That is the place of return for unbelievers, while those who obey the commands of Allāh are the creatures who will dwell in eternal (happiness).

The Apostle of Allāh, may Allāh bless Him and His Family, chose from their women (Rayḥāna, daughter of) 'Amr b. Khunāfa. Of their women, only one was killed. She had thrown a stone at him when he had come in front of the Jews in order to negotiate with them before the war broke out between them. Allāh protected him from that stone.

The conquest of the Banū Qurayẓa and Allāh's victory to the Prophet, may Allāh bless Him and His Family, was brought about through the Commander of the Faithful, and because of those whom he had killed and because of terror which Allāh, the Mighty and High, threw into their hearts with regard to him. This great virtue has already been described among his virtues, peace be on him, just as this quality has already been mentioned in the enumeration of his qualities, peace be on him.

(The Battle of Dhāt al-Salāsil)

(The part played) by the Commander of the Faithful, peace be on him, in the campaign of Wādī al-Raml - it is reported that it was named the campaign of Dhāt al-Salāsil - has been preserved by religious scholars, recorded by jurists, handed down by traditionists (aṣḥāb al-athār) and reported by historians (naqalat al-akhbār) as being one of the matters which may be attributed to his qualities, peace be on him, and described as one of his outstanding virtues in battle (jihād). (The account) has been agreed as a single unit in sense by all men.

The biographers of the Prophet (aṣḥāb al-siyar) have reported that one day the Prophet, may Allāh bless Him and His Family, was sitting down when a Bedouin came and squatted in front of him and said: "I have come to advise you." "What is your advice?" he asked.

"A group of Arabs," he told him, "have plotted to come and attack you at night in Medina." Then he described them to him.

Then (the Prophet) ordered the Commander of the Faithful, peace be on him, to call out: "The prayer is general (al-ṣalāt jāmi'a, i.e. all should attend the prayer)." The Muslims gathered and the Prophet went up on to the pulpit. He praised and glorified Allāh. Then he said: "People, there is an enemy of Allāh and of you. (News) has come for you that they will attack you at night in Medina. Who will go to the valley?"

One of the Emigrants stood up and said: "I will go there, Apostle of Allāh."

So he gave him the flag and gathered seven hundred men for him. Then he said to him: "Depart in the name of Allāh."

He arrived before the people at mid-morning. They said to him: "Who is the man?"

"I am a messenger of the Apostle of Allāh," he answered. "Either you declare: There is no God but Allāh alone, Who has no partner and Muḥammad is His servant and His Apostle; or I will strike you down with my sword."

"Go back to your master," they told him, "for we are in such numbers as you could have no power over."

The man returned and informed the Apostle of Allāh about that. The Prophet, may Allāh bless Him and His Family, (again) asked: "Who will go to the valley?"

Another man from the Emigrants stood up and said: "I will go there, Apostle of Allāh." He gave him the standard and he set out. Then he returned exactly as his first colleague had returned. Then the Apostle of Allāh, may Allāh bless Him and His Family, said: "Where is 'Alī b. Abī Ṭālib?"

The Commander of tile Faithful, peace be on him, stood up and said: "I am here, Apostle of Allāh."

"Go to the valley," he told him.

"Yes," he replied.

He had a turban which he could not put on until the Prophet, may Allāh bless Him and His Family, sent him on a difficult mission. He went to the house of Fāṭima, peace be on her, and he asked her for the turban.

"Where are you going?" she asked. "Where has my father sent you?" "To Wādī al-Raml," he answered.

She wept in anxiety for him. The Prophet came in while she was still in that state. "Why are you crying?" he said. "Are you afraid that your husband will be killed? No indeed, not if Allāh, the Exalted, wishes (him not to be)."

"Don't deprive me of heaven, Apostle of Allāh," 'Alī, peace be on him, said to him.

Then he set out. With him he took the standard of the Prophet. He went on until he reached people in the evening. He waited until morning and then prayed the morning prayer with his companions. He put them in ranks and leant on his sword as he advanced towards the enemy.

"Men," he called out, "I am the messenger of the Apostle of Allāh to you that you should declare: There is no God but Allāh and Muḥammad is His servant and His Apostle. If you do not, I will strike you down with my sword." "Go back like your colleagues went back," they said.

"By Allāh, I will not go back until you submit to Islam or I have struck you down with this sword of mine," he answered. "I am 'Alī b. Abī Ṭālib b. 'Abd al-Muṭṭalib."

The people became agitated when they realised who he was. Then they became courageous enough to fight against him, peace be on him. He killed six or seven of them. Then the polytheists fled and the Muslims were victorious. They collected up the booty and he set off back to the Prophet, may Allāh bless Him and His Family.

[It is reported on the authority of Umm Salama, the mercy of Allāh be on her, who said:]

The Prophet of Allāh, may Allāh bless Him and His Family, used to take a siesta in my house. When he woke up frightened by a dream, I told him: "Allāh is He Who will give you neighbourly protection."

"True," he said, "Allāh is the One Who will give me neighbourly protection. But Gabriel, peace be on him, told me that 'Alī is coming."

Then he went out to the people and ordered them to meet 'Alī. The Muslims positioned themselves in two ranks with the Apostle of Allāh, may Allāh bless Him and His Family. When ('Alī) saw the Prophet he dismounted from his horse and bent to (the Apostle's) feet to kiss them. The (Prophet) said to him, peace be on him: "Mount (your horse). Allāh, the Exalted, and His Apostle are pleased with you."

The Commander of the Faithful, peace be on him, wept with joy and went off to his house. The Muslims handed over the booty. Then the Prophet, may Allāh bless Him and His Family, asked some of those who were with him in the army: "What did you think of your commander?"

"We were aware of nothing from him except that he never led us in the prayer without reciting in it: Say: He is One Allāh (CXII)," they answered.

"I will ask him about that," said the Prophet, may Allāh bless Him and His Family.

When he came upon him, he asked him, "Why in the statutory

prayers, did you only recite Sūrat al-Ikhlāṣ (CXII) with them?"

"Apostle of Allāh," he answered, "I loved it."

"Indeed Allāh has loved you as you have loved it," said the Prophet, may Allāh bless Him and His Family. Then he said: "'Alī if it was not for the fact that I am concerned that some factions will say of you what the Christians say of Jesus, son of Mary, I would say of you today words such as (after them) you would never pass a gathering of men without them taking the soil from your feet."

The conquest in this campaign was especially due to the Commander of the Faithful, peace be on him, after others had completely failed in it. 'Alī, peace be on him, was especially singled out for praise for it from the Prophet, may Allāh bless Him and His Family. These are virtues the like of which did not occur in anyone else. Many biographers of the Prophet (aṣḥāb al-siyar) have mentioned that it was with regard to this campaign that the Sūrat al-'Ādiyāt (the Swift-Runners) (C) was revealed to the Prophet and that it includes the report of the circumstances in which the Commander of the Faithful, peace be on him, acted there.

The Campaign against the Banū al-Muṣṭaliq

Then there are the reports which are well known among religious scholars of his heroism, peace be on him, against the Banū al-Muṣṭaliq. The conquest was due to him in that campaign after men from the Banū 'Abd al-Muṭṭalib had been struck down. The Commander of the Faithful, peace be on him, killed two of the enemy: they were Mālik and his son. The Prophet of Allāh took many prisoners whom he divided out among the Muslims. Among the prisoners captured on that day were Juwayra daughter of al-Ḥārith b. Abī Ḍirār. The battle-cry of the Muslims during the battle with the Banū al-Muṣṭaliq was: Ya Manṣūr, amit. "O He Who is victorious, bring death," The Commander of the Faithful, peace be on him, captured Juwayra and took her to the Prophet, may Allāh bless Him and His Family. Her father came to the Prophet after the rest of the tribe had submitted to Islam and said: "O Apostle of Allāh, my daughter should not be a prisoner because she is a noble woman." "Go and ask her choice," he told him.

"You are good and kind," he replied.

Then her father went to her and said: "My little child, do not disgrace your tribe." "I have chosen Allāh and His Apostle," she answered. "Allāh has now done this for you," her father told her.

It was settled and the Apostle of Allāh freed her and put her in the group of his wives.

(The Expedition to al-Ḥuḍaybiyya)

(The expedition to) al-Ḥuḍaybiyya followed (the campaign against) the Banū al-Muṣṭaliq. At that time the standard was given to the Commander of the Faithful, peace be on him, just as it had been on many occasions before that. His bravery in the ranks of the men on that day both in war and battle has appeared from what was reported and mention of it has become widespread. That was after the pledge of allegiance (bay'a) which the Prophet, may Allāh bless Him and His Family, took from his Companions and (they gave) their covenants to remain steadfast. The Commander of the Faithful, peace be on him, was the one who took the women's pledge of allegiance on behalf of the Prophet, may Allāh bless Him and His Family. On that day their pledge of allegiance took the form that he threw a robe between himself and them and he rubbed it with his hand and they made their pledge of allegiance to the Prophet, may Allāh bless Him and His Family, by rubbing the robe. Then the Apostle rubbed the robe of 'Alī, peace be on him.

Other things connected with (the expedition to) al-Ḥuḍaybiyya are (as follows). When Suhayl b. 'Amr saw them and came towards their position, he begged the Prophet, may Allāh bless Him and His Family, for peace. Inspiration came down on the Prophet in answer to that, and that he should make the Commander of the Faithful, peace be on him, his writer on that day and the one who would take down the peace treaty in his handwriting.

The Prophet, may Allāh bless Him and His Family, said to him: "'Alī, write down: In the name of Allāh, the Merciful, the Compassionate."

"This is something which is being written between us and you, Muḥammad," Suhayl b. 'Amr intervened. "Therefore begin with something which we accept and write: In Your name, O God."

The Prophet, may Allāh bless Him and His Family, said to the Commander of the Faithful, peace be on him: "Remove what you have written and write: In Your name, O God."

"If it was not for the fact that I obey you, Apostle of Allāh, I would not remove: In the name of Allāh, the Merciful, the Compassionate," the Commander of the Faithful, peace be on him, replied. Then he removed it and wrote: In Your name, O God.

Then the Prophet, may Allāh bless Him and His Family, told him: "Write: This is what the Apostle of Allāh and Suhayl b. 'Amr have agreed upon."

However Suhayl b. 'Amr again intervened, saying: "If I accepted this description of you in this document which is being made between us, I would have admitted prophethood to you, otherwise by agreeing to that I would be witnessing against myself or at least expressing it with my tongue. Remove this name and write: This is what Muḥammad b. 'Abd Allāh has agreed upon."

"Indeed, by Allāh, he is truly the Apostle of Allāh despite your arrogance," said the Commander of the Faithful, peace be on him.

"Write his name as the condition which must be carried out," retorted Suhayl. "Suhayl, woe on you, cease from your obstinate behaviour," the Commander of the Faithful, peace be on him, said to him.

"Remove it, 'Alī," the Prophet, may Allāh bless Him and His Family, ordered him.

"Apostle of Allāh," he said, "my hand will not move to remove your name from association with prophethood."

"Then put my hand on it," he said to him.

He did that and the Apostle of Allāh removed it with his own hand. Then he said to the Commander of the Faithful, peace be on him: "You will be asked to do the same and you will agree to it despite any pain (it causes you)."

The Commander of the Faithful, peace be on him, completed the document. When the truce had been completed, the Apostle of Allāh, may Allāh bless Him and His Family, slaughtered his sacrificial victim, which had been destined for Mecca, where he was.

The system of the organisation of this expedition had been dependent on the Commander of the Faithful, peace be on him. All that took place in it including the pledge of allegiance, the drawing up of the people in ranks for battle and then the truce and the writing of the document, had been due to the Commander of the Faithful, peace be on him. There was in what Allāh had arranged, the sparing of the shedding of blood and the well-being of the position of Islam.

The people have reported of the raid, two virtues with which he was specially singled out, in addition to what we have already mentioned.

We have added these to his great virtues and noble qualities.

[Ibrāhīm b. ‘Umar reported on the authority of those men he relies upon, on the authority of Qāyid, the retainer of ‘Abd Allāh b. Sālim, who said:]

When the Apostle of Allāh, may Allāh bless Him and His Family, set out on the ‘umra (the minor pilgrimage) of al-Ḥuḍaybiyya, he stopped at al-Juḥfa and did not find any water there. He sent Sa‘d b. Mālik with the water-skins. However Sa‘d returned with the water-skins after only going a little way. He said: “Apostle of Allāh, I was not able to continue. My legs stopped moving out of fear of the enemy.”

“Sit down,” the Prophet, may Allāh bless Him and His Family, told him.

Then he sent for another man. He went out with the water-skins but when he reached the place where the first had stopped, he also returned. The Apostle of Allāh asked him: “Why have you returned?”

"Apostle of Allāh," he answered, "by Him Who sent you with the truth as a prophet, I was not able to continue because of my fear."

The Apostle of Allāh summoned the Commander of the Faithful and sent him with the water-skins. Those who were thirsty came out but they were not complaining about his return since they had seen the return of those who had gone before him. 'Alī, peace be on him, went out with the water-skins. Eventually he reached al-Ḥarār and looked for water. Then be brought them back to the Prophet, may Allāh bless Him and His Family. There were shouts of joy for them. When he entered, the Prophet, may Allāh bless Him and His Family, declared: "Allāh is greater (Allāhu akbar)," and he prayed for goodness for him.

In this expedition, Suhayl b. 'Amr approached the Prophet and said to him:

"Muḥammad, our slaves have joined you, send them back to us."

The Apostle of Allāh was so angry that the anger could be seen in his face. He said: "Men of Quraysh, desist or Allāh will send on you a man whose heart Allāh has examined for faith who will strike your necks according to (the requirements of) religion."

One of those present asked: "Apostle of Allāh, is Abū Bakr that man?" "No," he answered.

"Then is it 'Umar?" he asked.

"No," he replied, "it is he who is patching sandals within the enclosure." The people hurried to the enclosure to see who the man was and there was the Commander of the Faithful, 'Alī b.

Abī Ṭālib peace be on him.

A group of men report this tradition on the authority of the Commander of the Faithful. In it they say that 'Alī, peace be on him, told this story and then he said: "I heard the Apostle say: Whoever vies against 'Alī deliberately, will take as his own a place in Hell-fire."

What the Commander of the Faithful, peace be on him, was repairing was the strap of one of the sandals of the Prophet, may Allāh bless Him and His Family. It had broken and he was patching the place and repairing it.

[Ismā'īl b. 'Alī al-'Ammī reported on the authority of Na'il b. Najīḥ, on the authority of 'Amr b. Shamir, on the authority of Jābir b. Yazīd, on the authority of Abū Ja'far Muḥammad b. 'Ali, on the authority of his father, peace be on them, who said:]

The strap of the sandal of the Prophet, may Allāh bless Him and His Family, had broken. He gave it to 'Alī, peace be on him, to repair. Then he walked with one sandal for the distance of about a bow-shot. He approached his Companions and said: "One among you will fight for the interpretation (of the Qur'ān) as he fought with me for its revelation."

"I am that man, Apostle of Allāh," said Abū Bakr.

"No," he replied.

"I, Apostle of Allāh," said 'Umar.

"No," he replied.

The people desisted and looked at one another. The Apostle of Allāh, may Allāh bless Him and His Family, said: "It is the one who is repairing the sandal." Then he indicated with his hand towards 'Alī b. Abī Ṭālib, peace be on him. "He will fight for the interpretation (of the Qur'ān) when my practice (sunna) is abandoned and neglected and the Book of Allāh is distorted and when those who have no right speak of religion, 'Alī, peace be on him, will fight them in order to revive the religion of Allāh, the Exalted."

The Campaign against Khaybar

After al-Ḥuḍaybiyya, there followed the campaign against Khaybar. In that too, beyond any doubt, success was due to the Commander of the Faithful, peace be on him. What has been gathered from the accounts of the reporters makes clear his great merit in this campaign, and uniquely characterizes him in the qualities shared by no other person.

[Yaḥyā b. Muḥammad al-Azdī reported on the authority of Mas'ada b. Yasa' and 'Abd Allah b. 'Abd al-Raḥīm, on the authority of 'Abd al-Mālik b. Ḥishām and Muḥammad b. Isḥāq and other traditionists (aṣḥāb al-āthār), who say:]

When the Apostle of Allāh, may Allāh bless Him and His Family, drew near to Khaybar, he said to the people: "Halt"

The people halted and he raised his hand towards the sky and said: "O Allāh, Lord of the seven heavens and what they shade, Lord of the seven earths and what they maintain, Lord of the devils and what they lead astray, I ask You for the good of this village and the good of what is in it and I seek refuge with You from its evil and the evil that is in it."

Then he went down under a tree in that place. He stayed there and we stayed there for the rest of that day. On the next day at mid-day, the herald of the Apostle of Allāh, may Allāh bless Him and His Family, summoned us and we gathered before him. There was a man sitting with him. He said: "This man came to me while I was sleeping. He drew my sword and said: 'Muhammad, who can save you from me today?' I told him: 'Allāh will save me from you.' Then he sheathed the sword and has remained sitting here without moving as you see."

"Apostle of Allāh, perhaps something has disturbed his reason," we suggested. "Yes," said the Apostle of Allāh, may Allāh bless Him and His Family, "leave him."

Then he turned away and did not pay any attention to him.

The Apostle of Allāh, may Allāh bless Him and His Family, besieged Khaybar for more than twenty days. At that time the standard was held by the Commander of the Faithful, peace be on him. He was suffering from pains in his eyes which kept him from the battle (for a time). The Muslims used to attack the Jews in front of their forts and at the sides. One day they overcame the gate but they had dug a trench around themselves. Marḥab came out on foot to oppose them in battle.

The Apostle of Allāh, may Allāh bless Him and His Family, summoned Abū Bakr and said to him: "Take the standard."

He took it with a number of the Emigrants and they fought without achieving anything. He returned vigorously denouncing the people who had followed him while they were just as vigorously blaming him.

The next day he gave it to 'Umar. The latter went a little way with it and then came back accusing his followers of cowardice while they were also accusing him of cowardice.

Then the Prophet, may Allāh bless Him and His Family, said: "This standard is not for anyone to carry whom they can accuse of cowardice to me. It is for 'Alī b. Abī Ṭālib."

"He has bad eyes," he was told.

"Show him to me and you will show me a man who loves Allāh and His Apostle and whom Allāh and His Apostle love. He takes things up in the right way and he will not flee," he said.

They brought 'Alī b. Abī Ṭālib, peace be on him, leading him to him.

"What is troubling you, 'Alī?" the Prophet, may Allāh bless Him and His Family, asked him.

"Sore eyes which prevent me from seeing and a pain in my head," he answered. "Sit down," he told him, "and put your head on my thigh."

'Alī, peace be on him, did that and the Prophet, may Allāh bless Him and His Family, prayed for him. He spat some saliva into his hand and rubbed it on his eye and his head. His eyes opened and the pain in the head which he had had was eased. He had said in his prayer: "O Allāh, make the heat and the cold obedient." He gave him the standard; it was a white standard. He said: "Take the standard and set forth with it. Gabriel is with you. Victory is in front of you and terror is spread into the hearts of the enemy. Be aware, 'Alī, that they have found in their Book that the name of the one who will destroy them is Īliyā. When you meet them, say: I am 'Alī, then they will forsake (the field) if Allāh, the Exalted, wishes."

The Commander of the Faithful, peace be on him, reported: I set out with it until I came to the fortress. Marḥab came out. He was wearing a helmet in which a stone had made a hole showing the white of his head. He was reciting:

Khaybar knows that I am Marḥab - the carrier of arms, a hero who has been tested.

I answered:

I am he whom my mother called a lion. Like a lion of the forests, fierce in strength,

With my sword I will make you weigh the weight of an ear torn off.

We exchanged blows. I came quickly against him and struck him. I cut through (the place where) the hole (was) in the helmet and through his head so that my sword reached his teeth. He fell dead.

In the account it is reported that when the Commander of the Faithful said: "I am 'Alī b. Abī Ṭālib," one of the rabbis of the people called out to them: "I swear by what was revealed to Moses that you are defeated." As a result such terror entered their hearts that they were not able to bear it.

When the Commander of the Faithful, peace be on him, killed Marḥab, those who had gone out with Marḥab withdrew and barred the gate of the fortress to keep him out. The Commander of the Faithful, peace be on him, advanced against it. He worked on it until he opened it. However, most of the people from the other side of the trench did not come across against him. Thus did the Commander of the Faithful, peace be on him, capture the gate of the fortress. Then he used it as a bridge across the trench so that they might go across and conquer the fortress. They seized booty. When they withdrew from the fortress the Commander of the Faithful, peace be on him, took the gate in his right hand and spread it out many metres over the ground. It used to take twenty men to lock that gate.

After the Commander of the Faithful, peace be on him, had brought about the conquest of the fortress and had killed Marḥab and Allāh had granted their property as booty to the Muslims, Ḥassān b. Thābit al-Anṣāri sought permission from the Apostle of Allāh to recite a poem about him. He told him: "Recite it."

He recited:

'Alī was ashen-eyed, needing medicine, even then he did not find (the help of anyone) to nurse him.

The Apostle of Allāh healed him with saliva. He blessed the healer (raqī) and He blessed the healed.

He said: I will give the standard today, to a dauntless man, brave, one who loves the Apostle as a follower.

He loves Allāh and Allāh loves him. Through him Allāh will overcome the fortress, returning it to Allāh.

He distinguished 'Alī by that apart from all other creatures and he named him his helper and his brother.

[The traditionists have reported on the authority of al-Ḥasan b. Ṣālih, on the authority of al-A'mash, on the authority of Abū Isḥāq, on the authority of Abū 'Abd Allāh al-Judalī, who said:]

I heard the Commander of the Faithful, peace be on him, say: "When I broke down the gate of Khaybar, I used it as a shield and I fought against them with it. When Allāh brought about their humiliation and I had made the gate a means of overcoming their fort, I threw it into their trench."

A man asked him: "How were you able to bear the weight of it?"

"It was only like my shield which was in my hands on other occasions," he answered.

The biographers of the Prophet (aṣḥāb al-siyar) report that when the Muslims left Khaybar, they tried to carry the gate. It could only be lifted by seventy men. Concerning the Commander of the Faithful, peace be on him, carrying the gate, the poet says:

Indeed a man who carried a huge gate at Khaybar in the campaign against the Jews was supported by great power.

He carried the great gate, a gate which was the door to the restless hearts, while the Muslims and the people of Khaybar were mustered.

He threw it down and it took seventy men to undertake the burden of picking it up again - all of these exerting themselves fully to do it.

At last they picked it up with much effort and difficulty and urging of one another to pick it up again.

One of the Shī'a poets also spoke of this, praising the Commander of the Faithful, peace be on him, and disparaging his enemies, as has been reported by Abū Muḥammad al-Ḥasan b. Muḥammad b. Jamhūr, who said: I recited this to Abū 'Uthmān al-Māzinī:

The Prophet sent with his victorious standard 'Umar b. Ḥantama, the blackest of black. He went forward with it until they came out against him.

Without spirit, he bent, he was filled with fear and he withdrew. He brought back to the Prophet a standard which he had refused (to take forward).

He did not fear the shame of it and the blameworthiness of it.

The Prophet wept for him and criticised him for it.

Then he called for a man, noble of vision, who would go forward. He advanced with it amid a group of men, while (the Prophet) prayed for him.

Surely he would not shun it nor be defeated? He brought the Jews to a sad state of withdrawal when he slaughtered.

The leader of their army, a man with a sharp sword, who struck out fiercely. Then he turned to (the rest of) the people after that and scattered them.

The flies flee and every eagle is a lion. Allāh oppressed them because of His love for the family of Muḥammad

And because of His love of those who support (the family) by shedding blood.

The Conquest of Mecca

The campaign against Khaybar was followed by situations which were not the same as those which had occurred before. We now (briefly) allude to them. The majority of these consisted of missions which the Prophet did not take part in. Nor was their importance the same as it had been before. This was due to the present weakness of the enemy and that some of the Muslims did not need the others. We have passed over the enumeration of these matters even though the Commander of the Faithful, peace be on him, played a great role both in word and deed in all of these events.

Then followed the conquest of Mecca. By it the situation of Islam was strengthened and the religion became powerful by virtue of what Allāh, may He be exalted, (had bestowed) on His Prophet, may Allāh bless Him and His Family. Through it the promise was fulfilled, which Allāh had earlier given in His words, may He be exalted: When the help of Allāh and the conquest comes, you will see the people enter into the religion of Allāh in group after group (CX 1-2). And Allāh, the Mighty and High, had said a long time before that: You will enter the sacred Mosque in safety with your heads shaven or trimmed and without fear (XLVIII 27).

Eyes were turned towards it and necks were stretched out (in expectancy) of it. Yet the Prophet of Allāh organised that affair by keeping his journey to Mecca secret and by keeping the purpose of his intentions towards the inhabitants of that city hidden. Allāh, the Most High, had demanded that he keep reports of it concealed from the Meccans so that he should surprise them when he entered the city. In the group to whom the secret was confided was the Commander of the Faithful, 'Alī b. Abī Ṭālib, peace be on him. He was the partner of the Apostle of Allāh, may Allāh bless Him and His Family, in the plan. Then the Prophet, may Allāh bless Him and His Family, spread it to a further group. The matter was arranged with regard to it according to circumstances, in all of which the Commander of the Faithful was unique in merit insofar as no other person participated in them to the same extent.

Among (the indications of) that (is the incident that occurred when) Hāṭib b. Abī Balta'a - who was from Mecca and had been present at Badr alongside the Apostle of Allāh, may Allāh bless Him and His Family - wrote to the Meccans, informing them of the secret that the Apostle of Allāh, may Allāh bless Him and His Family, was coming against them. Inspiration came to the Apostle of Allāh, informing him of what had been done and of Hāṭib's letter being sent to the people (of Mecca). The Apostle of Allāh, may Allāh bless Him and His Family, restored the situation through the Commander of the Faithful, peace be on him. If the situation had not been restored by him, the organisation on whose success the victory of the Muslims depended, would have been put in jeopardy. A report of this story has already been given earlier and there is no need for us to repeat it.

Abū Sufyān came to Medina to renew the treaty between the Apostle of Allāh, may Allāh bless him and grant him peace, and Quraysh, after the incident caused by a group of the Banū Bakr against (the tribe of) Khuzā'a when they had killed some of them. Abū Sufyān intended to restore his leading position among his people. He was afraid of the help of the Apostle of Allāh, may Allāh bless Him and His Family, might give to (al-Khuzā'a). Also he was afraid about what would happen to them (i.e. Meccans) on the day of the conquest. He came to the Prophet and spoke to him about it but he did not give any answer. He left him and met Abū Bakr and caught hold of him. He thought that he could gain his request from the Prophet, may Allāh bless Him and His Family, through him.

"I cannot do that," Abū Bakr answered because he knew that his asking about that would achieve nothing.

Then Abū Sufyān thought that 'Umar might have the same (influence) as he had previously thought Abū Bakr had had. He spoke to him about it but the latter pushed him away with a roughness and a harshness which would almost have corrupted one's view of the Prophet, may Allāh bless Him and His Family.

He turned aside to the house of the Commander of the Faithful, peace be on him. He asked permission to enter and permission was granted. With (the Commander of the Faithful) were

Fāṭima, al-Ḥasan and al-Ḥusayn, peace be on them.

"'Alī," he said, "you are the closest of the people to me in relationship and kin and so I have come to you. Do not send me back as much without hope as I came. Intercede for me with the Apostle of Allāh for what I came for."

"Woe upon you, Abū Sufyān," he replied. "When the Apostle of Allāh, may Allāh bless Him and His Family, has decided on a matter, we cannot speak to him about it."

Abū Sufyān turned to Fāṭima, peace be on her, and said: "Daughter of Muḥammad, can you tell your two sons to give me neighbourly protection among the people? For they are lords of the Arabs to the end of time."

"My sons have not reached the age to grant neighbourly protection among the people," she answered, "and no one will grant neighbourly protection against the Apostle of Allāh, may Allāh bless Him and His Family."

Abū Sufyān was bewildered and felt helpless. Then he went up to the Commander of the Faithful, peace be on him, and said: "Abū al-Ḥasan, I see that matters have become confused as far as I am concerned. (Please,) advise me." "I cannot see anything which will avail you," the Commander of the Faithful, peace be on him, told him. "However, you are the leader of the Banū Kināna. Therefore arise and grant protection among the people. Then go back to your land."

"Do you think that will help me at all?" he asked.

"No, by Allāh, I do not think so," he answered. "Yet, I can find nothing else."

So Abū Sufyān went and stood in the mosque and called out: "I have come to grant protection among the people."

Then he mounted his camel and departed. When he came back to Quraysh, they asked him: "What (was the situation you left) behind you?"

"I went to Muḥammad, may Allāh bless Him and His Family, and I spoke to him," he told them. "But he gave me no answer. Then I went to Ibn Abī Quḥāfa (Abū Bakr) and I found nothing better from him. Then I met Ibn al-Khaṭṭāb and I found him harsh and rough without any kindness in him. Then I went to 'Alī and I found him the gentlest of men to me. He advised me to do something, which I did. By Allāh, I do not know whether it will be of any avail to me or not." "What did he tell you to do?" they asked.

"He told me to grant protection among the people and I did so," he answered.

"Did Muḥammad permit that?" they asked.

"No," he replied.

"By Allāh, the man did no more than play with you," they told him. "It will not be of any use to you."

"No, by Allāh, but I could not find anyone else (to suggest anything)," he answered.

The attitude of the Commander of the Faithful, peace be on him, towards Abū Sufyān was the most correct in terms of the fulfilment of the Muslims' task and for the (success) of the plan. Thus he (Abū Sufyān) brought about for the Apostle of Allāh, may Allāh bless Him and His Family, something, in the attitude of the people, which he would not have been able to achieve, if he had not been able to demonstrate that

'Alī had given Abū Sufyān the truth about his position. Also he achieved this because of his gentleness towards him, so that when he left Medina, he thought that there was some (hope for him). Thus through his departure in those circumstances he ceased from attempting to make a plot by which he might have thrown some disorder into the plan of the Prophet, may Allāh bless Him and His Family. For, if he had left in despair in the way the two men (i.e. Abū Bakr and 'Umar) had filled him with despair, he would have renewed the people's view of fighting against (the Prophet), peace be on him, and of guarding against him in a way which did not occur to them, after Abū Sufyān brought (news of) what he had done to them. For he had stayed in Medina to intrigue to gain his purpose of seeking intercession with the Prophet, may Allāh bless Him and His Family. In that way, he had intended to bring about a situation which would keep the Prophet away from Quraysh and by delaying him from them, (the Prophet) would have missed his opportunity. The success which was brought about through Allāh, the Most High, was connected with the vision of the Commander of the Faithful, peace be on him, insofar as he saw by dealing with Abū Sufyān he would enable the Prophet, may Allāh bless Him and His Family, to occupy Mecca as the latter had intended.

When the Apostle of Allāh, may Allāh bless Him and His Family, ordered Sa'd b. 'Ubāda to enter Mecca carrying the standard, he became aggressive towards the people and showed the anger he felt against them. He entered Mecca shouting:

"Today is the day of slaughter, the day of capturing any daughter."

Al-'Abbās heard him and asked the Prophet: "Haven't you heard what Sa'd b. 'Ubada is saying? I am afraid that he will attack Quraysh fiercely."

"'Alī," said the Prophet, may Allāh bless Him and His Family, to the Commander of the Faithful, peace be on him, "go to Sa'd and take the standard away from him. You be the one who enters Mecca with it."

The Commander of the Faithful, peace be on him, went up to him and took it from him. Sa'd did not stop him from taking it from him. The loss in this matter which would have been caused by Sa'd, was restored by (the action of) the Commander of the Faithful, peace be on him. The Apostle of Allāh, may Allāh bless Him and His Family, did not regard any of the Emigrants or Anṣār as suitable to take away the standard from the leader of the Anṣār except the Commander of the Faithful, peace be on him. He knew that if anyone else had wanted to do that, Sa'd would have refused him, and in his refusal there would have been caused a disruption of the plan and a dispute between the Anṣār and the Emigrants. Since Sa'd would not have lowered his position for any of the Muslims or for all the people except the Prophet, may Allāh bless Him and His Family, and since it would not be sound judgement for the Apostle of Allāh to take the standard from (Sa'd) himself, he appointed someone who could really take his place and could not be distinguished from him (the Prophet), someone to whom no one else within the group should be shown greater obedience. There was no one else characterised by rank and merit for this except the Commander of the Faithful, peace be on him. In such a quality no one else had a share nor was anyone else his equal. It was a lesson from Allāh, the Most High, and His Apostle, with regard to the attainment of public interest through the despatch of the Commander of the Faithful, apart from anyone else, which indicated his choice for decisive affairs, just as it was a lesson from Allāh with regard to whom He chose for prophethood and the fulfilment of the public good by sending him. This revealed their (i.e. the Prophet and the Commander of the Faithful) being the best of all creatures.

The Apostle of Allāh, may Allāh bless Him and His Family, gave an instruction to the Muslims on setting out for Mecca that they should only kill those who fought against them. He guaranteed the security of those who clung to the veils of the Ka'ba except a group of them who had committed evil actions against him. Among these were Miqyas b. Ṣubāba, Ibn Khaṭal, Ibn Abī Sarḥ and two songstresses who had sung insulting songs about the Apostle of Allāh, may Allāh bless him and his family, and lamentations for the Meccans killed at Badr. The Commander of the Faithful, peace be on him, killed one of the songstresses and the other fled until refuge was found for her. A Persian struck her in al-Abṭah during the rule (imāra) of 'Umar b. al-Khaṭṭāb and killed her. The Commander of the Faithful, peace be on him, also killed al-Ḥuwayrith b. Nufayl b. Ka'b. He was one of those who had abused the Apostle of Allāh at Mecca. He, peace be on him, learnt that his sister, Umm Hāni', had given refuge to some people from Banū Makhzūm, including al-Ḥārith b. Hishām and Qays b. al-Sā'ib. He, peace be on him, set out for her house wearing an iron helmet. He called: "Send out those to whom you have given refuge."

By Allāh, they began to act out of fear of him just like birds who let their droppings fall (from the sky). Umm Hāni' came out to him and she did not recognize him.

"Servant of Allāh," she said, "I am Umm Hāni', a cousin of the Apostle of Allāh, may Allāh bless Him and His Family. I am the sister of 'Alī b. Abī Ṭālib, peace be on him. Therefore go away from my house."

"Bring them out," demanded the Commander of the Faithful, peace be on him. "By Allāh, I will complain about you to the Apostle of Allāh, may Allāh bless Him and His Family," she told him.

Then he took his helmet off his head. She recognized him and she came close to him so that she might embrace him.

"May I be your ransom," she said, "I swore that I would complain about you to the Apostle of Allāh, may Allāh bless Him and His Family."

"Go and make good your oath," he told her. "He is at the top of the valley."

Umm Hāni' reported: I went to the Prophet while he was in his tent washing. Fāṭima, peace be on her, was keeping him veiled (from view). When the Apostle of Allāh, may Allāh bless Him and His Family, heard the sound of my voice, he said: "Welcome to Umm Hāni'."

"By my father and mother (whom I would ransom for) you," I said, "I have come to complain to you of the treatment I have received today from 'Alī b. Abī Ṭālib."

"Have you given neighbourly protection to those to whom you (are reported to) have given neighbourly protection?" the Apostle of Allāh, may Allāh bless Him and His Family, asked.

Then Fāṭima, peace be on her, said: "You have only come to complain of 'Alī because he caused the enemies of Allāh and of His Apostle to be afraid."

"May Allāh, the Most High, be thanked for the efforts of 'Alī b. Abī Ṭālib," said the Apostle of Allāh, may Allāh bless Him and His Family. "I grant neighbourly protection to those whom Umm Hāni' gave neighbourly protection because of her position through (her brother) 'Alī b. Abī Ṭālib, peace be on him."

When the Apostle of Allāh, may Allāh bless Him and His Family, entered the (Sacred) Mosque, he found there three hundred and sixty idols. Some of them were attached to others by lead.

"Give me a handful of pebbles," he said to the Commander of the Faithful, peace be on him.

The Commander of the Faithful, peace be on him, picked up a handful and gave it to him. Then he threw it at them, saying: "Say: Truth has come and falsehood has disappeared. Indeed falsehood was ever disappearing." (XVII 81).

Every idol fell face downwards. Then he ordered them to be taken out, thrown down and broken.

In the actions of the Commander of the Faithful, peace be on him, which we have mentioned concerning the enemies of Allāh he killed in Mecca, the fear he caused to those who had been traitors and the help which he gave to the Apostle of Allāh, may Allāh bless Him and His Family, in cleansing the (Sacred) Mosque of idols, his great bravery and his ignoring of kinship in obedience to Allāh, the Mighty and High, - all this - is evidence for him being characterised by great merit which no one else shared as we have already said.

In connection with the conquest of Mecca is the despatch of Khālid b. al-Walīd by the Apostle of Allāh, may Allāh bless Him and His Family, to the Banū Ḥudhayfa b. 'Āmir. They were at al-Ghumayṣā'. He was supposed to summon them to Allāh, the Mighty and High. He only sent him because of the hostile connection which existed between him and them. In the Jāhiliyya, they had seized some women from the Banū al-Mughīra and killed al-Fākih b. al-Mughīra, the uncle of Khālid b. al-Walīd, and they had also killed 'Awf b. 'Abd al-Raḥmān b. 'Awf. It was for that reason that the Apostle of Allāh, may Allāh bless Him and His Family, had sent him. He also sent with him 'Abd al-Raḥmān b. 'Awf, who had a similar hostile relationship with them. If it had not been for that, the Apostle of Allāh, may Allāh bless Him and His Family, would not have deemed

Khālid appropriate for command over the Muslims. We have already mentioned matters connected with him insofar as he had opposed the covenant of Allāh and the covenant of His Apostle and he had worked in the service of the practice of the Jāhiliyya; he had put the authority of Islam behind him; he had renounced the Apostle of Allāh through his action and losses caused by him had to be restored by the Commander of the Faithful, peace be on him. We have explained all this earlier, so that there is no need to repeat it here.

The Campaign against Ḥunayn

Then there was the campaign against Ḥunayn when the Apostle of Allāh, may Allāh bless Him and His Family, sought for help, because of the great number of those gathered against him. (The Prophet), peace be on him, went out towards the enemy with ten thousand Muslims. The majority of them thought that they would be victorious when they saw their gathering, their great numbers and their weapons. On that day, Abū Bakr was full of wonder at the great number. He said: "Today we will never be defeated as a result of being few in number."

As it happened the affair turned out the very opposite to what they had thought and Abū Bakr had contributed to this by his wonder at their (great number). However, when they met the polytheists, it was not long before they (the polytheists) put them all to flight so that only ten men remained with the Prophet, nine of them were Hāshimites and the tenth was Ayman b. Umm Ayman. Ayman was killed, may Allāh have mercy on him. Eventually those who had fled began to return to the Apostle of Allāh, may Allāh bless Him and His Family. They returned one by one until they joined one another and there were (sufficient for) an attack on the polytheists. Concerning Abū Bakr's wonder at the great number, Allāh, the

Most High, revealed: At the Battle of Ḥunayn when your great number pleased you, it did not avail you in any way. The earth became too narrow for you (to escape) to the same extent (as before) it had been too wide for you. You turned your backs and fled. Then Allāh sent down calm (fortitude) on His Apostle and the Faithful (IX 25-26). He means by "the Faithful", the Commander of the Faithful, 'Alī, peace be on him, and those of the Banū Hāshim who remained with him. On that day they were eight, and with the Commander of the Faithful they were nine. Al-'Abbās b. 'Abd al-Muṭṭalib was on the right of the Apostle of Allāh, al-Faḍl b. al-'Abbās was on his left. Abū Sufyān b. al-Ḥārith was holding his saddle at the rear of his mule, while the Commander of the Faithful, peace be on him, stood before him with his sword. Nawfal b. al Ḥārith, Rabī'a b. al-Ḥārith, 'Abd Allāh b. al-Zubayr b. 'Abd al Muṭṭalib and 'Utba and Ma'tib the two sons of Abū Lahab stood around him. All the rest, save those we have mentioned, turned their backs in flight. Concerning this Mālik b. 'Ubāda al-Ghāfiqī recited:

None consoled the Prophet except the sons of Hāshim in the face of the swords of the battle at Ḥunayn.

The people fled, save for this group of nine. They were calling to the people: Where are you?

Then they stood with the Prophet to face death. They denied us any ornament except shame.

Ayman guarded the trusty one (i.e. Muḥammad) from the people (and died) a martyr, and thus gained (eternal) happiness as a reward.

Al-'Abbās b. 'Abd al-Muṭṭalib recited concerning this situation:

We, nine, helped the Apostle of Allāh in the battle. The rest who could flee fled and scattered.

Whenever al-Faḍl attacked with his sword against the people, my words (were):

"Again my son, lest they return"

The nine of us faced death itself because of what is given in the service of Allāh causes no (real) suffering.

(In the first poem) there is a reference to Ayman b. Umm Ayman, may Allāh have mercy upon him.

When the Apostle of Allāh, may Allāh bless Him and His Family, saw the flight of the people from him, he said to al-'Abbās, who was a man with a loud strong voice: "Call to the people and remind them of the covenant."

Al-'Abbās called out at the top of his voice: "People who made the pledge of allegiance at the tree, men of Sūrat al-Baqara, where are you fleeing? Remember the covenant which you made to the Apostle of Allāh, may Allāh bless Him and His Family."

However, the people went on and turned their backs (in flight). It was a pitch black night and the Apostle of Allāh was in the valley. The polytheists came against him from the mountain passes into the valley, and from the sides of the valley, and its narrow defiles, with their swords drawn, and with clubs and stones.

[They reported:] The Apostle of Allāh, may Allāh bless Him and His Family, looked toward the people (turning) part of his face (towards them) in the darkness. And he gave light as if he was the moon on the night of the full-moon. Then he called out to the Muslims: "Where are you who gave your pledge to

Allāh (to protect) him?"

The first heard and then others of them. Not a man of them heard but did not fling himself to the ground and crawl down to where they were in the valley. When they met the enemy, they fought against them.

[They reported:] One of the Ḥawāzin approached in front of the people on a red camel with a black standard in his hand fixed on a long spear. Whenever he gained a victory over the Muslims, he would turn them face downward. If any of the people escaped him, he would pass him on to the polytheists behind him and they would follow him.

He was reciting:

I am Abū Jarwal, there will be no ceasing today until we destroy or are destroyed.

The Commander of the Faithful, peace be on him, directed himself towards him. He struck the buttocks of his camel and brought it down. Then he struck him and overcame him. He recited:

Now the people know with whom the morrow belonged. In battle I am one who brings disgrace (to others).

The flight of the polytheists began with the killing of Abū Jarwal, may Allāh curse him. Then the Muslims felt rebuked and formed ranks against the enemy. The Apostle of Allāh, may Allāh bless Him and His Family, said: "O Allāh, you have made the first of Quraysh taste defeat, give the last of them pleasure (of victory)."

The Muslims and the polytheists began to fight together. When the Prophet, may Allāh bless Him and His Family, saw them, he put his saddle on my mount so that he might have a view of their group. Then he said:

Now war has been kindled. I am the Prophet, that is no lie. I am the descendant of 'Abd al-Muṭṭalib.

It was very soon after that the (enemy) turned their backs (in flight). The prisoners were brought in bonds to the Apostle of Allāh, may Allāh bless Him and His Family.

When the Commander of the Faithful, peace be on him, killed Abū Jarwal and the people shrank away because of him being killed, the Muslims began to ply them with their swords. The Commander of the Faithful, peace be on him, led them in this so that he killed forty men from these people. Thus was the defeat and the capturing of prisoners brought about at that time.

Abū Sufyān Ṣakhr b. Ḥarb b. Umayya took part in this campaign. He was among the number of those of the Muslims who had fled (at first).

[It is reported on the authority of Mu'āwiya b. Abī Sufyān that he said:] I met my father fleeing with the Meccans of the Banū Umayya. I yelled out to him:

"Son of Ḥarb, by Allāh, won't you endure with fortitude alongside your cousin?

You have not fought for your religion nor have you faced these bedouin Arabs in order to protect your womenfolk."

"Who are you?" he asked.

"Mu'āwiya," I answered.

"The son of Hind?" he said.

"Yes," I replied.

"May I ransom you with my father and mother," he exclaimed.

Then he stopped and the Meccans gathered with him. I joined them. Then we attacked the people and scattered them. The Muslims continued to fight the polytheists and take them prisoner until day began to break. Then the Apostle of Allāh, may Allāh bless Him and His Family, ordered that none of the people taken prisoner was to be killed.

During the days of the conquest (of Mecca) the tribe of Hudhayl had sent a man called Ibn al-Anza' to spy on the Prophet, may Allāh bless Him and His Family, so that he would gain information about him. He had gone back to Hudhayl with his report. At the battle of Ḥunayn, he was captured. 'Umar b. al-Khaṭṭāb passed by him. When he saw him, he went up to one of the Anṣār and said: "This is the enemy of Allāh, who came to us as a spy. Here he is a prisoner. Kill him."

The man from the Anṣār cut off his head. When the Prophet learnt of that, he disliked it and said: "Didn't I order you not to kill prisoners? Yet after that you killed Jamīl b. Mu'ammar b. Zuhayr while he was a prisoner."

Then the Prophet, may Allāh bless Him and His Family, sent to the Anṣār while he was still angry. He demanded: "What prompted you to kill him when the messenger had come to you (telling you) not to kill any prisoners?"

"We only killed him at the behest of 'Umar," they answered.

The Apostle of Allāh turned away (from them) until 'Umayr b. Wahb spoke to him about forgiving (them).

The Prophet of Allāh made the distribution of the booty of Ḥunayn, particularly among the Quraysh. He gave a generous share to reconcile the hearts of some of them like Abū Sufyān Ṣakhr b. Ḥarb, 'Ikrima b. Abī Jahl, Ṣafwān b. Umayya, al-Ḥārith b. Hishām, Suhayl b. 'Amr, Zuhayr b. Abī Umayya, 'Abd Allāh b. Abī Umayya, Mu'āwiya b. Abī Sufyān, Hishām b. al-Mughīra, al-Aqra' b. Ḥābis, 'Uyayna b. Ḥiṣn and their like.

It is reported that he gave the Anṣār only a small part but that he gave most of it to the people whom we have named. A group of the Anṣār became angry on account of that. The Apostle of Allāh, may Allāh bless Him and His Family, was informed of their words of discontent against him. He summoned them and they gathered. He told them: "Sit down but do not let anyone other than your own people sit with you."

When they were seated the Prophet, may Allāh bless Him and His Family, came out and the Commander of the Faithful, peace be on him, followed him. He sat down in their midst and said to them: "I will ask you about a matter and then you answer me about it".

"Speak, Apostle of Allāh," they said.

"Were you not going astray and then Allāh sent you guidance through me?" he asked.

"Indeed", they answered, "the grace for that belongs to Allāh and His Apostle."

"Were you not on the edge of the pit of Hell-fire and then Allāh rescued you through me?" he asked.

"Indeed", they answered, "the grace for that belongs to Allāh and His Apostle."

"Were you not few and then Allāh made you many through me?" he asked. "Indeed", they answered, "the grace for that belongs to Allāh and His Apostle."

"Were you not enemies (of each other) and then Allāh reconciled your hearts through me?" he asked.

"Indeed", they answered, "the grace for that belongs to Allāh and His Apostle."

The Prophet fell silent for a short time and then he said: "Will you answer me according to what is in your minds?"

"How else can we answer you?" they said. "Indeed it is our fathers and mothers (who have required) that we answer you by saying that you have outstanding merit, favour and stature over us."

"If you had wanted," he said, "you could have said: You came to us an exile and we gave you refuge. You came to us in fear (of your life) and we protected you. You came to us denounced as a liar and we believed in you."

They raised their voices in weeping. Their shaykhs and leaders stood up before him and kissed his hands and feet. Then they said:

"We are satisfied with Allāh and His Apostle. Here is our wealth (placed) before you. If you wish, divide it among your people. Those of us who spoke earlier (against you), only spoke out of jealousy, deception in the breast and sin in the heart. They had thought that (your action) was taken in anger against them and to reduce them. They seek forgiveness from Allāh for their sins. O Apostle of Allāh, forgive them."

Then the Prophet, may Allāh bless Him and His Family, said: "O Allāh, grant forgiveness to the Anṣār and the sons of the Anṣār, and the sons of the sons of the Anṣār. People of the Anṣār, are you not content that no one except you will return with grace and favour? For when you return (part of) your share (of the rewards of battle) will be (the presence of) the Apostle of Allāh (in your city)." "Indeed," they replied, "we are content."

The Prophet, may Allāh bless Him and His Family, said: "On that day the Anṣār were my close supporters and my family. If the people had gone along the valley and the Anṣār had gone along a mountain pass, I would have gone along the mountain pass of the Anṣār. O Allāh, grant forgiveness to the Anṣār."

On that day the Apostle of Allāh, may Allāh bless Him and His Family, had given al-'Abbās b. Mirdās four camels. He was angry at this and recited:

Do you divide my share of the booty and the share of al-'Ubayd between 'Uyayna and al-Aqra'?

At any gathering (of people) neither Ḥiṣn nor Ḥābis would take precedence over my leader.

I am no less a man than those two. Whoever you put down today will not be raised.

The Prophet, may Allāh bless Him and His Family, learned of what he had said and summoned him to attend him.

"You are the one who spoke these words: Do you divide my share of the booty and the share of al-'Ubayd between al-Aqra' and 'Uyayna," he said.

"No, may my father and mother be a ransom for you, you are

not the poet,"

interrupted Abū Bakr.

"How is that?" he asked.

"Rather he said between 'Uyayna and al-Aqra'," he replied.

"Arise, 'Alī," the Apostle of Allāh, may Allāh bless Him and His Family, told the Commander of the Faithful, peace be on him, "and cut out his tongue for (what) it said."

"By Allāh, because of these words you are harsher with me than at the battle with Khath'am when they came against us in our houses," al-'Abbās b. Mirdās cried out. He caught hold of the hands of 'Alī b. Abī Ṭālib (and said): "Take me away. If I knew anyone who would free me from this, I would summon him. So I say to you, 'Alī, will you be the one who cuts out my tongue?"

"I will only carry out with you what I have been ordered to do," he said.

Al-'Abbās reported: He set off and remained with me until he brought me to the enclosures. He told me: "Count out the numbers between four and a hundred." I said: "May I ransom you with my father and mother. How generous, considerate and learned you are!"

"The Apostle of Allāh gave you four camels," he said, "and thus made you one of the number of the Emigrants. If you wish, just keep them. However, if you wish, take a hundred and be included with the people (who were given) a hundred." "Advise me," I asked.

"I would advise you to take what the Apostle of Allāh, may

Allāh bless Him and His Family, has given you and be satisfied with that," he told me. "Then I will do so," I said.

When the Apostle of Allāh, may Allāh bless Him and His Family, had distributed the booty at Ḥunayn, a tall man with a lump of skin between his eyes, as a result of much prostration approached him. He greeted him without any specific reference to the Prophet. Then he said: "I have seen what you have done with this booty."

"How do you see it?" he asked.

"I consider that you have gone astray," he said.

At this, the Apostle of Allāh became angry and said: "Shame on you, since I have no injustice, who has it?"

"Shall we not kill him?" the Muslims asked.

"Leave him," he said. "He will have followers who will dart from this religion like the arrow darts from the bow. Allāh will bring about their death at the hand of the man most loved by Him after me."

The Commander of the Faithful, 'Alī b. Abī Ṭālib, peace be on him, killed him among the Khawārij he killed at the battle of al-Nahrawān.

Consideration should be given to the qualities displayed by the Commander of the Faithful, peace be on him, in this campaign. If you ponder them and think about their implications, you will find that he, peace be on him, carried out every outstanding action which took place in it. Thus he is uniquely characterised by qualities which nobody else in the community (umma) shares. It was he, peace be on him, who stayed with the Apostle of Allāh when all the rest of the people fled except the small group who remained alongside him, peace be on him. We already have thorough knowledge of his precedence in courage, bravery, fortitude and vigour over al-'Abbās and al-Faḍl, his son, and Abū Ṣufyān b. al-Ḥārith and the rest of the group. (We have this) by the example of his actions on other occasions at which none of them were present. Reports of him are famous concerning his battle with men of equal rank and his killing of heroes. None of these has been known for anything similar to his exploits. No death of an enemy (in battle) is traced back to them by any famous report. Thus it can be realised that their remaining steadfast was through him, peace be on him. If it had not been for him, a crime would have been committed against religion which would not have been set right. By his taking up that attitude and his endurance with the Prophet, may Allāh bless him and grant him peace, the return of the Muslims to the battle was made possible and their encouragement to attack the enemy. His killing Abū Jarwal, the foremost of the polytheists, was the reason for the defeat of the people and the victory of the Muslims. Through the killing by him, peace be on him, of the forty whom he killed, weakness came upon the polytheists and thus he was the cause of the their desertion and anxiety, and the victory of the Muslims.

(The Muslims' flight) was contributed to by the lack of judgement of this man (when he caused them to be overconfident) through expressing wonder at their great numbers. (It was this man) who preceded 'Alī to the rank of the caliphate (khilāfa) after the Apostle of Allāh, may Allāh bless Him and His Family. Thus he was the cause of their initial defeat, or at least one of the causes. Then it was his colleague who caused prisoners of the enemy to be killed after the Prophet, may Allāh bless Him and His Family, had forbidden them to be killed. Thus he committed a great crime against Allāh, the Exalted, and against His Apostle. (On the other hand, 'Alī) was a help to the Prophet, may Allāh bless Him and His Family, in reconciling the Anṣār, by gathering them together and speaking to them. Religion was strengthened by him and by him was removed fear of discord which overshadowed the people because of the distribution of the booty. Thus he shared with the Apostle of Allāh, may Allāh bless Him and His Family, in that merit which no one else participated in. In the matter of al-'Abbās b. Mirdās, he carried it out in such a way that he was the cause of the strengthening of faith in his heart and the removal of doubts about religion from his soul and his accepting of His Apostle, peace be on him, by obeying his command and being content with his judgement. Then the Apostle of Allāh, may Allāh bless Him and His Family, made him the one who would carry out the judgement on the man who protested against his decision, as a sign of the right of the Commander of the Faithful, peace be on him, in his actions, and in the correctness in his fighting. He called attention to the duty of obedience (to 'Alī) and warned against disobedience (to him). Indeed truth was in his heart and loins and he testified to it by being the best of creatures. This is in contrast to the actions carried out by his rivals who usurped his position. It shows the contradictory nature of their actions and excludes them from merit (leading them) to a low position which would cause such a man to perish, or would almost (cause it). This is apart from the greatness (of 'Alī's actions which are above) the actions of even those loyal men in that campaign and their closeness in the battle which they fought in. By this they are excluded from the praise which we have given to him by virtue of their deficiency which we have described.

Expeditions to Awṭās and al-Ṭā'if

When Allāh, the Exalted, had scattered the gathering of the polytheists at Ḥunayn, they separated into two groups. The Bedouin and those who followed them went to Awṭās while Thaqīf and those who followed them went to al-Ṭā'if. The

Prophet, may Allāh bless Him and His Family, sent Abū ʻĀmir al-Ashʻarī to Awṭās with a group of men which included Abū Mūsā al-Ashʻarī. He sent Abū Sufyān Ṣakhr b. Ḥarb to al-Ṭā'if.

Abū ʻĀmir went forward carrying the standard and fought until he was killed protecting it. The Muslims said to Abū Mūsā: "You are the cousin of the commander and he has been killed. So take up the standard so that we might fight before it."

Abū Mūsā took it up and he and the Muslims fought until Allāh gave them victory.

Abū Sufyān, on the other hand, came against Thaqīf and they made a direct attack on him. He was put to flight and he returned to the Prophet, may Allāh bless Him and His Family. He said: "You sent me with men who would not even have been able to lift the buckets of Hudhayl and the Bedouin. They were of no use to me."

The Prophet, may Allāh bless Him and His Family, turned away from him in silence. Then he went, himself, to al-Ṭā'if and laid siege to it. He sent out the Commander of the Faithful, peace be on him, with some horsemen. He ordered him to plunder everything he found and to destroy every idol he found.

He went forward until the horsemen of Khathʻam met him amid a great group.

One of their men called Shihāb came forward in the darkness just before dawn.

He called: "Is there anyone who will fight me in single combat?"

"Which (of you) will be for him?" the Commander of the Faithful, peace be on him, asked them.

No one rose. So the Commander of the Faithful rose to go against him. Then Abū al-'Āṣ b. al-Rabī' jumped up and said: "You will be too much for him, Commander of the Faithful."

"Indeed," he replied, "but if I am killed, you take command over the men."

The Commander of the Faithful went forward against him while reciting:

Duty is required of every leader that he water the straight lance (with blood) or it is broken.

Then he struck him down and killed him. He went along with those horsemen until he had broken the idols. Then he returned to the Apostle of Allāh, may Allāh bless him-and his family, while the latter was besieging the inhabitants of al-Ṭā'if.

When the Prophet, may Allāh bless Him and His Family, saw him, he magnified Allāh for his victory. Then he took him by the hand and went aside with him and spent a long time in confidential talk with him.

['Abd al-Raḥmān b. Ṣubāba and al-Ajlaḥ both report on the authority of Abū al-Zubayr, on the authority of Jābir b.'Abd Allāh al-Anṣārī:]

When the Apostle of Allāh, may Allāh bless Him and His Family, had been alone with 'Alī, peace be on him, on the campaign against al-Ṭā'if, 'Umar b. al-Khaṭṭāb came to him and said: "Why do you take him aside and speak to him alone, apart from us?"

"'Umar," he replied, "I have not made him my confidant. Rather Allāh has made him His confidant."

'Umar opposed him, saying: "This is just the same as you said to us before al-Ḥuḍaybiyya that we would enter the Sacred Mosque safely if Allāh wished it. Then we did not enter it and we were turned away from it."

"I did not tell you that you would enter it in that year," the Prophet, may Allāh bless Him and His Family, shouted at him.

Later Nāfi' b. Ghaylān b. Ma'tib came out from the fortress of al-Ṭā'if with some horsemen from Thaqīf. The Commander of the Faithful, peace be on him, met him at Baṭn Wajj. There he killed him and the polytheists were put to flight. Terror seized the people and a group of them came down to the Prophet, may Allāh bless Him and His Family, and submitted to Islam. The Prophet's siege had lasted a little more than ten days.

In this campaign Allāh, may He be glorified, also characterised the Commander of the Faithful, peace be on him, with qualities which none of the other people shared. During it, the conquest was brought about at his hands; he killed those men of Khath'am whom he killed apart from anyone else; there occurred the confidential conversation which the Apostle of Allāh, may Allāh bless Him and His Family, attributed to Allāh, may His name be exalted. By this is clearly demonstrated his outstanding merit, his special consideration by Allāh, the Exalted, by which he was separated from the rest of men. The intensity of his opponents' reaction to these events indicates their awareness of his inner significance and Allāh's revelation of the reality of His secret communications with him. In that there is a lesson for those who have minds.

The Expedition to Tabūk and the Commander of the Faithful's Deputising for the Prophet at Medina

With regard to the expedition to Tabūk, Allāh, may His name be exalted, revealed to His Prophet, may Allāh bless Him and His Family, that he should go there himself and summon the people to set out with him. He told him that in the expedition there would be no need for war and there would be no fighting against the enemy since these matters would come to him without the sword. It was a device by which to test and try his Companions' (willingness) to set out, so that in that way they could be distinguished and their secret feelings revealed to him. The Prophet, may Allāh bless Him and His Family, summoned them to set out for the lands of the Byzantine (Empire). However, their fruit had ripened and the heat was oppressive for them. Most of them were slow in obeying him out of a desire for delay, out of greed for their own livelihoods and their improvement, and out of fear of intense heat, of the extent of the distance and of meeting the enemy. But some of them, despite finding it burdensome, arose to set out while others lingered behind.

When the Prophet, may Allāh bless Him and His Family, was ready to go out, he appointed the Commander of the Faithful, peace be on him, as his deputy over his family, his children and his place of emigration. He told him: "'Alī, Medina will only be properly looked after by myself or by you."

He said that because he, peace be on him, knew the wicked intentions of the Bedouin and many of the Meccans, and those around them whom he had attacked and whose blood he had shed. He was concerned that they would seek (to control) Medina when he was away from it and occupied in Byzantine territory. Since there was no one to take his place there, there would be no safety from their treachery, from the corruption they would cause in (Medina) the place of emigration, and from their overreaching themselves to actions which would hurt his family and his successors. He, peace be on him, knew that no one could take his place in terrifying the enemy, guarding the place of emigration and protecting those who were there except the Commander of the Faithful. Thus he clearly appointed him as his deputy, and gave an explicit nomination of him to the Imamate after him.

This is indicated by the account that has made clear that when the Hypocrites learnt that the Apostle of Allāh, may Allāh bless Him and His Family, had appointed 'Alī, peace be on him, as his deputy over Medina, they were envious of him because of that. After (the Prophet's) departure, ('Alī's) position there began to distress them; for they knew that (the city) would be protected and that there would be no opportunity for a man with hostile or covetous intent. That grieved them and they would have preferred ('Alī) to leave with (the Prophet) because of the occurrence of corruption and confusion which they hoped for during the absence of the Apostle of Allāh, may Allāh bless Him and His Family, from Medina and while it would be free of a man to guard it who would cause terror and fear. Therefore they accused him of (seeking) luxury and ease by remaining with the people while those of them who had departed were undergoing hardships, through journeying and (risking) danger. They spread rumours about him, peace be on him, and said: "The Apostle of Allāh, may Allāh bless Him and His Family, did not appoint him as deputy as an act of honour, privilege and love. He only left him behind because of his finding him burdensome."

With this rumour they slandered him like Quraysh had slandered the Prophet by (attributing to him) madness sometimes, and poetry at other times, by (accusing him of) magic at times and of being a pagan soothsayer at others. They knew that (the facts) were opposite and contrary to that, just as the Hypocrites knew that (the facts) were opposite and contrary to the slanders they were spreading against the Commander of the Faithful, peace be on him. The Prophet had specifically recommended the Commander of the Faithful, peace be on him, to the people. He was the most lovable of the people to him, the happiest of them in his view, the most favoured by him, and the closest to him.

When the Commander of the Faithful, peace be on him, learned of the rumours spread by the Hypocrites against him, he wanted to show them to be liars and to reveal their shameful action. So he followed the Prophet, may Allāh bless Him and His Family, and told him: "Apostle of Allāh, the hypocrites are alleging that you left me behind because of finding (me) burdensome and because of hatred."

"Go back to your position, brother," the Prophet said to him. "Medina will only be properly looked after by myself and by you. You are my deputy (khalīfa) among my family (ahl al-bayt) and in the place of my emigration and my people. Are you not content, 'Alī, that you have the same rank with regard to me as Aaron had with regard to Moses, except that there is no prophet after me?"

This statement by the Apostle of Allāh is his designation of him for the Imamate and his setting him apart from the rest of the people for succession (khilāfa). Through it he indicated a merit in him which no one else shared and by it he required for him all the ranks which Aaron received from Moses except those which custom specifies to be required from (natural) brotherhood. He also excluded him from prophethood. Do you not see that (the Prophet), peace be on him, gave him all the ranks of Aaron with the only exceptions which his expressed word and reason would exclude? Everyone who has contemplated the meaning of the Qur'ān, who has pondered on the accounts and reports, has realised that Aaron was the brother of Moses, peace be on him, through his father and mother, his partner in his affair, and his helper in his prophethood and in propagating the messages from his Lord Allāh, may He be praised, his loins were strengthened through him and he was his deputy (khalīfa) over his people. His (authority) over them was from the Imamate; for the requirement of obedience to him (Moses) was like the Imamate of him (Aaron) and the requirement of obedience to him. He (Aaron) was the most lovable of the people to him (Moses) and the most meritorious of them in his view. Allāh, the Mighty and High, has said, putting words in the mouth of Moses, peace be on him: My Lord, enlarge my breast for me and let my affair give joy to me. Loosen the knot of my tongue so that they may understand my speech. Make Aaron, my brother, my helper from my family. Strengthen my loins through him and make him a partner in my affair so that we may praise You much and mention You frequently. (XX 25-34). Allāh, the Exalted, answered his request and gave him his request and desire when He said: Your request has been granted, Moses. (XX 36). And Allāh, the Exalted, said, putting the words into the mouth of Moses: Moses said to his brother Aaron: Be my deputy over my people, be righteous and do not follow the path of the corrupters. (VII 142).

When the Apostle of Allāh, may Allāh bless Him and His Family, gave 'Alī the same rank with regard to himself as Aaron had with regard to Moses, he required for him by that everything which we could mention except what custom specifies for natural brotherhood, and the exception of prophethood which was expressly stated. This is a virtue which no other creatures shares with the Commander of the Faithful, peace be on him. Nor does anyone else equal him in its significance, nor does anyone come near to it in any circumstance. If Allāh, the Mighty and High, had known that His Prophet, may Allāh bless Him and His Family, would have any need of fighting and support on this expedition, He would not have allowed him to leave behind the Commander of the Faithful, peace be on him, as we have already mentioned. However He realised that the public interest (maṣlaḥa) lay in making him his deputy and that ('Alī) taking his place in (Medina) the place of emigration was the best action. (Allāh) had organised creation and religion as He had decreed concerning that and He brought it about as we have outlined and explained.

(The Campaign against 'Amr b. Ma'dīkarib)

When the Apostle of Allāh, may Allāh bless Him and His Family, returned from Tabūk to Medina, 'Amr b. Ma'dīkarib came to him. The Prophet said to him: "Submit to Islam, 'Amr, and then Allāh will protect you from the greatest terror."

"What is the greatest terror, Muḥammad?" he asked. "For I have no fear." "'Amr," he told him, "it is not as you think and suppose. Indeed there will be one great shout among the people. Not one person will remain who does not attend, nor a living person who does not die, except as Allāh wishes. Then there will be another great shout among them and those who are dead will assemble and all get into ranks. The heavens will split open and the earth will be crushed. The mountains will be cut asunder at the crushing and the fire will hurl the mountains like sparks. No one who has a soul will remain except his heart be stripped bare while he mentions his sins and is occupied with his soul, except as Allāh wishes. Then, where will you be, 'Amr, at this?"

"Indeed I am hearing of a terrible event," said 'Amr.

Then he believed in Allāh and His Apostle. People from his tribe also believed with him and then they returned to their tribe.

'Amr b. Ma'dīkarib looked towards Ubayy b. 'Ath'ath al-Khath'amī. He seized him by the neck and brought him to the Prophet, may Allāh bless Him and His Family.

"Give me back this sinner who has killed my father," he said.

"Islam leaves unavenged acts committed in the Jāhiliyya," replied the Apostle of Allāh, may Allāh bless Him and His Family.

'Amr departed as an apostate. He made a raid on people from the Banū al-Ḥārith b. Ka'b and went on to his own tribe. The Apostle of Allāh, may Allāh bless Him and His Family, summoned 'Alī b. Abī Ṭālib, peace be on him. He put him in charge of some of the emigrants and despatched him to the Banū Zubayd. He sent Khālid b. al-Walīd with a group of Bedouin and ordered him to head against (the tribe of) Ju'fā. When the two men ('Alī and Khālid) met, 'Alī b. Abī Ṭālib, peace be on him, was to be the commander of the people.

The Commander of the Faithful, peace be on him, set out. He put Khālid b. Sa'īd b. al-'Āṣ in charge of his vanguard. Khālid (b. al-Walīd) put Abū Mūsā al-Ash'arī in charge of his vanguard. When Ju'fā heard about the army, they split into two groups. One group went to Yemen and the other group attached themselves to the Banū Zubayd.

The Commander of the Faithful, peace be on him, learnt of that and wrote to Khālid b. al-Walīd: "Stop where my messenger reaches you." He did not stop, so ('Alī) wrote to Khālid b. Sa'īd b. al-'Āṣ: "Intervene so that you stop him." Khālid (b. Sa'īd) met him and stopped him.

The Commander of the Faithful, peace be on him, caught up

with him and upbraided him severely for his opposition to his orders. Then he went on until he came upon the Banū Zubayd in a valley called Kisr. When the Banū Zubayd saw him, they said to ʻAmr: "How are you, Abū Thawr? When this young man meets you, he will take tribute from you."

"He will know that he has met me," he said.

Then ʻAmr went forward and cried out: "Who will meet me in combat?"

The Commander of the Faithful, peace be on him, rose to go against him but Khālid b. Saʻīd also stood up and said: "Abū al-Ḥasan, (I would ransom) you with my father and mother, let me meet him in combat."

"If you consider that you owe any obedience to me, remain in your place," the Commander of the Faithful, peace be on him, told him.

He stayed and the Commander of the Faithful went forward. There was a great clamour. ʻAmr was put to flight and his brother and cousin were killed. His wife, Rukāna daughter of Salāma, was taken, and his (other) womenfolk were captured.

The Commander of the Faithful, peace be on him, departed and left Khālid b. Saʻīd behind in charge of the Banū Zubayd to collect their taxes and to provide security for those who, having submitted to Islam, returned to him from their flight. ʻAmr b. Maʻdīkarib returned. He asked permission (to visit) Khālid b. Saʻīd and the latter gave him permission. Then he returned to Islam. He spoke to him about his wife and children and he gave them to him.

When ʻAmr stood at the door of Khālid b. Saʻīd, he found (there) an animal which had been slaughtered. He gathered the bones of it together and struck them with his sword, cutting through them all. His sword was called Ṣimṣama. When Khālid b. Sa'īd gave 'Amr his wife and children, 'Amr gave him al-Ṣimṣama.

(Earlier) the Commander of the Faithful, peace be on him, had chosen a slave-girl from among the prisoners. Now Khālid b. al-Walīd sent Burayda al-Aslamī to the Prophet, may Allāh bless Him and His Family. He told him: "Get to (the Prophet) before the army does. Tell him what 'Alī, peace be on him, has done in choosing a slave-girl for himself from the khums (fifth of the booty that was to go to the Prophet and others, including the family of the Prophet) and bring him dishonour."

Burayda went and came to the door of the Apostle of Allāh. There he met 'Umar al-Khaṭṭāb. The latter asked him about how their expedition had gone and about why he had come. He told him that he had only come to bring dishonour to 'Alī and he mentioned his choosing a slave-girl from the khums for himself.

"Carry out what you have come to do," 'Umar told him, "for he (the Prophet) will be angry at what 'Alī, peace be on him, has done on account of his daughter."

Burayda went in to the Prophet, may Allāh bless Him and His Family. He had with him the letter from Khālid with which he had been sent. He began to read it. The face of the Prophet began to change.

"Apostle of Allāh," said Burayda, "if you permitted the people (to act) like this, their fay' (booty to be distributed) would disappear."

"Woe upon you, Burayda," the Prophet, may Allāh bless Him and His Family, told him. "You have committed an act of hypocrisy. 'Alī b. Abī Ṭālib is allowed to have what is allowed to me from their fay'. 'Alī b. Abī Ṭālib, peace be on him, is the best of men for you and your people and the best of those whom I will leave behind after me for the whole of my community. Burayda, I warn you that if you hate 'Alī, Allāh will hate you."

Burayda reported: I wanted the earth to split open for me so that I could be swallowed into it. Then I said: "I seek refuge in Allāh from the anger of Allāh and the anger of the Apostle of Allāh. Apostle of Allāh, forgive me. I will never hate 'Alī and I will only speak good of him."

The Prophet, may Allāh bless Him and His Family, forgave him.

In this expedition, the Commander of the Faithful (demonstrated) qualities which were beyond comparison with the qualities of anyone else. In particular, victory in it was brought about by his hand. It also showed his great merit and his sharing with the Prophet, may Allāh bless Him and His Family, in the fay' which Allāh had permitted to the latter. Thus it showed his special designation for something which none of the other people could have and it set him apart by reason of the Apostle of Allāh's love for him and his preference for him which had been hidden to those who had no previous knowledge of it. There is also his warning Burayda and others against hating him and against enmity towards him, and his urging him to love him and accept his authority (wilāya). In addition the response to the plot of his enemies in their attempt to vilify him indicates that he was the best (afḍāl) of creatures in the view of Allāh, the Exalted, and of him (the Prophet), peace be on him, and the one with the most right for his position (of authority) after him. In himself he was the most special of (the Muslims) with (the Prophet) and the most influential of them with him.

(The Campaign of (Dhāt) al-Salāsil)

Then there was the campaign of (Dhāt) al-Silsila. That was when a Bedouin came to the Prophet, may Allāh bless Him and His Family. He squatted in front of him and said: "I have come to advise you. A group of Arabs have gathered together at Wadī al-Raml and they have plotted to come and attack you at night in Medina." Then he described them to him.

The Prophet, may Allāh bless Him and His Family, ordered the call to be given: "The prayer is general (al-ṣalāt jāmi'a i.e. all should attend the prayer)." The Muslims gathered and he went up on to the pulpit. He praised and glorified Allāh. Then he said: "There is an enemy of Allāh and an enemy of yours who has plotted to attack you at night. Who will (go against) them?"

A group of the poor people stood up and said: "We will go against them, Apostle of Allāh. Therefore appoint whoever you wish over us."

He drew lots among them and the lot fell upon eighty from among them and others. He summoned Abū Bakr and said to him: "Take the flag and depart against the Banū Sulaym. They are near al-Ḥarra."

He departed and with him went the people until he drew near their land. There were many stones and trees there and the people (i.e. the Banū Sulaym) were in the middle of the valley and the descent to it was difficult. When Abū Bakr got to the valley, he intended to go down but the people came out against him and put him to flight. They killed a great number of the Muslims and Abū Bakr fled from the people.

When they came to the Prophet, may Allāh bless Him and His

Family, he gave the command to 'Umar b. al-Khaṭṭāb and sent him against them. They lay hidden under the stones and trees. When he went to descend, they came out against him and put him to flight.

The Prophet, may Allāh bless Him and His Family, was grieved at this. 'Amr b. al-'Āṣ said to him: "Send me against them, Apostle of Allāh. For warfare is deception and perhaps I can deceive them."

He sent him with a group of men and commissioned him (to carry out the task). When he got to the valley, they came out against him and put him to flight. They killed a number of those who accompanied him.

(After this), the Apostle of Allāh, may Allāh bless Him and His Family, delayed for several days praying (for Allāh's help) against them. Then he summoned the Commander of the Faithful, peace be on him. He gave him the command and said: "I have sent him as one who will attack, not one who will flee." Then he raised his hands to the heavens and said: "O Allāh, if You know that I am Your Apostle, then protect him for me. Act through him, act." Thus he prayed for the will of Allāh for him.

'Alī b. Abī Ṭālib set out and the Apostle of Allāh, may Allāh bless Him and His Family, went out to say farewell to him. He went with him to the mosque of the allies (al-aḥzāb). 'Alī, peace be on him, was riding a shorn-haired bay. He was wearing two Yemenī garments and carrying a spear. The Apostle of Allāh, may Allāh bless Him and His Family, said farewell to him and prayed for him.

He had sent among those who had been sent with him, Abū Bakr, 'Umar and 'Amr b. al-'Āṣ. ('Alī) set off towards Iraq deviating from the (usual) route so that they would think that he was heading with (his men) in another direction. Then he took them along a little known track and brought them along so that he approached the valley from (the direction of) its entrance. When he was near the valley, he ordered those with him to tie up their horses and he made them stop in their place. He said to them: "Do not leave your position." Then he went forward in front of them. He stood at a distance from them.

When 'Amr b. al-'Āṣ saw what he had done, he had no doubt that victory would be his. (Resenting this, he) said to Abū Bakr: "I know that place better than 'Alī, peace be on him. There, there is something which will attack us more fiercely than the Banū Sulaym. There are hyenas and wolves. If they come out against us, I am afraid that they will cut us down. Speak to him to let us go up the valley."

Abū Bakr went forward and spoke to him. He spoke at length but the Commander of the Faithful, peace be on him, did not answer a single word. He went back to them and said: "No, by Allāh, he did not say a single word in reply."

Then 'Amr b. al-'Āṣ said to 'Umar b. al-Khaṭṭāb: "You are more powerful with him."

So 'Umar went and spoke to him. He treated him exactly as he had treated Abū Bakr. He returned to them and told him that he had not answered him.

'Amr b. al-'Āṣ spoke to (the men): "It is not fitting that we should lose our lives.

So come with us up the valley."

"No, by Allāh," retorted the Muslims, "we will not do so. The Apostle of Allāh ordered us to listen to 'Alī, peace be on him, and to obey him. Shall we abandon his command and listen to you and obey you?"

They continued in this manner so that the Commander of the Faithful, peace be on him, felt (a feeling of) pride. He was able to surround the people while they were still unaware. Allāh, the Exalted, gave him power over them.

Sūrat al-'Ādiyāt ḍabḥan (C) was revealed to the Prophet, may Allāh bless Him and His Family. The Prophet, may Allāh bless Him and His Family, announced the news of the victory to his Companions and ordered them to meet the Commander of the Faithful, peace be on him. They went to meet him with the Prophet, may Allāh bless Him and His Family, at their head. The Muslims positioned themselves in two ranks. When ('Alī) saw the Prophet, he dismounted from his horse. The Prophet said to him: "Mount (your horse). Allāh and His Apostle are pleased with you."

The Commander of the Faithful, peace be on him, wept with joy. Then the Prophet, may Allāh bless Him and His Family, said: "'Alī, if it was not for the fact that I am concerned that some factions of my community would say (of you) what the Christians say of the Messiah, Jesus, son of Mary, I would say of you today such as (after them) you would never pass a gathering of men without them taking the soil from under your feet."

Victory in this expedition was entirely due to the Commander of the Faithful after the corruption which had occurred through the others. He was singled out for special praise by the Prophet with regard to it, for virtues which in no way occurred in anyone else. He distinguished him with a rank in which no one else had any share.

THE ROLE OF THE COMMANDER OF THE FAITHFUL IN THE LAST YEAR OF THE PROPHET'S LIFE

(The Deputation of Christians from Najrān and the Contest of Prayer)

When Islam had spread after the conquest (of Mecca) and the raids already described, which followed it, and its authority had become strong, delegations began to visit the Prophet, may Allāh bless Him and His Family. Some of them submitted to Islam while others sought protection so that they might return to their people (to tell) their people about his view towards them. Among those who came in a delegation to him were Abū Ḥāritha, the bishop of Najrān, with thirty of the Christians who included the deputy (al-'āqib), the chief (al-sayyid) and 'Abd al-Masīḥ. They arrived at Medina at the time of the afternoon prayer. They were wearing robes of silk and crosses.

The Jews approached them and they began to interrogate each

other. The Christians said: "You are not believing in anything (correctly)." And the Jews replied to them: "You are not believing in anything (correctly)." Concerning that, Allāh, may He be praised, revealed: The Jews say that the Christians are not believing in anything (correctly) and the Christians say that the Jews are not believing in anything (correctly) .... etc. to the end of the verse (II 113).

When the Prophet had prayed the afternoon prayer, they came forwards. At their head was the bishop. He said to him: "Muḥammad, what do you say about the Lord, the Messiah?"

"He is a servant of Allāh," replied the Prophet, "whom Allāh chose and he answered Him."

"Do you know, Muḥammad, whether a father caused him to be born?" asked the bishop.

"He was not born as a result of intercourse so he could not have a father," answered the Prophet.

"How can you say that he is a servant who has been created, when you can only consider a servant who has been created to be born as a result of intercourse and so to have a father?" he asked.

Allāh, may He be praised and exalted, revealed these verses in Sūrat 'Āl 'Imrān (III) in answer to him: The likeness of Jesus according to Allāh is like the likeness of Adam. Allāh created him from earth. Then Allāh said to him: "Be." That is the truth from your Lord. Therefore do not be one of those who go beyond the bounds (of reason). If anyone disputes with you concerning him, after knowledge has been given to you, say to him: Come, let us call our sons and your sons, our women and your women, and ourselves and yourselves. Then let us call on Allāh to witness against each other and let us make the curse of Allāh fall on those who lie (III 59-61).

The Prophet, may Allāh bless Him and His Family, recited it to the Christians and challenged them to a contest of prayer to Allāh (mubāhala). He said: "Allāh, the Mighty and High, has informed me that dread torment will come down on him who has spoken falsely after the contest of prayer (mubāhala). By this the truth will be distinguished from the false."

The Bishop held a meeting of consultation with 'Abd al-Masīḥ and the deputy. Their unanimous view was to wait until the early morning of the next day. When they both returned to their men, the bishop told them: "Watch Muḥammad tomorrow morning. If he comes out with his children and his family, then be warned against the contest of prayer (mubāhala) with him. However, if he comes out with his Companions, then make the contest of prayer with him, for he believes in something other (than the true religion)."

On the next morning, the Prophet, may Allāh bless Him and His Family, came and took 'Alī b. Abī Ṭālib by the hand, while al-Ḥasan and al-Ḥusayn, peace be on them, were walking in front of him and Fāṭima, peace be on her, walked behind him. The Christians came out, at their head their bishop. When the bishop saw that the Prophet, may Allāh bless Him and His Family, was advancing with those who were with him, he asked about them. He was told: "That is his cousin 'Alī b. Abī Ṭālib, who is his son-in-law and the father of his two grandsons and the most lovable of creatures to him. Those children are the sons of his daughter by 'Alī, peace be on him. They are the most lovable of creatures to him. That girl is his daughter, Fāṭima, peace be on her, the dearest of people to him and the closest to his heart."

The bishop looked at the deputy, the chief and 'Abd al-Masīḥ and said: "Have you seen that he has come with the special members of his children and his family so that he may make the contest of prayer with them, trusting in his truthfulness. By God, he would not have come with them while he was afraid that the proof would be against him. Therefore be warned against the contest of prayer with him. By God, if it was not for the position of Caesar (i.e. the Byzantine emperor), I would submit to him. But (now) make peace with him on what can be agreed between you and him. Return to your land and think about it yourselves."

"Our view conforms with your view," they replied.

"Abū al-Qāsim," the bishop called out, "we will not make a contest of prayer with you but we will make peace with you. Therefore make peace with us as we propose."

So the Prophet made peace with them on the condition (of the payment) of two thousand protective breastplates, each breastplate being forty standard dirham (in value). If they varied in value, it would be taken into account. The Prophet, may Allāh bless Him and His Family, had a document written (laying out the terms) by which he had made peace with them. The document is as follows:

In the name of Allāh, the Merciful and the Compassionate.

In terms of gold and silver, produce and slaves, nothing will be taken from them except two thousand protective breastplates, each breastplate being worth forty dirham. If they vary in value, it will be taken into the account. They will pay one thousand of them in the month of Ṣafar and one thousand of them in the month of Rajab. (In addition,) they will provide forty dīnārs for a dwelling house for my agent (rasūl), not more than that. Also in every incident that occurs in Yemen, it will be required of them, (that is) of everyone who lives in a permanent settlement (dhī'adan), to pay as guaranteed equally (by both parties) thirty breastplates, thirty horses and thirty camels as guaranteed equally (by both parties). They will have the neighbourly protection of Allāh (jiwār Allāh) and the protection (dhimma) of Muḥammad b. 'Abd Allāh. Whoever of them takes interest after this year will be denied my protection.

This is a document made on behalf of Muḥammad, the Prophet, the Apostle of Allāh, may Allāh bless Him and His Family, and the people of Najrān and their followers.

The people took the document and departed.

In the story of the people of Najrān there is a clear explanation of the outstanding merit of the Commander of the Faithful, peace be on him, in addition to the clear sign of the Prophet, may Allāh bless Him and His Family, and the miracle which indicates his prophethood. Do you not see the Christians' admission of his prophethood, and his convincing them to refrain from the contest of prayer, and making them realise that if they had taken part in such a contest, dread punishment against them would have been permissible? Similarly he, peace be on him, was confident in victory and success over them by the proof (he would bring) against them. Allāh, the Exalted, gave judgement in the verse of the contest of prayer on behalf of the Commander of the Faithful, peace be on him, that he was of the same (station) as the Apostle of Allāh, thus revealing the great extent of his outstanding merit and his equality with the Prophet, the blessings and peace of Allāh be on Him and His Family, in terms of perfection and protection (iṣma) from sin. Indeed Allāh made him and his wife and his two sons, who were so close to each other in age, a proof for His prophet and evidence for His religion. He gave textual evidence of the judgement that al-Ḥasan and al-Ḥusayn were his sons and that Fāṭima was his "womenfolk" referred to in the statement and those addressed in the call for the contest of prayer and dispute. This is a merit which no one else of the community shares with them, nor even approaches them in it, nor has anything like it in its significance. It is associated with the outstanding special qualities of the Commander of the Faithful, peace be on him, which we have already mentioned earlier.

The Prophet's Farewell Pilgrimage and the Declaration at Ghadīr Khumm.

Among the stories relating the outstanding merit of the Commander of the Faithful, peace be on him, and giving special emphasis to his virtues, which came after the (visit of the) delegation from Najrān, is that which distinguishes him from all the rest of men - (that is) the Farewell Pilgrimage and the reports of what took place during it. During it the Commander of the Faithful had the most elevated position.

The Apostle of Allāh, may Allāh bless Him and His Family, had sent him, peace be on him, to Yemen to collect the fifth share (khums) of their gold and silver and collect the breastplates and other things which the people of Najrān had agreed to pay. He went there to carry out the requests of the Apostle of Allāh, may Allāh bless Him and His Family. In accordance with his instructions and speedily demonstrating his obedience, he performed his duty. The Apostle of Allāh trusted in no one else as he trusted in him for that task. Nor did he consider anyone among the people appropriate to undertake it except him. He made him, peace be on him, occupy a similar position to himself in that. He appointed him as his deputy, in confidence of him and secure in the knowledge that he would carry out the difficult tasks which were imposed upon him.

Then the Apostle of Allāh, may Allāh bless Him and His Family, decided to go on the pilgrimage and to carry out the duties which Allāh, the Exalted, had decreed. He summoned the people to (join) him and his call went out to the furthest points in the land of Islam. The people began to prepare to set out with him. A great crowd came to Medina from the outskirts, and around, and the area nearby. They began to make preparations to set out with him.

He, may Allāh bless Him and His Family, set out with them with five days remaining in (the month of) Dhū al-Qa'da. He had written to the Commander of the Faithful, peace be on him, about going on the pilgrimage from Yemen but he had not mentioned the kind of pilgrimage he had decided to make.

In fact (the Prophet), peace be on him, had set out as a qārin (a pilgrim who would make the lesser pilgrimage ('umra) and the greater pilgrimage (ḥajj) together without any break in the state of ritual consecration necessary for both pilgrimages), by driving the sacrificial animal with him. He put on the pilgrim garment and entered into the state of ritual consecration (aḥrama) at Dhū al-Ḥulayfa. The people did the same with him. He began the ritual call of the pilgrimage (talbiya) on the night he reached al-Baydā' which is half-way between the two sanctuaries (of Medina and Mecca). Then he went on to Kirā' al-Ghamīm. The people with him were riding and on foot. Those on foot found the journey arduous. (The hardships of) travelling and tiredness beset them. They complained of that to the Prophet, may Allāh bless him and grant him peace, and asked him if they could be carried by mounts. He told them that he could not find (an animal) for each of them and instructed them to fasten their belts and to mix sand with milk (to rub on their feet). They did that and they found relief in it.

(Meanwhile) the Commander of the Faithful, peace be on him, set out with the soldiers who had accompanied him to Yemen. He had with him the breastplates which he had collected from the people of Najrān. When the Apostle of Allāh, may Allāh bless Him and His Family, was nearing Mecca on the road from Medina, the Commander of the Faithful, peace be on him, was nearing it on the road from Yemen. He went ahead of the army to meet the Prophet, may Allāh bless Him and His Family, and he left one of their number in charge of them. He came up to the Prophet as the latter was looking down over Mecca. He greeted him and informed him of what he had done and of what he had collected and that he had hurried ahead of the army to meet him. The Apostle of Allāh, may Allāh bless Him and His Family, was pleased at that and delighted to meet him.

"'Alī, have you consecrated yourself for the pilgrimage?" he asked him.

"You did not write to me about the way you would consecrate yourself, Apostle of Allāh," he answered. "I did not know. Therefore I made my intention according to your intention and said: O Allāh, let my intention be the intention of Your Prophet. I have driven thirty-four sacrificial animals with me."

"Allāh is greater (Allāhu akbar)," replied the Apostle of Allāh, may Allāh bless Him and His Family. "I have driven sixty-six. You will be my partner in my pilgrimage, my rituals and my sacrifice. Therefore remain in your state of ritual consecration and return to your army. Then hurry with them to me so that we may meet in Mecca, if Allāh, the Exalted, wills."

The Commander of the Faithful, peace be on him, said farewell to him and returned to his army. He met them nearby and found that they had put on the breastplates which they had had with them. He denounced them for that.

"Shame on you!" he said to the man whom he had appointed as his deputy over them. "Whatever made you give them the breastplates before we hand them over to the Apostle of Allāh, may Allāh bless Him and His Family? I did not give you permission to do that."

"They asked me to let them deck themselves out and enter into the state of consecration in them, and then they would give them back to me," he replied.

The Commander of the Faithful, peace be on him, took them off the people and put them back in the sacks. They were discontented with him because of that. When they came to Mecca, their complaints against the Commander of the Faithful, peace be on him, became numerous. The Apostle of Allāh ordered the call to be given among the people: "Stop your tongues (speaking) against 'Alī b. Abī Ṭālib, peace be on him. He is one who is harsh in the interests of Allāh, the Mighty and High, not one who deceives in His religion."

At this the people refrained from mentioning him and they realised the high position he enjoyed with the Prophet, may Allāh bless Him and His Family, and his anger against anyone who wanted to find fault with him.

The Commander of the Faithful, peace be on him, had entered into his state of consecration following the Apostle of Allāh, may Allāh bless Him and his family. Many of the Muslims had set out with the Prophet without driving victims for sacrifice. Allāh revealed: Complete the greater pilgrimage (ḥajj) and the lesser pilgrimage ('umra) (II 196). The Apostle of Allāh explained: "The lesser pilgrimage ('umra) has been brought into the (rites of the) greater pilgrimage (ḥajj) until the Day of Resurrection."

He knitted the fingers of both hands together and then he said: "If I had anticipated the consequence of my commandment, I would not have driven sacrificial victims."

Then he ordered the call to be given: "Those of you who have not driven sacrificial victims, should break your state of consecration so that you only made it to perform the lesser pilgrimage ('umra). But those of you who drove sacrificial victims must remain in that state of consecration."

Some of the people obeyed that but others opposed it. Discussions took place among them concerning it. There were some who maintained: "The Apostle of Allāh, may Allāh bless Him and His Family, has dishevelled hair and is dusty; shall we dress in clothes, have intercourse with women and use perfume?" And others said: "Are you not ashamed to come with heads dripping with water from ritual ablutions (after intercourse) while the Apostle of Allāh, may Allāh bless Him and His Family, remains in a state of ritual consecration?"

The Apostle of Allāh denounced those who opposed that and explained: "If I had not driven sacrificial victims, I would have broken my state of ritual consecration and only made it for the lesser pilgrimage ('umra). Therefore those of you who have not driven sacrificial victims, should break your state of consecration."

Some of the people withdrew their opposition but others still maintained it. Among those who maintained their opposition to the Prophet, may Allāh bless Him and His Family, was 'Umar b. al-Khaṭṭāb.

The Apostle of Allāh summoned him and asked him: "Why are you still in a state of ritual consecration, 'Umar? Did you drive sacrificial victims?" "I did not drive any." he replied.

"Then why have you not broken your state of consecration when I told those who had not driven sacrificial victims to break it?" he asked.

"By Allāh, Apostle of Allāh," he answered, "I could not break my state of ritual consecration while you were still in yours."

"You will never believe in it until you die." the Prophet, may Allāh bless Him and His Family, said.

Thus it was that ('Umar) maintained his denial of mut'at al-ḥajj (the joining of the lesser pilgrimage and the greater pilgrimage together with an intervening period of a few days when the pilgrim breaks the state of ritual consecration and is allowed all things in normal life). In the time of his leadership, he went up on the pulpit and forbade it once more and threatened punishment for its performance.

When the Apostle of Allāh carried out his rituals of the pilgrimage, he made 'Alī his partner in his sacrifice of animals: Then he began his journey back to Medina. ('Alī) and the Muslims went with him. He came to a place known as Ghadīr Khumm. At that time, it was not a place suitable for a halt because it lacked water and pasturage. However, he, peace be on him, stopped there and the Muslims with him. The reason for his halting at this place was that a revelation had been received by him concerning the appointment of the Commander of the Faithful, 'Alī b. Abī Ṭālib, peace be on him, as successor for the community after him. The revelation concerning that had been received earlier but without the designation of the time (for it to be made public). He had delayed (making it public) until the presence of a time in which he would be secure from any dispute among them concerning it. Allāh, the Mighty and High, had informed him that if he went beyond Ghadīr Khumm, many of the people would separate from his party (heading) for their towns, homes and valleys. Allāh wanted him to gather them together to hear the designation of the Commander of the Faithful, peace be on him, and to confirm the proofs of it to them. Therefore Allāh, the Exalted, revealed: O Apostle, make known what has been revealed to you from your Lord (V 67), that is concerning the succession of 'Alī and the designation of the Imamate for him. If you do not do it, you will not have made known His message. Allāh will protect you from the people (V 67). Thus He confirms the duty he had concerning that and the fear that had caused him delay and He guarantees to him protection and defence against the people.

The Apostle of Allāh, may Allāh bless Him and His Family, stopped at the place we have mentioned because of what we have described and explained about the command for him to do that. The Muslims stopped around him. It was a scorching day of intense heat. He ordered ('Alī), peace be on him, to go and stand under a great tree that was there and he ordered the travellers to be gathered in that place and to be put in (rows) one after another.

Then he ordered the crier to call out: "The prayer is general (al-ṣalat jāmi'a i.e. everybody should gather)." The travellers (all) gathered before him. Most of them wrapped their cloaks (riḍā') around their feet because of the scorching hot ground. When they had gathered, he climbed above the travellers so that he was high above them and he summoned the Commander of the Faithful, peace be on him. He made him come up with him so that he stood on his right. He then began to address the people. He praised and glorified Allāh, and preached most eloquently. He gave the community news of his own death, saying: "I have been summoned and it is nearly the moment for me to answer. The time has come for me to depart from you. I leave behind me among you two things which, if you cleave to them, you will never go astray - that is the Book of Allāh and my offspring from my family (ahl al-bayt). They will never scatter (from you) until they lead you to me at the (sacred) waters (of Heaven)."

Then he called out at the top of his voice: "Am I not more appropriate (to rule) you than yourselves?"

"By Allāh, yes!" they answered.

He went on speaking continuously without any interruption and taking both arms of the Commander of the Faithful, peace be on him, and raising them so that the white of his armpits could be seen, he said: "Whoever I am the master (mawlā) of, this man, 'Alī, is his master. O Allāh, befriend whoever befriends him, be hostile to whoever opposes him, support whoever supports him and desert whoever deserts him."

Then he, peace be on him, went down. It was the time of the midmorning heat. He prayed two rak'as. The sun then began to decline (at mid-day) so the mu'adhdhin (the one who calls the prayer) called for the statutory prayer (of mid-day). He led them in the mid-day prayer. Then he, peace be on him (went to) sit in his tent. He ordered 'Alī, peace be on him, to sit in his tent opposite him, and he ordered the Muslims to go in group after group to congratulate him on his position and to acknowledge his command over the faithful. All the people did that. Then he ordered his wives and the rest of the wives of the faithful who were with him to go to him and acknowledge his command over the faithful. They did that.

Among those who were profuse in their congratulations on his position was 'Umar b. al-Khaṭṭāb. He gave a public appearance of great joy at it, saying: "Bravo, bravo, 'Alī, you have become my master and the master of every believing man and woman."

Ḥassān b. Thābit came to the Apostle of Allāh, may Allāh bless Him and his family, and said: "Apostle of Allāh, will you permit me to recite what would please Allāh with regard to this position?"

"Recite in the name of Allāh, Ḥassān," he told him.

He stood on elevated ground. The people spread out to listen to his words and he began to recite:

On the day of al-Ghadīr he summoned them and made them answer at Khumm. Listen to the Apostle as he calls.

He said: "Who is your master (mawlā) and friend (walī)?" They answered without showing any signs of opposition:

"Allāh is our master (mawlā) and you are our friend (walī). You will never find any disobedience from us to you."

He said to him: "Arise, 'Alī, I am content that you should be Imam and guide after me.

Whomsoever I am master (mawlā) of, this man is his friend (walī). Therefore be faithful helpers and followers of him."

There he prayed: "O Allāh, befriend his friend and be hostile to whoever opposes 'Alī."

"May you always be supported by the Spirit of Holiness, Ḥassān," the Apostle of Allāh, may Allāh bless Him and His Family, said to him, "as long as you support us with your tongue."

The Apostle of Allāh made this condition in his prayer because he was aware that his attitude would end in opposition. If he knew that he would have remained sound (in belief) in future circumstances, he would have made the prayer for him absolute. Similar conditions were made by Allāh, the Exalted, in praising the wives of the Prophet. He did not praise them unconditionally because He was aware that some of them would change their condition later from the righteousness which entitled them to praise and honour. Thus He said: O Wives of the Prophet, you are not like any other women, if you are pious (XXXIII 32). He did not treat them in that the same way as he treated the family of the Prophet in terms of honouring and praise when they gave their food to orphans, the poor and prisoners. Therefore Allāh, may He be praised, sent down a revelation concerning 'Alī, Fāṭima, al-Ḥasan and al-Ḥusayn, peace be on them, after they had preferred (to give their food rather than have it) themselves despite their own need for it. For Allāh said: Out of love of Allāh, they feed the poor, the orphan and the prisoner. Indeed we feed you for the sake of Allāh. We do not want reward, nor thanks from you. We only fear our Lord on an inauspicious stern day. Then Allāh will guard them from the evil of that day. He will meet them with joy and splendour. He will reward them with gardens and silk for what they have endured. (LXXVI 8-12). He positively asserted reward for them unconditionally just as He stipulated conditions for others because He knew of the different circumstances as we have explained.

In the Farewell Pilgrimage, there was (an example) of the outstanding merit of the Commander of the Faithful, peace be on him, by which he was especially characterised as we have explained. In it he was uniquely set apart with the exalted rank in the way we have mentioned. He was the partner of the Apostle of Allāh in his pilgrimage, (and shared his) sacrificial animals and (shared with him) in the rites of the pilgrimage. Allāh, the Exalted, gave him the same intention as (the Prophet), peace be on them both, and agreement in worship. There was revealed concerning his position with (the Prophet), peace be on him, and his exalted station with Allāh, may He be praised, what extols his praise and requires the necessity of obedience to him by other men, by designating him for succession (khilāfa), and by making plain through him the call to follow him and forbidding opposition to him, and by the prayer for those who followed him in religion and provided help for him, the prayer against those who opposed him, and the curse against those who came forward in enmity against him. Thus it was demonstrated that he was the best of the creatures of Allāh, the Exalted, the noblest of His creation. This is also one of the things which no one else in the community had any share in, nor was there any substitute for it which might approximate it as is clear to anyone who thinks, and obvious to anyone who knows the significance of reality. May Allāh be He Who is praised.

The Circumstances of the Last Illness and Death of the Prophet

Among the circumstances which were given new significance by the Apostle of Allāh, may Allāh bless Him and His Family, and the events which occurred through the decree and ordinance of Allāh, which confirm his outstanding merit and characterise his exalted rank, are those which occurred after the Farewell Pilgrimage. That was when the (Prophet), peace be on him, realised through the nearness of (the end of) his allotted span (the need to put into effect) what he had already told his community. He, peace be on him, began to make speech after speech among the Muslims, warning them against discord after him and opposition to him. He confirmed his injunction to them to cleave to his sunna and those (matters) on which there was agreement and conformity. He urged them to follow his family, to obey them, to support, guard and hold fast to them in religion. He warned them against opposition and apostasy.

Among the things which were mentioned by him, peace be on him, is one which the reporters (of tradition and history) report with agreement and unanimity, that he, peace be on him, said: "People, I am a way-mark for you. You will come to me at the (heavenly) waters. Then indeed I will ask you about the two important things (which I left behind). Take care how you follow me with regard to them, for the Good and Knowing (Allāh) has informed me that they will never scatter (from you) until they meet me. I asked my Lord for that and He granted it to me. Indeed I have left among you the Book of Allāh and the offspring of my family (ahl al-bayt). Do not try to outdo them, for then you will be destroyed. Do not try to teach them, for they are more knowledgeable than you. People, may I not find you, after I (have gone), returning to being unbelievers with some of you striking down others, for then you will meet me with a host like a sea of flowing soldiers. Indeed 'Alī b. Abī Ṭālib, peace be on him, is my brother, my trustee (waṣī). After me he will fight for the (true) interpretation of the Qur'ān just like I fought for its revelation."

He, may Allāh bless Him and His Family, used to address meeting after meeting with words like these.

Then he commissioned Usāma b. Zayd b. Ḥāritha. He ordered and urged him to leave with many members of the community for where his father had been killed in the Byzantine (empire). He, peace be on him, decided to send out the foremost of the Emigrants and Anṣār in his army, so that at his death there would not be anyone in Medina who differed about the leadership and who had ambitions to become the leader of the people. In this way he (hoped to) set in order the situation for the man who was to succeed him and to prevent any opponent from opposing him in his right. He gave (Usāma) the command on the condition which we have mentioned and he endeavoured to send them out. He ordered Usāma to leave Medina with his army for al-Jurf, and he urged the people to go out to him and to go with him. He warned them against lingering and dilatoriness in (doing) it.

While matters were in that situation, the illness came upon him of which he (later) died. When he felt the sickness which had befallen him, he took the hand of 'Alī, peace be on him. A group of the people followed him and he headed for (the cemetery of) al-Baqī'. He told those who followed him: "I have been commanded to seek forgiveness for (the souls of) the people of (the cemetery of) al-Baqī'."

They went with him until he stopped in front of them. He, peace be on him, said: "People of the graves, let there be comfort for you in your situation (as opposed to the situation) in which discords have come upon the people like the cutting of the dark night when the first of them will follow the last."

Then he (spent) a long time seeking forgiveness for (the souls of) the people of (the cemetery of) al-Baqī'. (After this), he approached the Commander of the Faithful, peace be on him, and told him: "Gabriel, peace be on him, used to revise the Qur'ān with me once each year. This year he has revised it with me twice. I can only consider that it is because (the end of) my allotted span of life is at hand." Then he said: "'Alī, I was given the choice between remaining forever amid the treasuries of the world or of (going to) heaven. I have chosen to meet my Lord and (to go to) heaven. When I die, wash me. Cover my nakedness so that no one but a blind man could see it."

He returned to his house and remained there for three days in a weak condition. Then he went out to the mosque, wearing a turban on his head and leaning on the Commander of the Faithful, peace be on him, on his right hand and on al-Faḍl b. al-'Abbās on his other hand. He went up on the pulpit and sat there. Then he said: "People, the time of my departure from you has come. Whoever has any goods with me, let him come to me so that I may give them to him. Whoever has a debt which I owe him, let him inform me of it. People, between Allāh and any man there is nothing by which (Allāh) will give him better or by which Allāh will keep away from him evil, except works (al-'amal). People, by Him who sent me as a prophet with truth, let no one claim nor anyone desire that there should be salvation without works through (Allāh's) mercy. If I had disobeyed, I would have been hurled down (to damnation). O Allāh, have I conveyed (the message)?"

He went down and led the people in a short prayer. He returned to his house. At that time, he was in the house of Umm Salama, may Allāh be pleased with her. He remained there for a day or two. Then 'Ā'isha came to her to ask her to move him to her house so that she might undertake to nurse him. She had asked the wives of the Prophet about that and they had given her their permission. Thus he, may Allāh bless Him and His Family, was moved to the house in which 'Ā'isha lived. The illness remained with him for several days and grew more serious.

At the time of the morning prayer, Bilāl came while the Apostle of Allāh, may Allāh bless Him and His Family, was overcome by sickness. (He asked:) "Do I call the prayer, may Allāh have mercy on you?"

The Apostle of Allāh gave him permission to make his call and said: "Let one of the people pray before them, for I am too distracted by (the final hours of) my life."

"Order Abū Bakr," 'Ā'isha said.

"Order 'Umar," intervened Ḥafṣa.

When the Apostle of Allāh, may Allāh bless Him and His Family, heard their words and saw the eagerness of each of them to exalt her own father and their discord about that, he said: "Have you put the shroud on the Apostle of Allāh while he is still alive? Indeed you are like the mistresses of Joseph."

Then he, peace be on him, rose hurriedly fearing that one of the two men would go forward (to lead the prayers). He had ordered them to go with Usāma and he had had no idea that they would be disobedient. However when he heard what he heard from 'Ā'isha and Ḥafṣa, he knew that they had delayed in (obeying) his command. He hurried to prevent discord and remove doubt. He, blessings and peace be on him, arose despite the fact that he could barely lift himself off the ground through weakness. 'Alī b. Abī Ṭālib, peace be on him, took his hand and al-Faḍl b. al-'Abbās took the other. He leaned on them both and his feet dragged a trail along the ground because of his weakness.

When he came out into the mosque, he found that Abū Bakr had already got to the miḥrāb. He indicated with his hand that he should withdraw and Abū Bakr withdrew. The Apostle of Allāh, may Allāh bless Him and His Family, took up his place. He said the "takbir" and began the prayer which Abū Bakr had begun before without taking any account of what had already been performed.

After he had said the final greeting of the prayer, he returned to his house. He summoned Abū Bakr, 'Umar and a group of the Muslims who had been present at the mosque. He said: "Did I not order you to go with the army of Usāma?" "Yes, Apostle of Allāh," they replied.

"Why have you delayed from (carrying out) my order?"

"I had gone out but then I returned so that I might renew my covenant with you," Abū Bakr said.

"Apostle of Allāh, I did not go out because I did not want to ask travellers about you," 'Umar answered.

"Despatch the army of Usāma, despatch the army of Usāma," commanded the Prophet, may Allāh bless Him and His Family. He repeated it three times and then he fainted from the fatigue which had come upon him and the sorrow which possessed him.

He remained unconscious for a short time while the Muslims wept and his wives and the women and children of the Muslims, and all those present raised great cries of lamentation. The Apostle of Allāh, may Allāh bless Him and His Family, recovered consciousness and looked at them. Then he said: "Bring me ink and parchment so that I may write a document for you, after which you will never go astray."

Again he fainted and one of those present rose to look for ink and parchment.

"Go back," 'Umar ordered him. "He is delirious."

The man went back. (Later) those present regretted the dilatoriness (they had shown) in bringing ink and parchment and rebuked each other. They used to say: "We belong to Allāh and to Him we will return, but we have become anxious about our disobedience to the Apostle of Allāh, may Allāh bless Him and His Family."

When he, peace be on him, recovered consciousness, one of them said: "We will not bring you ink and parchment, Apostle of Allāh."

"May Allāh remove him who made you say 'no'," he said. "However, I will appoint a trustee over you in a better way through my family."

Then he turned his head away from the people. They rose to leave but al-'Abbās, al-Faḍl b. al-'Abbās and 'Alī b. Abī Ṭālib and his family, in particular, remained with him.

"If this matter is to be settled upon us after you, then tell us," al-'Abbās asked him. "If you know that we are to be overcome, then give us the decision." "You are those who will be found weak after me," he answered and then was silent.

The people (rose to leave), weeping with despair at (losing) the Prophet, may Allāh bless Him and His Family. When they had left, he, peace be on him, said: "Send back to me my brother and my uncle (i.e. 'Alī and al-'Abbās)."

They sent for someone to call them and he brought them. When he had them sitting close, he, blessings and peace be on him, said: "Uncle of the Apostle of Allāh, will you accept my testamentary bequest (waṣī), fulfil my promise and carry out my religion?"

"Apostle of Allāh, your uncle is an old man with the responsibilities of a large family," answered al-'Abbās. "You vie with the wind in liberality and generosity. You have made promises which your uncle could never fulfil."

Then he turned to 'Alī b. Abī Ṭālib, peace be on him, and said: "Brother, will you accept my testamentary bequest, fulfil my promises, carry out my religion on my behalf and look after the affairs of my family after me?"

"Yes, Apostle of Allāh," he replied.

"Come near me," he told him.

He went near to him and he embraced him. He took his ring from his finger and said: "Take this and put it on your finger."

Then he called for his sword, his breastplate and all his weapons and gave those to him. He looked for a turban which he used to wear around his stomach when he put on his weapons and went out to battle. It was brought to him and he gave it to the Commander of the Faithful, peace be on him. Then he said to him: "Go, 'Alī, in the name of Allāh, to your house."

On the next day, the people were denied access to him as he was seriously ill in bed. The Commander of the Faithful, peace be on him, did not leave him except to (fulfil) some necessities. Then he had to go to attend to some of his affairs. The Apostle of Allāh, may Allāh bless Him and His Family, recovered consciousness and he missed 'Alī. His wives were around him and he said: "Call my brother and my companion." The weakness returned to him and he fell silent.

"Call Abū Bakr," 'Ā'isha said.

Abū Bakr was summoned. He came and sat by his head. When he opened his eyes, he looked at him and then turned his head away from him. Abū Bakr arose and said: "If he had any need of me, he would have communicated it to me."

When he had gone, the Apostle of Allāh repeated his words a second time and said: "Call my brother and my companion."

"Call 'Umar for him," Ḥafṣa said.

'Umar was summoned. When he came and the Apostle of Allāh, may Allāh bless Him and His Family, saw him, he turned his head away from him. So he went away. Then he said: "Call my brother and companion."

"Call 'Alī," said Umm Salama, may Allāh be pleased with her, "for he does not mean anyone else."

The Commander of the Faithful was summoned. When he was

close to him, he indicated to him to bend down to him. Then the Apostle of Allāh, may Allāh bless Him and His Family, spoke privately to him for a long time. Then he rose and sat down beside him until the Apostle of Allāh, may Allāh bless Him and His Family, fell asleep.

When he had fallen asleep, ('Alī) went out.

"What did he entrust to you, Abū al-Ḥasan?" the people asked him.

"He taught me of a thousand doors of knowledge and each door opened for me (another) thousand doors," he answered. "He made a bequest to me of what I will undertake (qā'im) if Allāh, the Exalted, wishes."

He became critically ill and death was at hand. The Commander of the Faithful, peace be on him, was present with him. When his soul was about to depart, he said: "'Alī, put my head in your lap, for the order of Allāh (for my death) has come. When my soul departs, take it with your hand and rub your face with it. Then point me in the direction of the qibla. Carry out my command and pray over me as the first of the people. Do not leave me until you have buried me in my grave. Seek the help of Allāh, the Exalted."

'Alī, peace be on him, took his head and put it in his lap. Then he lost consciousness. Fāṭima, peace be on her, bent down to look into his face. She was weeping and calling to him, saying:

May he be watered by the white clouds (pouring water) on his face. (He was) the one who cared for orphans and the one who protected widows.

Then the Apostle of Allāh, may Allāh bless Him and His Family, opened his eyes and said in a weak voice: "These are words for your uncle, Abū Ṭālib. Do not recite them. Rather recite: Muhammad is no more than a messenger: many Were the messenger that passed away before him. If he died or were slain, will ye then Turn back on your heels? (III 144)."

She wept for a long time. He indicated to her to come close. She went close to him and he whispered something to her which lit up her face. Then he, blessings and peace be on him, died. The right hand of the Commander of the Faithful was under his jaw and his soul passed into it. He raised it to his face and rubbed it with it. Then he put him in the direction (of the qibla), closed his eyes, and laid him out on his waist-cloth (izār).

The report has been handed down that Fāṭima, peace be on her, was asked: "What did the Apostle of Allāh, may Allāh bless Him and His Family, whisper to you so that by it he made the grief and worry of his death leave you?"

She replied: "He told me that I would be the first of his family (ahl al-bayt) to join him and that it would not be a long time for me after him before I would be with him. That made (the grief) go from me."

When the Commander of the Faithful, peace be on him, wanted to wash him, he summoned al-Faḍl b. al-'Abbās and told him to get water for him to wash him after he had put a cover over his eyes. Then he split open his shirt from before the pocket to the midriff. He washed him, perfumed (his body) and shrouded him, while al-Faḍl passed him the water and helped him. When he had finished washing and preparing his body, he went forward and prayed alone. No one shared in the prayer with him. The Muslims in the mosque were talking about who would lead them in the prayer over him and where he would be buried. The Commander of the Faithful, peace be on him, came out to them and said: "The Apostle of Allāh, may

Allāh bless Him and His Family, is our Imam, both alive and dead. Therefore let group after group of you come in and let them pray over him without an Imam and then let them depart. Allāh only took the soul of the Prophet in one place and it would please him for his grave to be there. I will bury him in the room in which he died."

The people accepted that and were pleased with it.

When the Muslims had prayed over him, al-'Abbās b. 'Abd al-Muṭṭalib sent a man to Abū 'Ubayda b. al-Jarrāḥ. He used to dig graves for the Meccans. That was the custom of the Meccans. He also sent to Zayd b. Sahl, who used to dig graves for the Medinans and make a niche in the side of the grave. He summoned them both and said: "O Allāh, choose (one of them) for your Prophet."

The man was found to be Abū Ṭalḥa Zayd b. Sahl and he was told to dig a grave for the Apostle of Allāh, may Allāh bless him and grant him peace. He dug a tomb for him. The Commander of the Faithful, peace be on him, entered it (as did) al-'Abbās b. 'Abd al-Muṭṭalib, al-Faḍl b. al-'Abbās and Usāma b. Zayd, so that they might carry out the burial of the Apostle.

At this, the Anṣār called out from behind the house: "'Alī, we remind you of Allāh and our right today with regard to the Apostle of Allāh lest it should go (from us). Let a man from among us come in so that we may have a share in the burial of the Apostle of Allāh, may Allāh bless Him and His Family." "Let Aws b. Khawalī come in," he answered.

He was an excellent man, who had taken part in Badr, from the Banū 'Awf of Khazraj. When he came in, 'Alī, peace be on him, told him: "Go down into the grave."

He went down. The Commander of the Faithful put the (body

of) the Apostle of Allāh, blessings and peace be on them both, into his hands and lowered it into his grave. When it reached the earth, he told him to come out. He came out and 'Alī, peace be on him, went down into the grave. He uncovered the face of the Apostle of Allāh, may Allāh bless Him and His Family, and put his cheek on the earth in the direction of the qibla towards his right. Then he put clay soil on him and then poured the earth over him.

That was on Monday with two days remaining in (the month of) Ṣafar in the eleventh year after his emigration, the blessings and peace of Allāh be on him. He was sixty-three years of age.

Most of the people did not attend the burial of the Apostle of Allāh, may Allāh bless Him and His Family, because of the dispute which was taking place between the Emigrants and the Anṣār over the matter of succession (khilāfa). Most of them also missed the (funeral) prayer over him on that account as well. Fāṭima began to call out: "How evil has this morning become for him!" Abū Bakr heard her and said: "Your morning is an evil morning."

The people seized the opportunity of 'Alī b. Abī Ṭālib, peace be on him, being occupied with the Apostle of Allāh, may Allāh bless Him and His Family, and the isolation of the Banū Hāshim from them because of the tragedy which had befallen them with regard to the Apostle of Allāh, may Allāh bless Him and His Family. So they hurried to take control of the affair. What was agreed on was agreed in favour of Abū Bakr because of the dislike of the newly-converted Meccans (ṭulaqā') and (the dislike of) those whose hearts had been reconciled, of delaying the matter until Banū Hāshim had finished.

Thus was the matter settled and (the people) pledged allegiance to Abū Bakr because of his presence at the place. Well-known factors motivated the people to accept this. Among them were their own desires. This book is not the place to mention them and we will explain in detail the discussion about them (elsewhere).

The report is handed down that when what had taken place for Abū Bakr had taken place and those who pledged allegiance to him, had pledged allegiance, a man came to the Commander of the Faithful, peace be on him, while he was arranging the grave of the Apostle of Allāh, may Allāh bless Him and His Family, with a shovel in his hand. He said to him: "The people have pledged allegiance to Abū Bakr. The Anṣār have given up because of their differences and the new Meccan converts (ṭulaqā') have hurried to make their covenant to the man out of fear of your attaining authority."

He put the tip of the shovel on the ground with his hand still on it and answered: In the name of Allāh, the Merciful, the Compassionate. Do the people reckon that they will abandon saying: 'We believe,' without being guilty of deceit? We have tested those before them. Allāh knows those who are truthful and He knows the liar. Do those who do evil deeds consider that they can outdo us? How wrong is their judgement. (XXIX 2-4).

Abū Sufyān came to the door of the Apostle of Allāh, may Allāh bless Him and His Family, while 'Alī and al-'Abbās were zealously attending to the arrangements for him, and he called out:

Banū Hāshim, the people have no desire for you. Special (to them) are (the clans of) Taym b. Murra and 'Adī.

Yet authority should only be among you and belong to you. Only Abū al-Ḥasan ('Alī) has (a right) to it.

Abū al-Ḥasan, take hold of it with a resolute hand. You are being deprived of the authority which you expected.

Then he called out at the top of his voice : "Banū Hāshim, Banū 'Abd Manāf, are you content that the despicable father of a young camel, the son of a despicable man, should have authority over you? No, by Allāh, if you wish, let me provide horses and men (who will be sufficient) for it."

"Go back, Abū Sufyān," shouted the Commander of the Faithful, peace be on him. "By Allāh, you do not seek Allāh in what you are suggesting. You are still plotting against Islam and those who believe in it. We are busy with the Apostle of Allāh, may Allāh bless Him and His Family. Each person gets what he has earned and he is (only) responsible for (walī) the crime he has committed."

Abū Sufyān went to the mosque. There he found the Banū Umayya gathered. He urged them (to take action) in the matter but they did not respond to him.

Discord was general and affliction was everywhere. Evil events had taken place by which Satan gained (greater) power and in which lying and hostile people co-operated. Through their denunciation of it, the people of (true) belief were abandoned. This is the interpretation of Allāh's words: Beware of discord which especially strikes against those of you who oppress (VIII 25).

In the outstanding virtues of the Commander of the Faithful, peace be on him, which we have enumerated after what we have already mentioned with regard to the Farewell Pilgrimage, there is evidence which indicates that he, peace be on him, was especially characterised by them in a way that nobody else of mankind shared. Each one of them was a special category (of virtue) which stood in its own right without needing anything else to (explain) its significance.

Surely you realise that his special distinction during the illness of the Prophet, may Allāh bless Him and His Family, up to the time that Allāh, the Exalted, took him, required merit in religion and affinity to the Prophet, may Allāh bless Him and His Family? (This can be seen) through the good deeds which made (the Prophet) rely and depend on him, and set him apart from all the people in order to look after him at (the end of) his life. (Thus you should realise) the special distinction of his love for him which no one else shared with him. (Then there is also) the testamentary bequest (waṣiyya) which he made to him after it had been offered to someone else and refused because the burdens of the duties involved in it, and the responsibility of carrying it out and fulfilling the trust (were too heavy) for that other person to carry out. He was characterised by having been brothered with the Apostle of Allāh, may Allāh bless Him and His Family, and by being with him during his illness when he summoned him. In him was deposited the knowledge of religion by which he made him separate from anyone else. He carried out the washing and preparation of his body for (his journey to) Allāh. He said the (funeral) prayer over him before any one else, and he had precedence over them in that through his rank with (the Apostle) and with Allāh, the Exalted. He guided the community as to the manner of the (funeral) prayer over him when the matter was doubtful to them. He showed them the place to bury him despite the difference of opinion that they had had concerning that. They submitted to what he told them to do and considered him (right) in that. Thus through all of that he must be regarded as unique in his merit. Through it he brought to completion the outstanding action for Islam which he had begun at its beginning (and continued) to the death of the Apostle of Allāh, may Allāh bless Him and His Family. As a result of it there occurred for him a consecutive chain of virtues. No blemish entered any of his actions in religion. No aspect of his merit, as we have recorded it, puts any limitation on the ultimate in qualities of faith and in the virtues of Islam. This should also be associated with his marvellous miracles which confounded nature. He is such that there cannot be found an equal to him except for a prophet who has been sent (with a message) and an angel who has been brought into close proximity (with Allāh), and such as are associated with them in the degree of their virtues in the eyes of Allāh, may He be praised. With regard to those who oppose these three categories, traditional knowledge ('āda) follows a contrary (path to them) with the agreement of those who have reason (to think), tongues (to speak) and are aware of the traditions ('ādāt). We ask Allāh for success and by Him we will be protected from error.

LEGAL DECISIONS OF THE COMMANDER OF THE FAITHFUL

As for the reports which have demonstrated his outstanding quality in the legal decisions (he has given) with regard to religion and the laws (he has propounded) for which all the believers were in need, they are too numerous to be counted and too illustrious to be dealt with (properly), as are those which have been confirmed with regard to his precedence in traditional knowledge ('ilm), his supremacy over the community in gnosis (ma'rifa) and understanding. (There are many reports that) the scholars of the Companions (frequently) used to resort to him in matters which were difficult for them and they would seek his help in them and submit to his judgement concerning them. I will endeavour to put forward a brief summary which will give some indication of the others, if Allāh, the Exalted, wills.

A. Judgements of the Commander of the Faithful during the Lifetime of the Prophet

With the regard to this, there are those of his judgements while the Apostle of Allāh, may Allāh bless Him and His Family, was alive which have been reported by the transmitters of tradition from the non-Shīʻa (ʻāmma) and from the Shīʻa (khāṣṣa). In these (the Prophet) guided him and attested to the correctness of the decisions which he gave. He called attention to his goodness and praised him for it. Thus he separated him from the rest of men as a result of his outstanding merit in that. In this way he showed his entitlement to authority after him and the necessity for him to take precedence over others with regard to the position of the Imamate. Similarly, revelation has taken that (matter) within its compass in terms of the evidence for its meaning and what can be understood from the interpretation of its contents. Thus Allāh, the Mighty and High, says: Is not he who guides you to truth more entitled to be followed than one who does not go aright unless he is guided? For what is wrong with you, how do you judge? (X 35). Then there is His statement, may He be praised: Are those who know and those who do not know equal? Only those who possess hearts (ūlū al-albāb) remember (XXXIX 9). There is the statement by Him, the Mighty and High, in the story of Adam when the angel said: Are you creating in it one who will spread corruption there and shed blood while we (constantly) repeat Your praise and hallow You? He replied: I know what you do not know. And He taught Adam all the names (or things) and then He presented them to the angels. He said: Tell me the names of these if you are truthful. They answered: May You be praised, we have no knowledge except what You have taught us. You are the One Who knows and the Wise. Then He said: Adam, tell them their names. When he had told them their names, He said to them: Have I not told you that I know the unseen in the heavens and the earth and I know what you are showing and what you are keeping hidden (II 30-33). Allāh, the Exalted, informed the angels that Adam was more entitled to the vice-regency (khilāfa) than they were because He had informed him of the names and he was the most excellent of them in knowledge of things informed (to him). He, may His names be hallowed, (also) said in the story of Ṭālūt: Their prophet said to them: Allāh has sent Ṭālūt to you as a king.

They asked: Shall he have (the right of) kingship over us while we are more entitled to kingship than he is? He has not brought any extent of wealth. He replied: Allāh has chosen him to be over you and has increased him extensively in knowledge and substance. Allāh bestows His kingship on whom He wishes. Allāh is (all) embracing and One Who knows (II 247).

Thus (Allāh) made the manner of his right to precedence over them, by virtue of what He granted him in the scope of his knowledge and substance, and His having chosen him above all of them. These verses are in agreement with rational evidence that the one who is more knowledgeable has more right in the area of the Imamate than those who do not equal him in knowledge. Thus they also give evidence for the necessity of the precedence of the Commander of the Faithful, peace be on him, over all the rest of the Muslims in the succession (khilāfa) of the Apostle of Allāh, may Allāh bless Him and His Family, and in the Imamate of the community because of his precedence, peace be on him, over them in knowledge and wisdom and their falling short of his rank in that.

1. His Judgements in Yemen

Among those reports which have been handed down about his legal decisions, peace be on him, while the Prophet, may Allāh bless Him and His Family, was still alive and present, is the following:

When the Apostle of Allāh, may Allāh bless Him and His Family, wanted to invest him with the office of judge in Yemen and to send him to them so that he might teach them the laws, explain to them what was permitted and forbidden, and judge for them according to the laws of the Qur'ān, the Commander of the Faithful, peace be on him, asked him: "Apostle of Allāh, you are inviting me to (undertake) the office of judge while I am still a young man without knowledge of all (the matters of) judgement."

"Come nearer to me," he told him. He went nearer and he struck him in the chest with his hand and said: "O Allāh, guide his heart and strengthen his tongue."

The Commander of the Faithful reported: "I never doubted in my ability to judge between two men after that occurrence."

When the administrative house (dār) in Yemen was occupied by him and he began to take care of the office of judging and giving decisions among the Muslims, which the Apostle of Allāh, may Allāh bless Him and His Family, had entrusted to him, two men were brought before him. Between them was a maidservant over whom both of them had equal rights of possession as a slave. They had both been ignorant of the prohibition of having intercourse with her and had both had intercourse with her in the same month of her menstrual cycle. (They had done this) in the belief that this was permissible, because of their recent acceptance of Islam and their lack of knowledge of the laws which were in the law of Islam (sharī'a). The maidservant had become pregnant and given birth to a boy. They were in dispute as to (who was the father).

He drew lots with their names on for the boy. The lot fell upon one of them. He assigned the boy to him but required him to pay half his value as if he had been a slave of his partner. He said: "If I knew that you had both embarked on what you have done after the proof had been given you of it being prohibited, I would have exerted (every effort) to punish you both."

The Apostle of Allāh, may Allāh bless Him and His Family, learned of this case. He accepted it and he acknowledged the judgement on them within Islam. He said: "Praise be to Allāh

Who has created among us, the family (ahl al-bayt), one who can judge according to the practice and method of David in judging." In that he was referring to judgement according to inspiration (ilhām) which would have been taken in the sense of revelation (waḥy) and the sending down of a text for it if there had been any explanation of such (an occurrence ever having taken place).

Among the cases brought before him, peace be on him, while he was in Yemen, is the report of (the case in which) a pit was dug for a lion. It fell into it and the people gathered round to look at it. One man was standing on the edge of the pit. His foot slipped and he hung on to another man. That man hung on to a third, and the third to a fourth. They all fell into the pit and were all killed. He, peace be on him, gave the judgement that the first was the prey of the lion and he (and his family) were responsible for the payment of a third of the blood-price for the second. Similarly the second (and his family) were responsible for the payment of a third of the blood-price for the third and the third (and his family) were responsible for the payment of a third of the blood-price for the fourth.

The report of that reached the Apostle of Allāh, may Allāh bless Him and His Family. He said: "Abū al-Ḥasan has given judgement in their regard with the judgement of Allāh, the Mighty and High above (on) His throne."

Then there was brought before him (the case in which) it is reported that a girl was carrying (another) girl on her shoulder in a game. Another girl came along and pinched the girl who was carrying (the other one). She jumped because of being pinched. The girl who was being carried fell and broke her neck. She died. He, peace be on him, judged that the girl who did the pinching was, responsible for a third of the blood-price, the girl who jumped was responsible for (another) third of it and the remaining third was inoperative because the riding of the girl, who broke her neck, on the girl who jumped was in fun.

The report of that reached the Apostle of Allāh, may Allāh bless Him and His Family. He accepted it and testified to the correctness of it.

He, peace be on him, gave judgement on (a case where) a wall had fallen on some people and killed them. Among their number there was a slave-woman and a free woman. The free woman had had a small child, born of a free man, and the slave-woman had had a small child, born of a slave. The free child could not be distinguished from the slave child.

He drew lots between them; he adjudged freedom as belonging to the one of them for whom the lot for freedom was drawn and he adjudged slavery for the one for whom the lot for slavery was drawn. Then he freed (the slave child) and made him retainer (lit. client mawlā) (of the free child). In this way he also decided about their inheritance with the decision going in accordance with (the norm for) the free one and his retainer.

The Apostle of Allāh, may Allāh bless Him and His Family, accepted his judgement in this decision and he declared its correctness through his acceptance of it, as we have mentioned and described.

2. A Case outside Yemen during the Life of the Prophet

Reports have been handed down that two men brought a dispute before the Prophet, may Allāh bless Him and His Family, about a cow which had killed a donkey.

"Apostle of Allāh," said one of them, "this man's cow has killed my donkey." "Go to Abū Bakr," the Apostle of Allāh told them, "and ask him about that."

They came to Abū Bakr and told him their story.

"Why have you left the Apostle of Allāh, may Allāh bless Him and His Family, and come to me?" he asked them.

"He told us to do that," they answered.

"A beast has killed a beast and therefore its owner has no responsibility (for the dead beast)," he said.

They returned to the Apostle of Allāh, the blessing of Allāh be on him, and told him of that. He said to them: "Go to 'Umar b. al-Khaṭṭāb and tell him your story. Ask him for a judgement about that."

They went to him and told him their story. He asked: "Why have you left the Apostle of Allāh and come to me?"

"He told us to do that," they answered.

"Why did he not tell you to go to Abū Bakr?" he asked.

"We were ordered to do that," they told him, "and we went to him." "What did he say to you about this case?" he enquired. "He said such and such," they replied.

"My view agrees with Abū Bakr's," he said.

They returned to the Prophet, may Allāh bless Him and His Family, and gave him a report of that. He said: "Go to 'Alī b. Abī Ṭālib so that he may judge between you."

They went to him and told him their story.

"If the cow entered into the stable of the donkey, then the owner (of the cow) must pay the price of the donkey to the owner (of the donkey)," he declared. "But if the donkey entered into the stable of the cow, and (the cow) killed it, the owner (of the donkey) has no payment due from the owner (of the cow)."

They went back to the Prophet, may Allāh bless Him and His Family, and told him about his judgement between them. He, may Allāh bless Him and His Family, said: "'Alī b. Abī Ṭālib, peace be on him, has given judgement between you with the judgement of Allāh, the Exalted." Then he said: "Praise be to Allāh who has created among us, the family (ahl al-bayt), one who can give judgement in the manner of David."

Some of the non-Shī'a ('āmma) authorities report that this judgement between the two men was made by the Commander of the Faithful, peace be on him, in Yemen.

B. Judgements of the Commander of the Faithful during the Rule of Abū Bakr

(This is) a brief summary of the legal decisions given by (the Commander of the Faithful), peace be on him, during the rule of Abū Bakr. Among these is the account which has been handed down by both non-Shī'a and Shī'a authorities:

A man was brought before Abū Bakr. He had drunk wine, so Abū Bakr wanted to administer the prescribed punishment (ḥadd) on him. However the man pleaded: "I drank it without having knowledge that it was forbidden because I grew up among people who regarded it as lawful. I did not know that it was forbidden until now."

Abū Bakr became unable to deliver a decision in the matter. He did not know the way to judge him. Some of those present advised him to seek for information from the Commander of the Faithful, peace be on him, about the decision in that matter. He sent someone to ask him about it.

The Commander of the Faithful advised: "Tell two trustworthy Muslims to go around the gatherings of the Emigrants and Anṣār to ask them whether any of them had recited to (the man) the verse (of the Qur'ān) forbidding (wine) or had reported it to him on the authority of the Apostle of Allāh, may Allāh bless Him and His Family. If two of them give testimony of that, then he should carry out the prescribed punishment on him. If no one can give testimony on that, he should tell him to repent and let him go."

Abū Bakr did that. Not one of the Emigrants and Anṣār gave evidence that they had recited the verse (of the Qur'ān) forbidding (wine) or had reported it to him on the authority of the Apostle of Allāh, may Allāh bless Him and His Family. So he told him to repent and let him go. He submitted to (the authority of) 'Alī in judging it.

*****

They have reported that Abū Bakr was asked about Allāh's words: Fākihatan wa abbān (LXXX 31). He did not know the meaning of al-abb in the Qur'ān and said: "Any sky which looks down (on me) or any land which holds me up ....

rather what shall I do, if I say something about the Book of Allāh, the Exalted, which I do not know. As for al-fākiha, (fruit), we know its meaning but as for al-abb Allāh knows better."

The Commander of the Faithful, peace be on him, was informed of that statement of his about it. "May Allāh be praised, did he know that al-abb is fresh herbage (kalā') and pasture (mar'an) and that His words, wa fākihatan wa abbān, are the enumeration by Allāh, the Exalted, of his favours to His creatures through the things which He has provided for them to eat and created for them and their animals; (these are some of) the things by which their spirits are kept alive and their bodies exist."

*****

Abū Bakr was asked about al-kalāla (IV 176). He answered: "I will give my opinion about it. If I am right, then it is from Allāh. If I am wrong, then it is from myself and from Satan."

The Commander of the Faithful was informed of that. He said: "What makes him satisfied with opinion in this situation? Did he not know that al-kalāla is brothers and sisters from (the same) father and mother, and from just the father and also from the mother in the same way. Allāh, the Mighty and High, said: If they seek a decision from you, say: Allāh gave a decision to you in terms of the brothers and sisters (al-kalāla). If a man dies without children and he has a sister she shall have half of what he left (IV 176). He, the Mighty (also) said: If a man is succeeded by brothers and sisters (al-kalāla) or by a wife while he had a brother or a sister, each one will have a sixth. If there are more than that, then they shall have a third (IV 12)."

*****

The report is handed down that one of the Jewish rabbis came to Abū Bakr and said: "You are the successor (khalīfa) of this community."

"Yes," he replied.

"We find in the Torah that the successors (khulafā') of prophets are the most knowledgeable of the communities," he said. "Therefore tell me about Allāh, the Exalted. Where is He? In heaven or on earth?" "In heaven on the throne," answered Abū Bakr.

"Then I should consider that the earth is without Him and I should consider according to this statement that He is in one place and not in another," the Jew stated.

"That is doctrine of atheists (zanādiqa)," declared Abū Bakr. "Go away from me or I will kill you."

The rabbi turned away in amazement and mockery at Islam. The Commander of the Faithful, peace be on him, met him.

"Jew, I know what you have asked about and did not get an answer for," he said. "We say that Allāh, the Mighty and High, is the whereness of whereness, there is no where for Him. He avoids any place containing Him while He is in every place, without contact with anything and without being next to anything. He encompasses knowledge of what is there and nothing of it is outside His provenance. I am telling you about what is written in one of your books which attests the truth of what I have told you. If you know it, do you believe in it?" "Yes," replied the Jew.

He said: "Didn't you find in one of your books that Moses, the son of 'Imrān, peace be on him, was sitting down one day when an angel came to him from the East. Moses asked him: 'From where have you come?' It answered: 'From Allāh, the Mighty and High.' Then an angel came to him from the West. He asked: 'From where have you come?' It answered: 'From Allāh, the

Mighty and High.' Then another angel came to him and said: 'I have come to you from the Seventh Heaven, from (being with) Allāh, the Mighty and High.' Another angel came to him and said: 'I have come to you from the Seventh Firmament, from (being with) Allāh, the Mighty and High.' Then Moses said: 'May Allāh be praised, no place is without Him and He is not nearer to one place than another.'"

The Jew replied: "I testify that this is the truth and you have more right to (occupy) the place of your Prophet than the one who has control over it."

Reports like these are numerous.

C. Reports of the Judgements of (the Commander of the Faithful) during the Rule of 'Umar b. al-Khaṭṭāb

Among these is what has been handed down by non-Shī'a ('āmma) and Shī'a (khāṣṣa) authorities concerning the story of Qudāma b. Maẓ'ūn. The latter had drunk wine and 'Umar wanted to carry out the prescribed punishment on him. However, Qudāma had said: "It is not necessary to give me the prescribed punishment because Allāh has said: There is no crime in what those who have believed and performed good works have tasted as long as they have feared Allāh, believed and performed good works (V 93)."

So 'Umar withdrew the prescribed punishment.

The Commander of the Faithful, peace be on him, learned of that. He went to 'Umar and said: "You failed to administer the prescribed punishment on Qudāma for drinking wine."

"He recited the verse of Qur'ān to me," said 'Umar and recited it.

"Qudāma is not one of the people (referred to) in the verse" retorted the Commander of the Faithful, peace be on him. "Nor can anyone use it (as a pretext) for committing actions which Allāh has forbidden. Those who have believed and performed good actions cannot make what is forbidden lawful. Send for Qudāma and make him repent from what he said. If he repents, then administer the prescribed punishment on him. If he does not repent, kill him, for he has abandoned the religion (milla)."

Then 'Umar became aware (of the real situation). Qudāma knew of the discussion and (publicly) showed his repentance and his withdrawal (of his assertion). 'Umar withdrew the punishment of death but he did not know how he should administer the prescribed punishment on him. He asked the Commander of the Faithful, peace be on him: "Show me how the prescribed punishment (should be administered) on him."

"Give him the prescribed punishment of eighty (lashes)," he said. "For when the drinker of wine drinks it, he becomes drunk. When he becomes drunk, he talks nonsense. When he talks nonsense, he spreads calumnies."

Therefore 'Umar had him given eighty lashes and he gave judgement according to his advice in that matter.

*****

It is reported that during the time of 'Umar, a man seduced a mad woman. Evidence for that was established against her. Therefore 'Umar ordered her to be flogged according to the prescribed punishment. She was brought past the Commander of the Faithful (on her way) to be flogged.

"Why is the mad woman of the family of so-and-so being dragged along?" he asked.

"A man seduced her and fled and the evidence for fornication has been established against her. So 'Umar ordered her to be flogged," he was told.

"Take her back to him," he told them, "and ask him: Don't you know that this is a mad woman and the Apostle of Allāh, may Allāh bless Him and His Family has said: The order (of punishment) should be withheld from the mad person until he recovers. Her reason and her soul have been overcome."

She was taken back to 'Umar and he was told what the Commander of the Faithful, peace be on him, had said. He said: "Allāh has rescued (me) from it. I was almost destroyed through whipping her." And he withdrew the prescribed punishment from her.

*****

It is reported that a pregnant woman who had committed adultery was brought before 'Umar. He ordered her to be stoned. The Commander of the Faithful, peace be on him, told him: "Take care that you have a (right to take) action against her, that is not a (right to take) action against what is in her womb. For Allāh, the Exalted, says: Nor does any bearer of a burden bear the burden of another (VI 164)."

"I have not lived (to see) a problem with which Abū al-Ḥasan is not (competent to deal)," said 'Umar. Then he asked: "What shall I do with her?"

"Take care of her until she gives birth," he said. "When she has given birth and you have found someone to nurse her child, then administer the prescribed punishment on her." `

Thus was 'Umar relieved of (his cares). In that decision, he relied on the Commander of the Faithful, peace be on him.

*****

It is reported that ('Umar) summoned a woman who had been conversing with men at her (house). When his messengers came to her, she was frightened and afraid. She had a miscarriage and her child fell to the ground crying but then died.

'Umar was informed of that. He gathered the Companions of the Apostle of Allāh, may Allāh bless Him and His Family, together and asked them about the law concerning that. They all said: "We consider that you were acting correctly. You only wanted good and there is no (blame for) anything against you in that."

Ṭhe Commander of the Faithful, peace be on him, was sitting without saying anything about that. 'Umar asked him: "What is your view about this, Abū al-Ḥasan?"

"You have heard what they said," he answered.

"But what is your view?" he insisted.

"The people have said what you heard," he replied.

"I adjure you to give your view," he said.

"If people have (been trying to) come close to you, they have deceived you," he said. "If they thought about their advice then they have disregarded (the fact that) the blood-wit is required of you as the one responsible for the death and you thereby incur the blood-wit ('āqila), because the killing of the child was (as a result of) a mistake connected with you."

"By Allāh, you have advised differently from them," he said. "By Allāh, I will not delay until the blood-wit is paid by (my clan) Banu 'Ādī"

The Commander of the Faithful, peace be on him, had brought that about.

*****

It is reported that during the time of 'Umar, two women were disputing over a child. Each of them claimed that it was her child without any proof but no one else contested their claim to it. The decision with regard to that was not clear to 'Umar. He resorted to the Commander of the Faithful, peace be on him, with regard to it.

He summoned the two women and warned them both, making them both afraid. But they both persisted in their dispute and difference. In the face of their both persisting in dispute, he, peace be on him, said: "Bring me a saw."

"What are you going to do?" the two women asked.

"I will cut it into two halves," he said, "and each of you can have a half."

The one remained silent but the other said: "O Allāh, O Allāh, Abū al-Ḥasan, if there is no escape from that, then let her have it."

"Allāh is greater (Allāhu akbar)," he said. "This is your son not hers. If it had been her son, she would have had pity on him and been anxious (about him)."

The other woman admitted that the right (to the child) belonged to her colleague and the child was not hers. Thus was 'Umar relieved (of his cares) and he blessed the Commander of the Faithful for the trouble that he had saved him from through (his) judgement.

*****

[It is reported on the authority of Yūnus, on the authority of al-Ḥasan:]

A woman was brought before 'Umar. She had given birth six months earlier and he now intended to stone her. The Commander of the Faithful, peace be on him, said to him: "If you quarrel with the Book of Allāh, I will dispute with you. Allāh, the exalted says: The (period) of pregnancy and weaning (of a child) is thirty months (XLVI 15). And He, the High, (also) says: Mothers suckle their children for two complete years for anyone who wants to carry out (the full period of) suckling (II 233). When the woman has carried out the suckling for two years, and the (period of) pregnancy and suckling (of the child) is thirty months .... At the moment (she has only fulfilled) the responsibility (of suckling) for six months (and therefore cannot be killed)."

'Umar freed the woman and confirmed the decision concerning that. The Companions acted according to it and the Successors (al-tābi'ūn) (to the Companions) and those who adopted it right up to the present time.

*****

It is reported that witnesses gave evidence against a woman that they had found her at one of the watering places of the Bedouin and a man who was not her husband (ba'l) was having intercourse with her. 'Umar ordered her to be stoned as she had a husband (ba'l). She declared: "O Allāh, You know that I am innocent."

"Do you impugn the witnesses as well?" remarked 'Umar.

"Let them bring her back and let them question her," said the Commander of the Faithful, peace be on him. "Perhaps she has an excuse."

She was brought back and questioned about the circumstances (of what she had done). She said: "My family had some camels. I went out with my family's camels and took with me some water. There was no milk in the camels. A neighbour of ours had camels with him and there was milk in his camels. My water was used up and I asked him to give me a drink. He refused to give me a drink unless I submitted myself to him. I refused. When my life was about to depart I submitted myself to him unwillingly."

"Allāh is greater (Allāhu akbar)," declared the Commander of the Faithful, peace be on him. "Whoever is compelled (to do something) without desiring (to do it) is not a transgressor and no sin is (counted) against him (II 173)."

When 'Umar heard that he freed her.

*****

Among the reports about (the Commander of the Faithful), peace be on him, with regard to the idea of giving judgement, and the soundness of (his) opinion, his guidance of the people to their (true) interests and his realisation of what would be likely to corrupt the people without his informing them of the proper course is the following:

[Shabāba b. Suwār has reported on the authority of Abū Bakr

al-Hudhalī, who said: I heard one of our scholars saying:]

The foreigners (a'ājim) from Hamdhān, al-Rayy, Iṣfahān, Qūmus and Nahāwand sent letters to each other. They sent messengers to one another (saying): "The king of the Arabs who has brought them their religion and produced their Book has died." They were referring to the Prophet, may Allāh bless Him and his family. "Their king after him was an insignificant king and he has died." They were referring to Abū Bakr. "Another arose after him who has lived longer so that he has reached as far as you in your lands and he has sent his soldiers to attack you." They were referring to 'Umar b. al-Khaṭṭāb. "He will not desist from you until you expel those of his soldiers who are in your land, go against him and attack him in his land. Therefore make an alliance (to do) this and make a covenant (to carry) it (out)."

When the report (of this) came to the Muslims in Kūfa, they sent it to 'Umar b. al-Khaṭṭāb. When the report reached him, he was very afraid on account of it. He went to the mosque of the Apostle of Allāh, may Allāh bless Him and His Family. He went up on the pulpit and praised and glorified Allāh. Then he said: "Men of the Emigrants and the Anṣār, Satan has gathered groups (of men) against you. With them he has dared to attempt to put out the light of Allāh. Indeed the people of Hamdhān, the people of Iṣfahān, the people of al-Rayy and Qūmus, of Nahāwand, despite difference in language, colour and religion, have made a covenant and an alliance to drive your brother Muslims from their land and to come against you and attack you in your land. Give me advice but be brief and not too lengthy in words This is a day for (such advice), after which there will be a day (to speak at greater length)."

They began to consult. Ṭalḥa b. 'Ubayd Allāh stood up - he was one of the orators of Quraysh. He praised and glorified Allāh. Then he said: "Commander of the faithful, affairs have begun to bridle you; times have brought hardship to you; misfortunes have tested you and experiences have taught you. You, the one blessed with authority (amr) and fortunate in nature, have been given authority. Therefore you have knowledge, you have been given information and you know it well. You have only avoided (evil) consequences of Allāh's decision as a result of choosing good. So attend to this matter according to your own view and do not avoid that." Then he sat down.

"Speak," 'Umar urged (the people).

'Uthmān b. 'Affān stood up. He praised and glorified Allāh. Then he said: "I think that you should direct the Syrians from Syria and the Yemenīs from Yemen, and that you should go with the inhabitants of these two sanctuaries (Mecca and Medina) and with the people of the two camp towns of Kūfa and Baṣra. Then all the polytheists would meet all the Muslims. Commander of the faithful, you would not seek to survive after the Arabs, nor would you enjoy with any delight the world, nor would you seek refuge from it in a well-fortified fortress. Therefore attend to (the matter) with your own view and do not avoid that." Then he sat down.

"Speak," 'Umar urged (the people).

The Commander of the Faithful, 'Alī b. Abī Ṭālib, peace be on him, spoke praising Allāh until he had finished the introductory praises and he glorified Him and called for blessings on His Apostle, may Allāh bless Him and his family. Then he said: "If you sent the Syrians from Syria, the Byzantines would come against their children. If you sent the Yemenīs from Yemen, the Abyssinians would come against their children. If you sent (the people) from the two sanctuaries, the bedouin would rebel against us on (every) flank and side. Thus the families of Arabs which you leave behind you are more important to you than what is in front of you. As for what you have mentioned of the number of foreigners and your fear of their groupings, we never fought in the time of the Apostle of Allāh, may Allāh bless Him and His Family, with regard to number. We only used to fight with regard to the help (of Allāh). As for what you have been informed of their gathering to come against the Muslims, Allāh is more averse to their coming than you are to it. It is more appropriate for Him to change what He is averse to. When the foreigners look at you, they say (to themselves) that this is the man of the Arabs. If you break him, you break the Arabs and it would be much more difficult for (them to continue) their eager (advance). Thus you united them against yourself and those who did not use to support them are (now) supporting them. However, I consider that you should make them remain in their camp-town and write to the people of Baṣra. Let them divide into three groups. Let one of their groups look after their offspring as guards of them. Let another group undertake (the task of resisting) the people who have made this covenant, to break them up. Let (the third) group go to their brothers as reinforcements for them."

"This is the best view," said 'Umar. "I would like to follow it." Then he began to repeat the words of the Commander of the Faithful, peace be on him, setting it out in admiration of it and as his choice. [Al-Shaykh al-Mufīd, may Allāh be pleased with him, said:]

Consider, may Allāh support you, this view which was announced with the merit of sound judgement when the thoughtful leaders (ūlū al-albāb wa-al-'ilm) were in dispute. Reflect upon the success which Allāh brought to the Commander of the Faithful, peace be on him, in all circumstances and the way the people used to resort to him in difficult matters. Then add that to what has been established of his merit in religion which was not possible for the other prominent people so that they were in need of him because of his knowledge. You will find out about it in the chapter on miracles, which we have already mentioned. May Allāh be the friend of success.

This has been a brief outline of the judgements delivered by (the Commander of the Faithful), peace be on him, during the rule of 'Umar b. al-Khaṭṭāb. There were similar (judgements) during the rule of 'Uthmān b. 'Affān.

D. Reports of the Judgements of the Commander of the Faithful during the Rule of 'Uthmān b. 'Affān.

Among these is the report which non-Shī'a ('āmma) and Shī'a (khāṣṣa) historians (naqalat al-āthār) relate.
An old man married a woman. The woman became pregnant but the old man claimed that he had not had intercourse with her and denounced her pregnancy. The matter was unclear to 'Uthmān. He asked the woman: "Did the old man make you lose your virginity while (you) were a virgin?"

"No," she replied.

"Administer the prescribed punishment on her," ordered 'Uthmān.

"A woman has two orifices," the Commander of the Faithful, peace be on him, interposed, "the orifice for the menstrual flow and the orifice for urine. Perhaps the old man was close to her and his semen managed to flow into her menstrual orifice. Then she became pregnant through him."

He asked the man about that and he answered: "I used to discharge semen while kissing her but without ever going to the extent of making her lose her virginity."

"The pregnancy is due to him," declared the Commander of the Faithful, peace be on him, "and the child is his child. I consider that he should be punished for his (wrongful) denunciation."

'Uthmān carried out his judgement in that and was amazed at him.

*****

They have reported that a man had a concubine and he gave her a child. Then he separated from her and married her to one of his slaves. The master died. She was freed by virtue of her being in the possession of her son. Her son also inherited her husband. The son died and she inherited her husband from her child. They came before 'Uthmān as a result of a dispute. She was claiming: "This is my slave." He was claiming: "She is my wife and I will not release her (from the marriage)."

"This is a difficult problem," said 'Uthmān.

The Commander of the Faithful, peace be on him, was present. He said: "Ask her whether he has had intercourse with her after her inheritance." "No," she replied.

"If I was aware that he had done that, I would have punished him," he said. "Go. He is your slave without any rights over you. If you wish to keep possession of him, or to free him, or to sell him, that is your right."

*****

They reported that in the time of 'Uthmān a slave woman who was in the process of buying her freedom (makātiba) committed fornication. She had already purchased three-quarters of her freedom. ‘Uthmān asked the Commander of the Faithful whether he should have her flogged according to the amount (required) for a free woman or the amount required for a slave. He also asked Zayd b. Thābit. The latter said that she should be flogged according to the amount (required) for a slave. “How can she be flogged according to the amount (required) for a slave when she has already purchased three-quarters of her freedom?” asked the Commander of the Faithful, peace be on him. “Should you not whip her according to the amount (required) for a free woman as she is much more of that?”

“If that is the case,” said Zayd, “then she ought to inherit according to the amount (required) for a free woman.”

“Indeed, that is necessary,” replied the Commander of the Faithful, peace be on him.

Zayd was silenced but ‘Uthmān disagreed with the Commander of the Faithful, peace be on him. He followed Zayd’s statement without paying attention to the proof which had been given to him (by the Commander of the Faithful).

*****

Mentioning further examples such as these would make the book unduly long.

However the reports about them are well known.

E. Reports of the Judgements of (the Commander of the Faithful), peace be on him, after the Pledge of Allegiance of the General Populace to him and the Death of ‘Uthmān

The traditionists (ahl al-naql wa ḥamalat al-āthār) report that a woman gave birth on the bed of her husband to a child who had two heads and bodies attached to one waist. His family were confused as to whether it was one or two. They went to the Commander of the Faithful, peace be on him, to ask him about that so that they might know the law with regard to him. The Commander of the Faithful, peace be on him, told them: "Watch him when he goes to sleep. Then wake up one of the bodies and heads. If they both wake up at the same time, then they are a single human being. If one of them wakes up and the other remains asleep, they are two persons and their rights in inheritance are the rights of two persons."

*****

[Al-Ḥasan b. 'Alī al-'Abdī reported on the authority of Sa'd b. Ṭarīf, on the authority of al-Asbagh b. Nubāta, who said:]

While Shurayḥ was in a session of judgements, a person came to him and said:

"Abū Umayya, let me speak to you privately, for I have a (great) need."

He ordered those around him to leave him and they went away. Only his close associates (khāṣṣa) who attended him remained. He said: "Say what your need is."

"Abū Umayya," (the person) told him, "I have what men have and what women have. The judgement rests with you about whether I am a man or a woman."

He answered: "I have heard a decision about that from the Commander of the Faithful, peace be on him, which I remember. Tell me from which of the two orifices does your urine come?"

"From them both," answered the person.

"From which does it (finally) finish?" he asked.

"From them both together," was the reply.

Shurayḥ was amazed.

The person said: "I will tell you something (else) about my affair which is (even) more amazing."

"What is that?" asked Shurayḥ.

"My father married me (to a man) on the assumption that I was a woman. I became pregnant from my husband and I bought a slave girl to look after me. I had intercourse with her and she became pregnant from me."

Shurayḥ struck one of his hands against the other in amazement and said: "This is a matter which must be taken before the Commander of the Faithful, peace be on him, for I have no knowledge of the ruling concerning it."

He got up and the person followed him and those present with him. He went in to the Commander of the Faithful, peace be on him. He told the story to him and the Commander of the Faithful, peace be on him, summoned the person. He asked about (the story) which Shurayḥ had told him. (The person) admitted it.

"Who is your husband?" he asked.

"So-and-so b. so-and-so," was the reply, "and he is present in the town."

He had him summoned and asked him about what (the other) had said.

"It is true," he said.

"You have to be braver than a lion-hunter when you face this sort of situation," he said. Then he called Qanbar, his retainer (mawlā) and said: "Take this person into a house and with (the person) four just women and order them to strip (the person) naked and to count the ribs after making sure that the pudenda are covered." The man (i.e. Qanbar) said: "Commander of the Faithful, men and women will not be secure from this person."

So (the Commander of the Faithful) ordered that a straw-dealer should cover him with straw and he left him alone in a house. Then he went into it and counted the ribs. There were seven on the left side and eight on the right side. He declared: "This is a man."

He ordered his hair to be cut and that he be dressed in a hat, sandals and a cloak (ridā'). He separated him from his (former) husband.

[Some traditionists reported:] When the person made the claim he made about two orifices, the Commander of the Faithful, peace be on him, ordered two just Muslims to go to an empty house and take the person with them. He ordered two mirrors to be set up one of them facing the pudenda of the person and the other facing the (first) mirror. He ordered the person to show its nakedness by facing the mirror so that the two just men could not see it (directly). He ordered the two just men to look into the mirror facing (the first) mirror. When the two just men realised the truth of what the person had claimed about (having) two orifices, he considered its status (to be established) by counting the ribs. When he declared him to be a man, he ignored his claims of being pregnant as being a mistake and he did not act in accordance with it. He declared the pregnancy of the slave girl as due to him and he associated him with it.

*****

They reported that one day the Commander of the Faithful, peace be on him, went into the mosque and found a young man weeping (there) with some people around him. The Commander of the Faithful, peace be on him, asked about it. He said: "Shurayḥ has judged a case against me and he has not done me justice."

"What is (the nature of) your affair?" he asked.

"These people" he said and he indicated a group who were present, "took my father out on a journey with them. They came back but he did not come back. I asked them about him and they said that he had died. I asked them about the money (māl) that he had taken with him and they said: 'We do not know of any money.' Then Shurayḥ made them swear an oath and ordered me to stop interfering with them."

The Commander of the Faithful, peace be on him, told Qanbar: "Gather the people and summon the shuraṭ al-khamīs." (Shurtat al-Khamis were six thousand of 'Alī's followers who had pledged themselves to serve him until death, They can be regarded as a combination of bodyguard, police force and front-line soldiers.)

Then he sat down and summoned the group (to come before him) and the young man with them. He asked him about what he had said and he repeated his claim and began to cry, saying: "By Allāh, I accuse them of (killing) my father, Commander of the Faithful. They tricked him so that they could take him with them out of a desire to (get) his money."

Then, the Commander of the Faithful, peace be on him, questioned the people. They told him exactly what they had told Shurayḥ: "The man died and we do not know of any money of his."

Then he looked into their faces and said to them: "What do you think? Do you think that I do not know what you have done with the father of this youth? Then I would have little knowledge."

He ordered them to separate from each other and they separated from each other within the mosque. Each one of them was made to stand next to one of the pillars in the mosque. Next he summoned 'Ubayd Allāh b. Abī Rāfi', his scribe at that time, and told him to sit down. Then he called one of them. He told him: "Tell me on which day did you leave your houses while the father of this boy was with you? And (do it) without raising your voice." "On such and such a day," he said.

"Write it down," he told 'Ubayd Allāh.

"In which month was it?" he asked.

"In such and such a month," was the answer.

"Write it down," he instructed.

"In which year?"

"In such and such a year."

"Write it down."

'Ubayd Allāh wrote all that down.

"Of what sickness did he die?" he asked.

"Of such and such a sickness."

"In which place did he die?"

"In such and such a place."

"Who washed and shrouded his corpse?" "So-and-so."

"With what did you shroud him?"

"With such and such."

"Who said the prayer over him?"

"So-and-so."

"Who put him into the grave?"

"So-and-so."

'Ubayd Allāh b. Abī Rāfi' was writing all that down. When he came to the statement about the burial, the Commander of the Faithful, peace be on him, said: "Allāh is greater (Allāhu akbar)." (He said it) in a way that the people in the mosque could hear. Then he ordered the man to be taken back to his place.

He summoned another of the men and made him sit close to him. He questioned him in the same way as he had questioned the first man and he gave answers which disagreed with (the answers of) the first man throughout his interrogation. (All the time) 'Ubayd Allāh was writing them down. When he had finished his questioning, he said: "Allāh is greater," in a way that the people in the mosque could hear. He ordered that the two men be taken out of the mosque to the prison but they were to stand and wait at the door.

He summoned the third and questioned him in the same way as he had questioned the first. He gave answers which contradicted what both of them had said and he confirmed that to him. He said: "Allāh is greater." Then he ordered him to be taken out to his two colleagues.

He summoned the fourth of the men. His words were confused and he stuttered. (The Commander of the Faithful) warned him and made him afraid. (The man) confessed that his colleagues had killed the man and taken his money and that they had buried him in such and such a place near Kūfa. The Commander of the Faithful, peace be on him, said: "Allāh is greater." Then he ordered him to be taken to prison.

He summoned one of the men (already questioned) and said to him: "You have claimed that the man died in bed. Yet you killed him. Tell me the truth about your situation, otherwise I will punish you as a warning to the others that I should be told the truth in your case." He confessed to killing the man with a similar confession to his colleague.

Then he summoned the rest (of them) and they confessed the murder. They were at a loss to do anything. Their statements about the man's murder and the theft of his money concurred. He ordered some of his men to go with some of them to the place where they had buried the money and to get it out and hand it over to the young man, the son of the murdered man.

"What do you want (to be done to them) now that you know what they did to your father?" he asked him.

"I want the judgement between us to take place before Allāh, the Mighty and High," he said. "So I will spare their blood in this world."

Therefore the Commander of the Faithful, peace be on him, desisted from carrying out the prescribed punishment for murder but still punished them severely.

"Commander of the Faithful," Shurayḥ asked him, "how (did you manage to come to) this decision?"

He said: "David, peace be on him, passed some boys playing and calling out to one of them, 'Religion is dead.' The boy would then answer them. David, peace be on him, approached them. He said: 'Boy, what is your name?' 'My name is Religion is Dead,' he answered. 'Who gave you this name?' David, peace be on him, asked. He replied: 'My mother.' Then David asked: 'Where is your mother?' He answered: 'In her house.' 'Go with us to your house,' said David. He went with him to her and brought her out of her house. 'Maidservant of Allāh', he said, 'what is the name of your son?' 'His name is Religion is Dead,' she answered. 'Who gave him this name?' David, peace be on him, asked her. 'His father,' she replied. 'What was the reason for that?' he asked. She said: 'He went out on a journey with some people while I was pregnant with this boy. The people came back but my husband did not come back. I asked them about him and they told me that he had died. I asked them about his money and they told me that he did not leave any money. I asked them if he had made any instruction in his will. They said that he had. He had said that I was pregnant and if I bore a girl or a boy, I should name him Religion is Dead. Therefore I named him as I was instructed in his will as I did not wish to oppose him.' David, peace be on him, asked her: 'Do you know the people?' 'Yes,' she replied. He said to her, 'Come with me with these' - meaning the people who were in front of him. Then he had them brought out of their houses. When they were (all) present, he judged them according to this judgement. The murder was proved against them and he got the money from them. Then he said to her: 'Maidservant of Allāh, name this child of yours Religion is Alive.'"

*****

It is reported that a woman desired a young man and she tried to seduce him but the young man refused. She went away and got an egg. She put the white (of the egg) on her dress. Then she began to make accusations against the young man and had him brought before the Commander of the Faithful, peace be on him. She claimed: "This young man has treated me shamefully. He has raped me."

She took her dress and showed the white (on it) from the egg, saying: "This is his semen on my dress."

The young man began to cry, pleading and swearing his innocence from her accusations.

"Order someone to heat water until it is very hot," the Commander of the Faithful, peace be on him, told Qanbar. "Then bring it to me while it is still like that."

The water was brought and he ordered it to be thrown on the woman's dress. They threw it on it and the water collected up the white of the egg and they came together. He ordered it to be taken and given to two of his followers. He said: "Taste it and spit it out."

They tasted it and found that it (tasted like) egg. He ordered the young man to be freed and the woman to be flogged as a punishment for her false accusation.

*****

[Al-Ḥasan b. Maḥbūb reported: 'Abd al-Raḥmān b. al-Ḥajjāj told me: I heard Ibn Abī Layla saying:]

The Commander of the Faithful, peace be on him, judged a case which no one had dealt with before. That was that two men had travelled together on a journey. They sat eating together. One of them took out five loaves of bread and the other three. A man passed them and greeted them. They invited him to eat and he sat eating with them. When he had finished eating, he put down eight dirhams, saying: "This is compensation for your food which I have eaten."

The two men began to dispute over it. The one with three loaves said: "This (should be shared) between us, half each."

"Rather I should have five and you should have three," said the one with five loaves.

They came before the Commander of the Faithful, peace be on him, and told him their story. He said: "This is a matter in which meanness and rivalry is not proper. Reconciliation would be better."

"I will only be satisfied by the giving of judgement," said the one who had had three loaves.

"Since you will only be satisfied by the giving of judgement," said the Commander of the Faithful, peace be on him, "you have one of the eight and your companion seven."

"May Allāh be praised," he exclaimed, "how can this matter come to be like that?"

"I have told you," he said. "Didn't you have three loaves?"

"Yes," he answered.

"And your companion had five?"

"Yes."

"That is twenty-four (when multiplied) by three," he said. "So you ate eight, your companion eight and your guest eight. Thus he gave you eight dirhams. Seven of which belong to your companion (as he supplied seven-eighths of the guest's food) and one to you (as you supplied one-eighth of the guest's food)."

The two men departed (reflecting on) the perspicacity of the judgement of their case.

*****

The scholars of (religious) practices (siyar) report that during the time of the Commander of the Faithful, peace be on him, four men drank alcohol. They became drunk and began to cut each other with knives. Each of them was wounded. An account of their (action) was brought to the Commander of the Faithful, peace be on him, and he ordered them to be put into prison until they became sober. Two of them died in prison but two survived. The families of the two (dead) men came to the Commander of the Faithful, peace be on him, and demanded: "Give us the right to retaliate against these two men, Commander of the Faithful. For they have killed two of our colleagues."

"How do you know that?" he asked. "Perhaps (the dead men) killed each other." "We do not know," they answered. "So judge them according to what Allāh has taught you."

He said: "The blood-wit of the two men who were killed is the responsibility of the tribes of the four men after the account has been settled by the payment for the two who are alive of the blood-wit for their wounds."

That was a judgement in a case for which there was no way of establishing the truth other than by it. Don't you see that there was no evidence to distinguish the killer from the killed and no evidence of intention to kill? Therefore the judgement was made according to the rule of accidental killing and on the basis of confusion about (the actions of) the killer and killed.

*****

It is reported that six men went down to the Euphrates and dived into it to play. One of them drowned. Two of them testified that the (other) three had made him drown while the three testified that the two made him drown. He, peace be on him, adjudged the division of the blood-wit into fifths on the five. The two were to pay three-fifths according to the amount of testimony against them and the three were to pay two-fifths in accord with the amount of testimony against them.

There was no judgement in that with more right to (be considered) correct than the judgement he, peace be on him, gave.

*****

They reported that a man was about to die and he bequeathed part of his wealth without designating it. His heirs differed on that after his (death). They came before the Commander of the Faithful, peace be on him. He told them to exclude one-seventh of the wealth as the bequest and he recited the words of Him, the Exalted: It has seven gates, each of which is a divided part (XV 44).

He, peace be on him, judged (a case) concerning a man who, at his death, had made a bequest of a share of his wealth without specifying it. Similarly when he died, the heirs disputed about its significance. His judgement to them was to take out an eighth of his wealth and he recited the words of Allāh, the Exalted: The ṣadaqat (alms tax) is only for the poor and needy. (IX 60). There were eight categories for the (ṣadaqat) and to each category (he gave) a share of the ṣadaqat.

*****

He, peace be on him, judged a case concerning a man who made a bequest and said: "Free every slave of mine who has been long in my possession."

When he died, the executor did not know what to do. He asked about that and (the Commander of the Faithful) told him to free every slave (of the man) who had been in his possession for six months.

Then he recited His words, Exalted be His name: For the moon we have appointed stages until it becomes again like an old dry branch of a palm tree ('urjūn) (XXVI 39).

It has been established that the branch of a palm tree only becomes similar to the new moon in its strength six months after fruit has been taken from it.

*****

He gave judgement concerning a man who had made a vow to fast for a time but without mentioning any definite time. (He told him) to fast for six months and he recited the words of Him, the Mighty and High: It brings forth its fruit at every season by the permission of its Lord. (XIV 25)

That was every six months (so the time he interpreted to be

equivalent to six months).

*****

A man came to him and said: "Commander of the Faithful, I had some dates. My wife rushed (up to me) and took one of them and put it in her mouth. I vowed that she would never eat it nor spit it out."

He, peace be on him, said: "Let her eat half of it and spit out the other half. Then you will be free of your vow."

*****

He, peace be on him, gave judgement concerning a man who struck a woman and she had a miscarriage (when it was still) an embryo. (He ordered him) to pay the blood-wit for it of forty dīnārs and he recited the words of Him, the Mighty and High: We created man from an essence of clay. Then We made him a drop in a firm abode. Then We formed the drop into an embryo, and We formed the embryo into a clot of blood, and We formed the clot of blood into bones. We clothed the bones with flesh. Then we caused it to grow as a final act of creation. Blessed be Allāh the best of Creators. (XXIII 12-14). He explained that (the blood-wit for) the drop was twenty dīnārs, for the embryo forty dīnārs, for the clot sixty dīnārs, for the bone before it was established as a creature eighty dīnārs, for the form (of the child) before the soul entered it a hundred dīnārs. If the soul had entered it, then (the blood-wit) was a thousand dīnārs.

*****

This has been a sample of the judgements and difficult decisions pronounced by (the Commander of the Faithful), peace be on him. No one had given judgements on (such cases) before him. Nor did any of the non-Shī'a ('āmma) and Shī'a (khāṣṣa) know anything about them. His natural disposition ('itra) made him able to deal with them. If anyone else had been tested by having to give a decision about them, such a man would have shown his deficiency in (knowing) the truth about them, just as (the Commander of the Faithful) had made it clear.

In this brief outline of the legal decisions (of the Commander of the Faithful) which we have put forward here, there is sufficient for our purposes, if Allāh wills.

MEMORABLE WORDS AND SPEECHES OF THE COMMANDER OF THE FAITHFUL

His Words about Allāh

(This is) a brief account of some of the words of (the Commander of the Faithful), peace be on him, concerning the necessity of knowing Allāh, the Exalted, His unity and the denial of anthropomorphism (tashbīh), together with a description of Allāh's justice, the different kinds of wisdom and the evidence and proof of these.

[Abū Bakr al-Hudhalī reported on the authority of al-Zuhrī, on the authority of 'Īsā b. Zayd, on the authority of Ṣāliḥ b. Kaysān:]

The Commander of the Faithful, peace be on him, said, in urging the knowledge of Allāh, may He be praised, and (the acknowledgement) of His unity:

"The first act of worshipping Allāh is to know Him. The basis of knowledge of Him lies in (the acknowledgement of) His

Unity. The support for (the acknowledgement of) His Unity is the denial of any comparison of Him, the High, (with man) in terms of stating that human qualities (ṣifāt) subsist in Him. (This is) because of the testimony of reason that everyone in whom human qualities subsist is created (maṣnū'). Whereas the testimony of reason (requires) that He, the High and Exalted, Who is the Creator (ṣāni'), is not created. Through the creation of Allāh which points towards Himself, through reason which establishes the belief in knowledge of Him, through reflection which confirms the proof of His (existence), Allāh has caused His creation to be evidence of Himself. Through it, He has revealed His Majesty. He is One, Unique in His eternity, without partner in His Divinity, without equal in His Divinity. By virtue of the contradictory nature of things which contradict each other, there is knowledge that nothing is contrary to Him. By virtue of the nature of comparability in matters which can be compared, there is knowledge that nothing can be compared to Him."

(The Commander of the Faithful said this) in a speech which, if it was fully reported, would make this book too long.

*****

Among the speeches recorded on his authority, peace be on him, about the denial of any comparison of Allāh (with human qualities) is that which al-Sha'bī reported. He said that the Commander of the Faithful, peace be on him, heard a man saying: "By Him Who is veiled with seven layers (of heaven)." Then he raised his stick towards the sky.

"Woe upon you," he said, "Allāh is too exalted to be veiled from anything and for anything to be veiled from Him. Praise be to Him, Whom no place contains, yet from Whom nothing on earth or in heaven is hidden."

"Shall I redeem my oath, Commander of the Faithful?" the man asked.

"No," he answered, "you did not swear by Allāh. Therefore no atonement for perjury is required of you, for you were only swearing by something else."

*****

The historians (ahl al-sīra wa-'ulamā al-naqala) report that a man came to the Commander of the Faithful, peace be on him, and asked: "Commander of the Faithful, tell me about Allāh, the Exalted. Did you see Him when you worshipped Him?"

"I am not one who worships someone whom I have not seen" he answered.

"Then how did you find Him when you saw Him?" he asked.

"Woe upon you," he said, "the eyes do not see Him in terms of human eye-sight. Rather the hearts see Him through the inner realities of faith (īmān). (He can be) known through evidence and can be characterised by signs, which cannot be compared to people nor attained through sense perception."

The man went away saying: "Indeed, Allāh knows well how He should deliver His message."

In this account there is evidence that (the Commander of the Faithful) denied the possibility of direct vision of Allāh, the Mighty and High.

*****

[Al-Ḥasan b. Abī al-Ḥasan al-Baṣrī reported:]

A man came to the Commander of the Faithful, peace be on him, after his departure from the battle of Ṣiffīn. He asked him: "Commander of the Faithful, tell me: Was the battle which took place between you and these people a result of the decree and determination of Allāh?"

"You have never gone up a hill nor gone down into a valley without Allāh's decree and determination being present in the action," he answered.

"Then, Commander of the Faithful, I regard (all) my concerns as Allāh's responsibility," he said.

"Why?"

"If the decree and determination of Allāh drive us to act," he said, "then what is the point of rewarding us for obedience and punishing us for disobedience?" "Fellow," said the Commander of the Faithful, peace be on him, "have you thought that it was a sealed decree and determination? Don't think that. That sort of statement is the doctrine of idolaters, supporters of Satan and opponents of Allāh, the Merciful. (It is such people) and the Majīs with them who have adopted it. Allāh, exalted be His Majesty, gives commands as a matter of free choice (takhyīr), and gives prohibitions as a warning (against an action.) He puts the burden on us. He is not obeyed unwillingly nor is He disobeyed as one who can be overcome. He has not created the heavens and the earth and what is between them in vain. That is the opinion of those who disbelieve. There will be woe from Hell-fire for those who disbelieve. (XXXVIII 27)."

"What, then, is the decree and determination which you mentioned, Commander of the Faithful?" asked the man.

He answered: "It is the command to obey, the prohibition of

disobedience, the provision (to man) to draw near Him and to abandon those who disobey Him, the promise (of reward) and the threat (of punishment), the inspiration (He gives man) to do good and the fear of doing evil (which He arouses in man). All that is the decree of Allāh with regard to our actions and His determination of our deeds. As for anything else (which has been claimed), do not give it any consideration. For the consideration of it will invalidate your action."

"You have dispelled my worries, Commander of the Faithful," said the man.

"May Allāh dispel yours." And he began to recite:

You are the Imam, through obedience to whom we hope for forgiveness from Allāh, the Merciful, on the Day of the Return (to Him). You have explained what was unclear in our religion. May your Lord bounteously reward you with kindness.

*****

This account clarifies, through the words of the Commander of the Faithful, peace be on him, the meaning of (divine) justice and the prohibition of (belief in) the doctrine of determinism (jabr), (in addition to) establishing the wisdom in the actions of Allāh, the Exalted, and denying that there is any futility in them.

His Words about Knowledge ('Ilm)

(This is a selection of) some of the words of (the Commander of the Faithful), peace be on him, in praise of (traditional) knowledge ('ilm), about the categories of people, the merit of (traditional) knowledge, and about acquiring it and wisdom.

The traditionists (ahl al-naql) have reported on the authority of Kumayl b. Ziyād, may Allāh have mercy on him, that he said: One day the Commander of the Faithful took me by the hand in the mosque and led me out of it. When he had gone out into the desert, he breathed a deep sigh and said: "Kumayl, these hearts are containers (of knowledge); the best of them are those which best preserve (the knowledge). Therefore preserve what I say to you. There are three kinds of people: One who knows the Lord (for His own sake), one who acquires knowledge as a means of salvation and low class rabble, followers of every crower, who bend with every breeze. These men do not seek to be illuminated by the light of learning, nor do they resort to any sure authority (rukn).

"Kumayl, knowledge is better than wealth. Knowledge guards you while you guard wealth. Wealth is diminished by expenditure while knowledge is increased even by giving it away.

"Kumayl, the love of knowledge is a (kind of) religion which is professed (by a man) and through which he perfects his obedience (to Allāh) during his life and acquires a noble reputation after his death. Knowledge is a judge and wealth is something which is judged.

"Kumayl, those who amass wealth die even as they live while those who possess knowledge will continue to exist for as long as time lasts. Their individual entities will disappear but their images will remain in the hearts (of men).

"Here, indeed is much knowledge," and he pointed to his breast. "If I could come upon men who would carry it (ḥamala)... Indeed I came upon such as took it too quickly and (thus) did not protect it. Such a man would use the tools of religion for (success in) the world. He would seek to use the proofs of Allāh and His favours as a means of dominating His friends and His Book. Or (there was the sort of man) who submitted to the wisdom (of Allāh's knowledge) without having true vision of his own (need for) humility. At the first appearance of any problem, doubt would eat into his heart. Neither this man nor that one (was appropriate). (As each) eagerly sought pleasures and was easily dominated by passions or enamoured of amassing and hoarding wealth, they were not of the kind who would be shepherds of religion. They were both much more like cattle wandering without restraint in search of fodder. Thus in the (living) death of such carriers of knowledge would knowledge itself die.

"O Allāh, indeed the earth will never be without (a man who is) a proof (ḥujja i.e. an Imam) of You to Your Creation, whether (he acts) openly in the public eye or secretly out of fear. (In this way) the proofs of Allāh and His signs will not be brought to nought. Where are those men? They are men who are least in number yet greatest in Allāh's esteem. Through them Allāh preserves His proofs (to the world) until they hand them as a trust to their equals and sow them as seeds in the hearts of those like themselves. Through them knowledge has broken into the inner realities of faith and they have found the spirit of certainty to be something gentle and comforting. They have found easy what those who love the easy life have found to be hard and difficult. They are familiar with things which the ignorant distrust. They have travelled through this world with their bodies while their souls have been (always) associated with the Highest Abode. These are the representatives (khulafā') of Allāh on His earth and those who summon His worshippers to His (true) religion".

Then he breathed a deep sigh and said: "Oh, how I long to see them." He took his hand from mine and said to me: "Go now, if you wish."

*****

Among the words of (the Commander of the Faithful), peace be on him, urging people to knowledge (ma'rifa), explaining its merit, and the qualities of those who possess knowledge ('ulamā'), and (describing) how those who seek knowledge should be, is (this report) of a speech which scholars have handed down in (their) accounts. However, we have omitted the beginning of it, (starting at) his words:

"Praise be to Allāh, Who has guided us from error, Who has given us vision (and kept us away) from blindness, Who has (bestowed) on us the religion of Islam. (It is He) Who has caused prophethood to have been among us and Who has made us good men. He has made our ultimate pinnacle the ultimate pinnacle of prophets. He has made us the best community which has come for men. We enjoin the good and forbid the evil. We worship Allāh and we do not associate anything with Him, nor do we take any master (walī) apart from Him.

We are witnesses of Allāh and the Apostle was our witness (of Him). We seek intercession and are given intercession along with those with whom we sought intercession from Him. We ask and our request is granted. He forgives the sins of those whom we pray for. Allāh has elected us. We do not call on any master (walī) apart from Him.

"People, help one another to (acts of) good faith and piety. But do not help one another to sin and aggression. Fear Allāh. Indeed Allāh is severe in (His) punishment.

"People, I am the cousin of your Prophet and the closest of you to Allāh and His Apostle. Therefore question me, question me. It is as if knowledge ('ilm) has already wasted away among you. When any one who possesses knowledge perishes, then part of his knowledge perishes with him. Those among the people who possess knowledge ('ulamā') are like the full-moon in the sky whose light illuminates the rest of the constellations. Take hold of whatever knowledge appears to you. Beware of seeking it for four reasons: that through it you may vie with (other) possessors of knowledge; or that by it you may quarrel with the ignorant; or that as a result of it you act hypocritically in discussions; or that through it you may disregard the leaders of the people in favour of yourselves becoming leaders. Those who do (good) acts and those who do not will not receive equal punishment from Allāh. May Allāh benefit both us and you by what He has taught us. May (a man who has knowledge) use it only for the sake of Allāh. Indeed He is One Who hears, One Who answers."

*****

Among his statements, peace be on him, about the description of the one who possesses knowledge ('ālim) and the training of one who seeks to possess knowledge is what is reported by al-Ḥārith al-A'war. He said: I heard the Commander of the Faithful say: "It is the right of the one who possesses knowledge ('ālim) that he should not be questioned too much, nor be required to answer. Nor should he be troubled when he is tired, nor caught hold of by the sleeves when he rises (to leave). No (finger) should be pointed at him with regard to anything which is needed, nor should any secret of his be divulged. No one should speak slander in his presence. He should be given great respect in as much as he has preserved the command of Allāh. The student should only sit in front of him and should not expose him to too much of his company. If a student (seeking) knowledge, or anyone else, comes to him while he is in a group, he should make a general greeting to them all and give particular good wishes to him.

"Let him be respected whether he is present or absent. Let his right be known. Indeed the man who possesses knowledge receives greater reward than the man who fasts, the man who undertakes (other religious duties), the man who strives along the path of Allāh. When the one who possesses knowledge ('ālim) dies, a breach is made in Islam which can only be filled by his successor and the one who seeks after knowledge. The angels ask for forgiveness for him and those in heaven and on earth pray for him."

His Words concerning Heresy.

Among his speeches, peace be on him, concerning heretics (ahl al-bida') and those who speak of religion in terms of their own opinion while opposing the way of true believers (ahl al-ḥaqq) through what they say, is (the speech) reported by sound traditionists of the non-Shī'a ('āmma) and the Shī'a (khāṣṣa). The speech opens with the praising of Allāh and blessings on His Prophet, may Allāh bless Him and His Family, (and then goes on): "My responsibility for what I say is guaranteed and I am answerable for it. It will not wither the corn-seeds which men have sown, nor will roots be parched as a result of it.

"All goodness is within a man who knows his own Ability. Not knowing one's own ability is sufficient ignorance for man. A creature who is most hateful to Allāh is a man whom Allāh, the Exalted, has left to himself, (a man) who is deviating from the true path, (a man) enamoured of words of heresy. (In this heresy) he has become addicted to fasting and prayer. Yet he is seduction to those who are seduced by him, himself going astray from the guidance of those who came before him, and leading into error those who follow him. Thus he bears (responsibility) for the sins of others, being (himself) settled in his own sinfulness. (Such a man) has picked up the refuse of ignorance amid ignorant men without guidance. Unaware of the intense darkness of rebellion, he is blind to guidance. Yet men like himself call him knowledgeable ('ālim) while he is not constant in following it even for one complete day. He goes out early and seeks to make much of what is little (regarding it as) better than what is (truly) much, so that when he has quenched his thirst on polluted water and sought to increase (his knowledge) from what is vile, he sits as a judge responsible for the clarification of what is obscure to everyone else. He fears that those who came before him were without his wisdom and that the action of those who come after him will be like the action of those who came before him. If an obscure matter is brought before him, he gives an irrelevant comment on it according to his own opinion and then asserts (that) categorically. Thus he is enmeshed in doubts as if in the spider's web, not knowing whether he is right or wrong. He does not see that what is beyond (him) is within the reach (of others). If he made an analogy of one thing with another, he would never regard his opinion as being wrong. If a matter is obscure to him, he conceals it because he knows his own ignorance, deficiency, and the necessity (of hiding it) in order that it cannot be said that he does not know. Therefore he puts himself forward without knowledge. He is one who wanders aimlessly like riders without direction amid the uncertainties of unknown tracts of desert. Never does he excuse himself for what he does not know. Thus he gives a decision without ever having bitten into knowledge with a tooth that can bite. He scatters the traditions like the wind scatters sand. Inheritances (wrongly distributed) weep because of him, blood cries out for vengeance because of him. By his judgements he makes lawful the forbidden parts and forbids those that are allowed. He is invalid when he issues (judgements on cases) which come before him and he does not regret his inadequacy.

"People, it is required of you to obey and to know the one whom there is no excuse to be ignorant of. The knowledge with which Adam, peace be on him, descended, and everything with which the prophets were favoured down to your Prophet, the seal of the prophets, is in the offspring of your Prophet, Muḥammad, may Allāh bless Him and His Family.

Where has it brought you? Or rather where are you going, you who are descended from the loins of the men who were on the Ark? This (offspring of the Prophet) is like (the Ark of Noah). Therefore (adhere to them as) you would board it. Just as those who were in it were saved, so those who enter into (association with this family) will be saved through them. I guarantee that by a true oath and I am not one of those who make false claims. Woe on those who hold back, woe again on those who hold back. Haven't you been made aware of what your Prophet, may Allāh bless Him and His Family, said among you, when he said in the Farewell Pilgrimage: 'I leave behind me among you two important things which, if you cleave to them, you will never go astray - that is the Book of Allāh and the offspring from my family (ahl al-bayt). They will never scatter from you until they lead you to me at the (sacred) waters (of Heaven)'. Now take care how you oppose me with regard to these two (things). Otherwise there will be dread punishment. Indeed this (agreement with the Book and the family) is a sweet pleasant drink, so drink. But that (opposition) is salty and brackish, so avoid it.'"

His Words about this World and the Next

(Here is an extract from) his words, peace be on him, describing the world and warning against it.

"The world is just like a snake - a soft thing to touch but vicious in sting. Therefore avoid those things which please you in it because of the short length (of time) which they will be with you there. Be as familiar as you can with what is there while being as wary as you can of its possessions. For whenever one who possesses (the world) seeks to take ease from it, it diverts him from it to what is hateful."

*****

(These are some of) his words, peace be on him, regarding getting ready to go to the next world, preparing to meet Allāh, may His Name be exalted, and advice to the people about righteous deeds. The religious scholars report this in the traditions and the historians (aṣḥāb al-sīra wa-al-āthār) (also) report it:

Every night when the people were taking to their beds for sleep, he would call out in a voice which could be heard by all the people in the mosque and nearby: "May Allāh have mercy on you, prepare yourselves, for the call has been made among you for you to set out on the journey (to Allāh). Give scant (attention) to staying in this world and turn (to Allāh) with the best provisions you have. For in front of you is a mountain-pass which will be difficult to climb and halting-places full of terror, from which the one who travels (the road) and stops along it has no escape. Through Allāh's mercy, may you be saved from its horrors. After destruction there will be no haughtiness. How sad it will be for the negligent man that his own life will be a proof against him and (the evils of) his days will lead him to the distress which Allāh has made for (those of) us (who are like him). Beware of those who scorn grace and who will not be freed from vengeance after death. We only (exist) through Him and for Him and by virtue of His kind hand. He has power over everything."

*****

(These are some of) his words, peace be on him, concerning shaming the life of this world and seeking to carry out actions for the next world:

"Son of Adam, let not the greatest of your concerns be what happens to you today. For if it passes you by, it was not meant for you. Your concern should be now and on every day which comes to you, that Allāh will provide you with provision for it. You should know that you will never acquire anything beyond your own sustenance, save as one who looks after things on behalf of others. (If) your share (of wealth) in this world is abundant, then soon your heir will take it over and together with him your account on the Day of Resurrection will be lengthy. So be happy with what you have and make provision for the day of your return (to Allāh) which is ahead of you. The journey is long, the appointment is (on the day of) the Resurrection, the destiny is Heaven or the fire (of Hell)."

*****

Another speech of his, peace be on him, similar to that, is well known among the religious scholars and has been preserved by men of understanding and wisdom. "People, this world has turned its back and made known its departure. The next world has drawn near and given notice of its appearance. Indeed today is (like) the day horses are prepared (for a race) and tomorrow is (like) the day of the race. The destiny of the winner is Paradise while the fate (of the loser) will be Hell-fire. You are amid days of preparations for (men), behind whom the time of death is urging haste. Whoever dedicates his works to Allāh, will not have his hopes destroyed. Whoever allows the works (of the world) to delay him during the days of his preparations prior to the coming of the time of his death, his (worldly actions) will come to naught and his hopes will destroy him. Indeed act (righteously) with regard to both (what you) desire and (what you) fear. If your desire comes to you, thank Allāh and add it to (what you) fear. If (what you fear) befalls you, then be mindful of Allāh and add it to (what you) desire. Allāh has permitted those who do good (to enjoy) goodness. To those who thank Him, He gives increase (of blessings). There is no acquisition better than an acquisition for a day for which stores are stored, (a day) on which great sins are collected together and the intentions (of the heart) concerning them are tested. I have never seen one who aspires to Heaven asleep nor have I seen one who seeks to flee from Hell-fire asleep. One who does not benefit from certainty is harmed by doubt. The one who does not benefit from the presence of his heart and sight (will attain) his (sad) end without them. You have been commanded to set out (to the next world) and have been guided with provisions (for the journey). There are two things which I most fear for you -- the following of passion and the delay (of good actions) caused by hope. For following passion stops one from (attaining) the truth and the delay (of good actions) caused by hope makes one forget about (the need for such actions for) the next world. Indeed the world has set out on a journey away (from us) while the next world has set out on a journey towards (us). Both of them have children (who follow them). Therefore, if you can, be among the children of the next world and do not be among the children of this world. Today is (the day) for good actions without the account (to be settled). Tomorrow is (the day) for the account (to be settled) without (the opportunity for performing) good actions."

His Words about Companions, Ascetics and his Shī'a

Among the speeches which he, peace be on him, gave, mentioning the choice companions and ascetics, is that which Ṣa'ṣa'a b. Sūḥān al-'Abdī reported: He said that one day the Commander of the Faithful, peace be on him, prayed the morning prayer with them. When he had said the final greeting (of the prayer) he turned his head toward the qibla (i.e. in the direction of Mecca) as he mentioned Allāh. He did not turn to right or left until the sun's (shadow reached) the height of a spear on the wall of that mosque - meaning the Friday-mosque in Kūfa. Then he, peace be on him, turned his head towards us and said:

"I knew upright men in the time of my bosom companion, the Apostle of Allāh, may Allāh bless Him and His Family, who used to spend this night alternating between prostration and kneeling. In the morning they would have dishevelled hair, be dusty, and between their eyes, there would be (a lump) like the knee of the goat (as a result of prostration). When they remembered death, they quivered like trees quiver in the wind. Then their eyes would shed tears until their clothes became wet."

Then he, peace be on him, arose and he was speaking as if the people had remained heedless (of his words).

*****

(These are some of) his words, peace be on him, concerning his sincere Shī'a. The historians (naqalat al-āthār) report that one evening he, peace be on him, left the mosque. It was a moon-lit night. He headed towards the cemetery (jabbāna). A group of men followed him, standing behind him. He stopped and said: "Who are you?"

"Commander of the Faithful, we are your Shī'a," they replied.

He looked steadfastly at their faces and then said: "Why don't I see the mark of the Shī'a on you?"

"What is the mark of the Shī'a, Commander of the Faithful?" they asked.

"Yellow faces through staying awake at night," he replied, "bleary eyes through weeping, hunched backs through standing (in prayer), hollow stomachs through fasting, dry lips through prayer, and there is the dust of those who show humility on them."

His Words concerning Death

Among his words, peace be on him, warning and mentioning death is (the speech) which has become well-known. From it (is the following):

"Death is a greedy pursuer. As for the pursued, neither will the one who stays be able to weaken it, nor will the one who flees be able to escape it. Therefore go forward into battle and do not shrink away since there is no escape from death. Even if you are not killed, you will die. By (Allāh), in Whose hand is the life of 'Alī, a thousand sword blows on the head is easier than death in bed."

Concerning that are his words, peace be on him:

"People, you have become targets so that the Fates are shooting arrows down on you. Your properties have been plundered by the blows (of Fortune). Whatever food you have eaten has stuck in your throat. Whatever drink you have drunk has choked you. I testify by Allāh that you will not gain from this world any advantage which you can enjoy except by losing another which you were showing regard for.

"People, we have been created. Therefore be (eager) for eternity and not for transitory existence. For you will travel from one abode to another. So make provision for where you are going and where you will dwell for ever. Peace (be with you)."

Speeches Urging Men to Himself and his Family

(There are) among his speeches, peace be on him, those which urge men (to follow) him, give evidence of his own outstanding merit and of his being deprived of his right, and explain what oppression was committed against him, indicating it and drawing attention to it. (This is) what the Shī'a (khāṣṣa) and non-Shī'a ('āmma) have reported. It is mentioned by Abū 'Ubayda Ma'mar b. al-Muthanna and others whom the opponents of the Shī'a cannot accuse of (partiality) in their report. The Commander of the Faithful, peace be on him, said at the beginning of the address which he gave after the people's pledge of allegiance to his leadership (had been given) - that was after the murder of 'Uthmān - (the following):

"The ruler should only pay attention to his own soul. (If he pays attention to others) he will be distracted from Heaven and Hell will be in front of him. One who earnestly strives will be saved. One who seeks has hope. One who is remiss will be in Hell-fire. These are three (kinds of person). There are two (more): an angel who flies with his wings and a prophet whom Allāh has taken by his hand. There is no sixth (kind). The one who makes false claims will be destroyed. Those who rush heedlessly (into bad actions) will be made to fall. The right-hand side and the left-hand side lead (men) astray. The middle road is a path on which there still remains the Book, the sunna and the reports (āthār) of prophethood. Indeed Allāh, the Exalted, has treated the community with two medicines - the whip and the sword. There will be no hesitation by the Imam in applying them. Take cover in your houses and reconcile (the differences) which are between you. (There should be) repentance for what you have done. Whoever makes himself appear (falsely) to support truth will be destroyed. You were in some affairs, (in which you were inclined against me, it was an inclination for which) you had no excuse in my eyes. As for me, if I had wanted to say (it), I would have said: May Allāh forgive what has gone before. The two men (Abū Bakr and 'Umar) came first (in depriving me of my rights).

"Then the third stood like a crow, his concern for his stomach. Woe to him, if his wings have been clipped and his head cut off, it is better for him. Watch me. If you find something to denounce, denounce it. If you recognise it, then hasten (to carry it out). There is truth and falsehood. Each has its supporters. If the false becomes leader, then he will do as (was done) in the past. If truth becomes scarce, then perhaps for a short time it will recede but only to advance again. If your lives returned (to what they were before) you would be happy. I fear that you are now living in an intermediate period (without a prophet). I have only the ability to use reason (ijtihād) (to guide you). However, the pious of my family and the good ones of my offspring are the most forbearing of the people when they are young and the most knowledgeable of the people when they are older. We are the family of the House (ahl al-bayt), we know our knowledge from the knowledge of Allāh. We judge according to the law of Allāh, and we have taken (knowledge) from the words of the truthful one (i.e. the Prophet). If you follow our pronouncement, you will be guided by our clear vision. If you do not, Allāh will destroy you at our hands. We have the standard of truth. Whoever follows it, will attain it. Whoever delays from it will be drowned. Indeed through us, the vengeance of every believer will be realised. Through us, the rope of humiliation will be removed from your necks. It is through us, not you, that Allāh brings conquest. It is through us, not you, that He sets the seal (on life)."

*****

Another extract from his speech, peace be on him, urging (men) to himself and his family, peace be on him, are his words:

"Allāh singled out Muḥammad for prophethood, and chose him for the mission. He gave him information through inspiration. He set (him) among the people - He set him (there). We, the family of the House (ahl al-bayt), have the strongholds of knowledge, the gates of decision and the illumination of authority. Whoever loves us, his faith will benefit him and his works will bring him close (to Allāh). Whoever does not love us, his faith will not benefit him and his works will not bring him close to Allāh, even though he should strive night and day in prayer and fasting."

*****

In addition to that is what is reported by 'Abd al-Raḥmān b. Jundub on the authority of his father, Jundub b. 'Abd Allāh. The latter said: I visited 'Alī b. Abī Ṭālib, peace be on him, in Medina after the people had given the pledge of allegiance to 'Uthmān. I found him with head lowered and sorrowful. I asked him: "What has come upon your people?" "Beautiful endurance," he answered.

"Praise be to Allāh!" I said. "By Allāh, you are indeed enduring. Do what you said you would do among the people. Summon them to yourself and inform them that you are the closest and most appropriate of the people by virtue (of your relationship) with the Prophet, may Allāh bless Him and His Family, by virtue of your outstanding merit (faḍl) and your priority (in Islam). Ask them to help you against these men who have conspired against you. If ten out of a hundred answer you, you would be a powerful influence with the ten over the hundred. If they approached you, that would be as you would want. If they refused, you could fight them. If you are victorious, then the authority is Allāh's, Who gave it to his Prophet, blessing and peace be on him, and you are more appropriate for it than them. If you are killed in seeking it, then you would be killed as a martyr and you would be more deserving of Allāh's forgiveness and have more right to the inheritance of the Apostle of Allāh, may Allāh bless Him and His Family."

"Jundub," he said, "do you think that ten out of a hundred would pledge allegiance to me?"

"I would hope so," I replied.

"However," he retorted, "I do not expect two men from every hundred. I will tell you why. The people look to Quraysh. Quraysh says that the family of Muḥammad think that they have merit over the rest of the people and that they are the masters (awliyā') of the affair apart from (the rest of) Quraysh. (They say that) if they took charge of it, this authority would never leave them to go to anyone else. Since it is already with others, you should circulate it among yourselves. No, by Allāh, Quraysh will never give this authority to us voluntarily."

"Won't you go back and tell the people what you have just said?" I asked him. "Then summon them to yourself."

"Jundub," he said, "this is not the time for that."

After that, I returned to Iraq. Whenever I used to mention any of his virtues, accomplishments and rights to the people, they would treat me roughly and drive me away until the matter of my words was brought before al-Walīd b. 'Uqba who was our governor at that time. He sent for me and imprisoned me until someone spoke to him about me and then he freed me.

Speeches about those who refrained from Pledging Allegiance to him and those who broke their Pledge.

Among the speeches which he, peace be on him, made when 'Abd Allāh b. 'Umar b. al-Khaṭṭab, Sa'd b. Abī Waqqāṣ, Muḥammad b. Maslama, Ḥassān b. Thābit and Usāma b. Zayd withheld the pledge of allegiance from him is what al-Sha'bī reported:

When Sa'd and the others whom we have named withdrew from the Commander of the Faithful, peace be on him, and withheld their pledge of allegiance, he praised and glorified Allāh. Then he said:

"People, you have pledged allegiance to me in the same way as the pledge was made to those before me. Choice (khiyār) only belongs to people before they make their pledge of allegiance. When the pledge of allegiance is made, then they no longer have any choice. It is duty of the Imam to follow the right course and it is the duty of subjects to submit. However, this is a general pledge of allegiance. Whoever turns away from it turns away from the religion of Islam and does not follow the path of its people. Your pledge of allegiance to me was not a random matter (falta). My affair and your affair are not one. I want Allāh to be (the ultimate end) for you and you want me in the interests of yourselves. I swear by Allāh that I will give sincere advice to a rival and I will give justice to the oppressed. I have learnt matters about Sa'd, Ibn Maslama, Usāma, 'Abd Allāh and Ḥassān b. Thābit which I dislike. Truth (will be decided) between them and me."

*****

(These are some of) his words, peace be upon him, when Ṭalḥa and al-Zubayr reneged on their pledge of allegiance and set out for Mecca to meet 'Ā'isha to incite (people) against him and to make an alliance opposed to him. The religious scholars have preserved on his authority, peace be on him, that after he had praised and glorified Allāh, he said:

"Allāh sent Muḥammad, may Allāh bless Him and His Family, to all the people.

He made him a mercy for the worlds. He made manifest what he had been ordered to and spread the message of his Lord. The manifestation was carried out through him and that which was split was united in him. Roads were made safe through him and (the shedding of) blood was brought to an end by him. By him reconciliation was brought about between men with feuds and hostility, with hatred in their breasts and malice rooted in their hearts. Then Allāh took him to Himself, as a man to be praised who had not fallen short in the object for which he performed his mission. He had not achieved anything which fell short of his intention. After him there occurred the strife which there was over the leadership. Abū Bakr took control. Then after him (came) ‘Umar. Then ‘Uthmān took control. When there happened with regard to his affair what you already know, you came to me and said: ‘We will pledge allegiance to you.’ I said: ‘I will not do it.’ You said: ‘Yes.’ I said: ‘No.’ Then you seized my hand and stretched (yours) out towards it. I tried to withdraw it from you but you tugged at it and you pressed upon me like thirsty camels at the watering pools on a day when they are brought to them, so that I thought that you would kill me and that you would kill each other on my account. Therefore I stretched out my hand and you pledged allegiance to me of your own accord. The first of you to pledge allegiance to me were Ṭalḥa and al-Zubayr; they were acting voluntarily without any compulsion. It was not much later that they asked me to allow them to make the ‘umra (lesser pilgrimage). Allāh knows that they already intended treachery. I made them renew their covenant of obedience to me and (promise) that they would not harm the community with evil deeds. They gave their covenants to me. However, they did not fulfill their promises to me, they reneged on their pledge of allegiance to me and they broke their covenant to me. How surprising it is that they submitted to Abū Bakr and ‘Umar yet showed hostility to me. But I am not inferior to either of those two men. If I wanted to, I would say:

O Allāh, judge them both for what they have done against my rights and how they have attempted to diminish my authority. Give me victory over them."

*****

Elsewhere, he, peace be on him, spoke in a similar manner, (when) he said, after praising and glorifying Allāh:

"When Allāh, the Exalted, took His Prophet, blessings and peace be on him, we said: We are the family of his House, his group, his inheritors and his close friends and next of kin (awliyā), the creatures with most right with regard to him. There is no dispute about his right and authority. While we were in this position, the hypocrites rushed forward and took the authority of our Prophet by force away from us, and gave it to someone else. By Allāh, at that, our eyes all wept and our hearts (grieved). Because of it our breasts became worn (with sorrow) and our souls were afflicted with grief. I was humiliated. But I swear by Allāh that if it had not been for my fear of division among the Muslims and that most of them would return to unbelief and that religion would have been placed in jeopardy, we would have changed that as far as we could. But now you have pledged allegiance to me and those two men, Ṭalḥa and al-Zubayr, have pledged allegiance to me. Both you and they (have acted) spontaneously and according to (your own) choice. Yet both of them have arisen, heading for Basra to cause division in your unity (jamā'a) and to thrust misfortune into your midst. O Allāh, seize them for the way they have deceived this community and for their evil attitude towards the general populace."

Then he said (to the people): "May Allāh have mercy on you, hurry to seek out these two treacherous sinful perjurers before the opportunity of (preventing) the realisation of their criminal activities escapes."

*****

When he was informed of the journey of 'Ā'isha, Ṭalḥa and al-Zubayr from Mecca to Baṣra, he praised and glorified Allāh. Then he said:

"'Ā'isha, Ṭalḥa and al-Zubayr have set out. Each one of the two (men) makes claims for the caliphate separately from his colleague. Ṭalḥa only claims the caliphate because he is the paternal cousin of 'Ā'isha and al-Zubayr only claims it because he is the brother-in-law of her father. By Allāh, if the two are successful in what they intend, then al-Zubayr will execute Ṭalḥa or Ṭalḥa will execute al-Zubayr, this one disputing the (right to) kingship of the other. By Allāh, I know that she is one who rides a camel. She will not stop at any pasturage; she will not go along any mountain path, and she will not be able to stop anywhere except in rebellion against Allāh until her soul and (that of) those with her comes to its final end. A third (of those with her) will be killed, a third will flee, and a third will come back. Ṭalḥa and al-Zubayr know that they are wrong. They are not ignorant. How often does the ignorance of one who knows kill him and the knowledge that he has does not benefit him? By Allāh, the dogs of al-Haw'ab bark at her but does one who reflects interpret and one who ponders ponder? The sinful party has established itself. Where are the good?" (There is a tradition that the Prophet warned 'Ā'isha that when she heard these dogs barking she would know that she was doing wrong)

*****

When the Commander of the Faithful, peace be on him, headed for Baṣra, he stopped at al-Rabadha. The last (of the returning) pilgrims met him there. They gathered together to listen to some words from him, while he was still in his tent.

Ibn 'Abbās, may Allāh be pleased with him, reported:

I went to him and found him stitching a sandal. I said to him: "We have a great need (to know) what you will do in order to put right our affairs."

He did not speak to me until he had finished his sandal. He put it next to the other one and then he asked me: "(How much do you) value them?" "They have no value," I answered.

"More than that," he retorted.

"A fraction of a dirham," I suggested.

He said: "By Allāh, they are more lovable to me than these affairs of yours but for the fact that I must establish (what is) true and ward off (what is) false."

"The pilgrims have gathered together to listen to some of your words," I said. "Would you permit me to address them? If (my words) are good, they will be yours. If they are not, then they will be mine."

"No, I will speak," he answered, and he put his hands on my breast. The palms were rough and hard and it hurt me.

He got up. I seized hold of his clothes and said: "I commend Allāh and kinship to you."

"You should not (bother to) commend them to me," he replied and went out.

They gathered around him. He praised and glorified Allāh. Then he said: "Allāh sent Muḥammad, may Allāh bless Him and His Family, while there was no one among the Arabs who recited an (Arabic) scripture nor claimed prophethood.

He drove the people towards their salvation. By Allāh, I am still driving them towards it. I have not changed, I have altered nothing, I have betrayed nothing until the whole of it has passed away. What is between me and the Quraysh? By Allāh, I fought against them when they were unbelievers and I will fight against them when they bring sedition. This journey of mine (is made) on account of a covenant (made by the Prophet) to me. By Allāh, I will split open the false so that the truth may come out of its sides. Quraysh will not take vengeance on me, for Allāh has chosen us to be over them, and we will bring them under our control."

Then he recited:

By my life, you continued your drinking of pure milk and your eating of dry dates with yoghourt.

Yet we bestowed on you the highest rank even though you are not enough (for it). Around you, we give protection in the shield and spear.

*****

When he stopped at Dhū Qār, he took the pledge of allegiance from those who were present. After that he addressed them. He was profuse in his praise and glorification of Allāh and in calling for blessings on the Apostle of Allāh, may Allāh bless Him and His Family. Then he said:

"Affairs which we have (resolutely) endured have taken place earlier; (it was as if) there was a mote in our eyes in surrendering to the authority of Allāh, the Exalted, in matters by which he tested us. There is reward for that, for endurance of them was better than causing division among the Muslims and shedding their blood. We are the family of the House of Prophethood and the offspring of the Apostle, the creatures with the most right to the authority of the (prophetic) mission. (We are) the source of favour by which Allāh initiated this community. This Ṭalḥa and al-Zubayr are not from the family of prophethood nor from the offspring of the Apostle. When they saw that Allāh had restored our right to us after some time, they could not wait for one year, nor even one full month before they launched an attack, following in the footsteps of those before them, so that they might take away my rights and separate the unity (jamā'a) of the Muslims from me."

Then he made a prayer against them.

*****

['Abd al-Ḥamīd b. 'Imrān al-'Ijlī reported on the authority of Salama b. Kuhayl, who said:]

When the people of Kūfa met the Commander of the Faithful, peace be on him, at Dhū Qār, they welcomed him and said: "Praise be to Allāh, who has singled us out for (the honour of) granting you neighbourly protection and has honoured us by (enabling us to) support you."

Then the Commander of the Faithful, peace be on him, stood up among them to address them. He praised and glorified Allāh and said:

"People of Kūfa, you are the noblest of the Muslims, the most purposeful of them in following the correct course, the most upright of them in practice, the best of them in (your) participation in Islam, and the best among the Arabs in composition and origin. You are the fiercest of the Arabs in your love for the Prophet, may Allāh bless Him and His Family, and the members of his House. I only came to you out of my trust in you after Allāh because of the fact that you will give your lives against Ṭalḥa and al-Zubayr's renunciation (of their fealty to me), opposition to giving obedience to me, setting out with 'Ā'isha to create discord and taking her from her house until they had brought her to Baṣra. The common and confused people there were seduced. However I have been informed that men of merit and the choice men in religion among them had kept aloof and have shown their dislike for what Ṭalḥa and al-Zubayr have done."

He, peace be on him, fell silent and the Kūfans declared: "We are your supporters and helpers against your enemy. If you summon us to weaken their (hold) over the people, we would consider that good and we would hope (to do) it."

The Commander of the Faithful, peace be on him, called to them and praised them. Then he said:

"You know, Muslims, that Ṭalḥa and al-Zubayr gave their pledge of allegiance to me, willingly, without compulsion and of their own accord. Then they asked permission from me to go on the lesser pilgrimage ('umra). I gave permission to them. However, they went to Baṣra and killed Muslims and committed forbidden actions. O Allāh, they have cut themselves off from me, they have oppressed me and have broken their pledge of allegiance to me, they have gathered the people against me. Therefore, loose what they have bound, do not give (favourable) judgement on anything which they have done well and show them the evil (which will result) from their actions."

*****

Among his speeches, peace be on him, is (the speech he made) when he left Dhū Qār setting out for Baṣra. After praising and glorifying Allāh and calling for blessings on the Apostle of Allāh, may Allāh bless Him and His Family, (he said:)

“Allāh, the Exalted, has imposed the duty of struggling (on his behalf) (Jihād). He magnified it and He has made it a means of helping Him. By Allāh, neither the world nor religion will be properly maintained without it.

“Satan has gathered his party and has assembled his cavalry. He has brought doubt and deception into that when matters had been clear and restored.

“By Allāh, they have not blamed me correctly, nor have they done justice between me and themselves. They are demanding (restitution of) a right which they themselves abandoned, and (vengeance for) blood which they themselves shed. Even if I had been in partnership with them in it, they would have had a share in it. But if they have perpetrated it without me, the consequences of it are only theirs. Their greatest argument against me is against themselves. I have my clear vision which has not confused me.

“Indeed it is a wicked group in which there is kin and a scorpion’s sting whose vehemence lasts for a long time and the fever from it is possible. They are being suckled by a mother who is already dry. They revive a pledge of allegiance (i.e. to ‘Uthmān) which had already been forsaken by them in order that straying from truth might be restored to the place it (formerly) had. I am not to blame for what was done. I am innocent of (the crime) which was perpetrated.

“How disappointing is such a man to call on you! Who does he call? If he was asked: To whom is your call addressed and to whom do you answer? Who is your Imam and what is the practice (you call for), since falsehood has been removed from its place, his tongue would be silenced about what it had said.

“By Allāh, I shall make a tank overflow for them, from which I alone will draw. They will not be able to go away from it nor will they every be able to drink from it.

“I am content with Allāh’s proof against them and His blaming them, since I call to them and ask them to apologise. If they repent and accept (my call), then forgiveness will be given and the right course will have been accepted. There should be no ingratitude to Allāh. If they refuse, I will let them have the edge of the sword. There is sufficiency in it as a healer of a false man and a helper of a believer.”

His Words before and after the Battle of the Camel

(This is) from his speech, peace be on him, when he entered Baṣra and gathered his followers, to urge them to the struggle. Among the things he said, was: “Servants of Allāh, arise against these people, exposing your breasts to battle against them. They have reneged on their pledge of allegiance to me. They have expelled Ibn Ḥunayf, my governor, after grievous blows and violent punishment. They have killed al-Sabābija and retaliated against Ḥakīm b. Jabala al-‘Abdī.

“They have killed righteous men and pursued those who escaped to capture them behind every wall and under every hillock. They brought them and executed them in chains. What is their purpose? May Allāh fight them. Indeed they are liars.

“Arise against them and be fierce against them. Hurl yourself against them with endurance and with fore-thought, for you know that you are attacking and fighting them after you have disposed yourselves (to give) the most piercing thrust and the most severe blow and a contest of equals. Any individual among you who feels strong hearted at the (coming) engagement and sees any of his brothers failing should defend his brother who is a benefit to him just as he would defend himself. If Allāh wishes, he would do the same for him.

*****

(This is an extract) from his speech, peace be on him, when Ṭalḥa had been killed and the Baṣrans scattered.

"Through us you were raised to nobility. Through us you broke into a new dawn of light out of darkness like the darkness of a moonless night. Through us you were guided amid darkness. Ears which do not comprehend the severe warning (given them) have become deaf. How does one who is deaf to the loud cries (of Allāh) hear a weaker call (of myself)? The heart which palpitation (out of fear of Allāh) never leaves is strengthened. I have always expected the consequences of treachery from you and I have perceived in you the quality of the deceitful. The garments of religion have concealed me from you but the true nature of my purpose revealed you to me. I established the right way for you where you might recognize it. Yet without a guide, you were digging (aimlessly for the water of truth) and did not find such water.

"Today I am making things unknown to you speak out to you with clarity. The understanding of a man who has kept apart from me, has deserted him. I have never doubted in the truth from the time it was shown to me. The sons of Jacob were provided with the greatest evidence (for the truth) until they disobeyed their father and sold their brother (into slavery). Their repentance came after their confession of guilt, and through seeking the forgiveness of their father and their brother they were forgiven."

*****

Some of his words, peace be on him, spoken on his walking around the corpses (after the Battle of the Camel):

"Here are (members of) Quraysh who have cut off my kinship with them (literally, my nose). Yet my life has been restored. I had come forward to you warning you against seizing hold of the sword but you were like young men: You did not have any (real) knowledge of what you were seeing. However, it was destruction and an evil end. I seek refuge with Allāh from an evil end."

He passed Mu'īd b. al-Miqdād and said: "May Allāh have mercy on the father of this man. If he had been Alive, his judgement would have been better than this man's."

"Praise be to Allāh Who brought him down and made his side the inferior one," said 'Āmmār b. Yāsir. "Indeed, by Allāh, Commander of the Faithful, we do not esteem those who obstinately resist the truth, whether father or son."

"May Allāh have mercy on you and reward you well for your (adhering to the) truth," replied the Commander of the Faithful, peace be on him.

He passed 'Abd Allāh b. Rabī'a b. Darrāj who was among the slain. He said: "This hopeless man, what brought him out (in revolution)? Was it religion or support for 'Uthmān which brought him out (in revolution)? By Allāh, 'Uthmān had an unfavourable opinion of him and his father."

Then he passed Mu'īd b. Zuhayr b. Umayya and said: "If the sedition had been at the top of the Pleiades, this young man would have grasped at it. By Allāh, he was not there with a (brave) shout. The one who met him told me that he screamed with fear of the sword."

Then he passed Muslim b. Quraẓa and said: "Piety brought this man out (in revolution). Yet by Allāh he asked me to ask 'Uthmān about something which he used to claim (as his) before in Mecca. 'Uthmān gave it to him and said to me: 'If it had not been for you, I would not have given it to him.' Indeed this is what I knew. How sad for the brother of the clan. Then came the time for destruction as a result of helping 'Uthmān."

He went by 'Abd Allāh b. Ḥamīd b. Zuhayr and he said: "This is also one of those who went into battle against us with the claim that he was seeking Allāh by that. Yet he had written letters to me in which he made accusations against 'Uthmān. Then he gave him something and he was satisfied with that."

He went beside 'Abd Allāh b. Ḥakīm b. Ḥizām and said: "This man opposed his father in coming out in revolution even when his father would not help us. For the latter remained loyal in his pledge of allegiance to us even though he had held back (from helping us) and remained at home when he had doubts about the battle. The man who held back from us and the others today is not as blameworthy as he who fought against us is blameworthy."

Then he passed 'Abd Allāh b. al-Mughīra b. al-Akhnas and he said: "This man's father was killed on the day 'Uthmān was killed in his house. He came out in revolt enraged at the killing of his father. He is a young man and he became afraid because of his being killed."

Then he came to 'Abd Allāh b. Abī 'Uthmān b. al-Akhnas b. Sharīq and said:

"As for this man, it is just as if I was looking at him. The people had seized their swords as he fled running from the ranks. I turned away from him but he did not listen to the man who called to him until he killed him. This is one of the things which were hidden to the young inexperienced men of Quraysh. They had no knowledge of war. They were deceived and led into error. When they stopped, they were struck down and killed."

He walked on a little way and came to Ka'b b. Sūr. He said: "This is a man who came out against us with the Qur'ān (maṣḥaf) around his neck, claiming that he was a supporter of the community and urging the people to what was in (the Qur'ān) without himself knowing what was in it. Then he opened the Qur'ān for a decision at: Every obstinate tyrant is disappointed (XIV 15) (which he understood) as meaning Allāh had called (him) to kill me. However, Allāh killed him. Make Ka'b b. Sūr sit." So he was put in a sitting position. Then the Commander of the Faithful, peace be on him, said: "Ka'b, you have now discovered what my Lord truly promised me. Have you found what your Lord truly promised you?" Then he said, "Lay Ka'b to rest."

He came upon Ṭalḥa b. 'Ubayd Allāh and he said: "This is the man who broke the pledge of allegiance to me, the man who produced discord in the community, the man who gathered the people against me, the man who urged them to kill me and kill my offspring. Make Ṭalḥa b. 'Ubayd Allāh sit." So he was put in a sitting position. Then the Commander of the Faithful, peace be on him, said to him: "Ṭalḥa, you have discovered what my Lord truly promised me. Have you discovered what my Lord truly promised you?" Then he said, "Lay Ṭalḥa to rest."

He went on and one of those who was with him said to him: "Commander of the Faithful, were you speaking to Ka'b and Ṭalḥa after they had been killed?"

"By Allāh," he replied, "they heard my words just as the people of Qulayb heard the words of the Apostle of Allāh, may Allāh bless Him and His Family, on the day of the Battle of Badr."

*****

(This is some of) his speech at Baṣra after the defeat of the enemy. After praising and glorifying Allāh, he said:

"Allāh is One Who possesses extensive mercy, eternal forgiveness and Abundant pardon, (as He possesses) dread punishment. He dispenses His mercy and forgiveness to those of His creatures who obey Him and by His mercy those who are rightly guided are guided. He dispenses His vengeance, His severity and His punishment on those of His creatures who are disobedient. After guidance and clear explanations, those who have gone astray should not go astray. What is your view, people of Baṣra? You have reneged on your pledge of allegiance; you have publicly declared yourselves enemies against me."

A man stood up before him and said: "We think better now, for we see you have conquered and are powerful. If you punish us, that (would be because) we have committed a crime. If you forgive us, then forgiveness is more lovable to Allāh, the Exalted."

He said: "I forgive you but beware of sedition. You are the first subjects to have broken the pledge of allegiance and spread sedition in this community."

Then he sat down before the people and they pledged allegiance to him.

*****

He, peace be on him, wrote about the victory to the Kūfans:

In the name of Allāh, the Merciful, the Compassionate,

From the servant of Allāh 'Alī b. Abī Ṭalīb, Commander of the Faithful.

To the people of Kūfa.

Greetings, I commend to you the praise of Allāh, other than Whom there is no God. Allāh is a just arbitrator who does not change what is in people until they change what is in themselves. If Allāh wants evil for a people, there is no escape from it and they do not have a friend other than Him. I will tell you about ourselves and about those whom we went against - (that is) groups of the Baṣrans and the men of Quraysh and others who mixed with them in support of Ṭalḥa and al-Zubayr - and about their breaking of the agreement made with their oaths. I left Medina when news came to me about the men who had set off for (Baṣra), and about their gathering there and what they had done to my governor 'Uthmān b. Ḥunayf. (I went on) until I came to Dhāqān. There I sent al-Ḥasan b. 'Alī, 'Āmmār b. Yāsir and Qays b. Sa'd (to you) and I summoned you to (support) the right of Allāh and His Apostle, may Allāh bless Him and His Family, and my right. Your brothers soon set out to come to me. I went with them until we reached the outskirts (ẓahr) of Baṣra. I sought to excuse them through summoning them, and I presented them with proof. I (endeavoured to) diminish the stumbling and slipping caused by the apostates among Quraysh and others. I summoned them to repent from breaking their pledge of allegiance to me and the covenant which they had made to Allāh. They refused (everything) except to fight against me and to fight against those with me, and to persist in their quarrelsome error. I rose against them in battle. Allāh killed those of them who were killed as perjurers and He drove back those who withdrew to their town. Ṭalḥa and al-Zubayr were killed as a result of their perjury and rebellion. The woman (i.e.

'Ā'isha) was worse for them than the she-camel of Thamūd. They deserted and turned their backs (in flight). They were cut off from all means of protection. When they saw what had happened to them, they asked me to forgive them. I accepted that from them and sheathed the sword from them. I carried out (the requirements of) truth and the sunna among them and appointed 'Abd Allāh b. al-'Abbās as governor of Baṣra. Now I am coming to Kūfa, Allāh, the Exalted, willing. I have sent Zahar b. Qays al-Ju'fī to you so that you can ask him and he will tell you about us and them. Truth has brought them back to us and Allāh has been restored to them while they were reluctant. Greetings and the mercy and blessings of Allāh.

*****

Among the words he, peace be upon him, spoke when he came to Kūfa from Baṣra (are the following):

"Praise be to Allāh Who has aided His friend (walī), deserted His enemy, Who has given power to the truthful who was entitled and has brought low the false liar. People of the city, it is your duty to show respect to Allāh and obedience to those of the family of Your Prophet to whom Allāh has enjoined obedience. They are more appropriate (awlā) to be obeyed than those who make false claims saying, '(Come) to us. (Come) to us.' Such men were pretending to have our merit and were striving against our authority and sought to divest us of our right and keep it away (from us). They have tasted evil misfortune for what they dared (to do) and they will discover the error. (There are) among you men who have desisted from supporting us. I blame them. Desert them and make them hear (words) which they will dislike until they admit their bad behaviour towards us. Then we will see in such men things which we will like."

His Words about the Campaign against Mu'āwiya and the Battle of Ṣiffīn

Among the speeches which he, peace be on him, made when he undertook to set out for Syria to fight Mu'āwiya b. Abī Sufyān (is the following):

After praising and glorifying Allāh and calling for blessings on the Apostle of Allāh, may Allāh bless Him and His Family, (he said):

"Servants of Allāh, fear Allāh and obey Him and your Imam. Righteous subjects are saved by the just Imam. But sinful subjects are destroyed by the sinful Imam. Mu'āwiya has begun to usurp the right which belongs to me, and to break the pledge of allegiance to me, seeking to harm the religion of Allāh, the Mighty and High. Muslims, you know what the people did before when you came to me seeking for me to be in authority over you, so that you took me out of my house to pledge allegiance to me. I was reluctant with you in order to test your integrity. Then you repeated your words many times and I repeated (my reluctance) with you. You crowded upon me like thirsty camels at their pools of water in your anxiety to pledge allegiance to me so that I was afraid that some of you would kill others. When I beheld this from you, I considered my position and your position. I said: If I do not agree to their request, to undertake authority over them, they will not find anyone among them to take my place and act with my (degree of) justice among them. So I said: By Allāh, that I should rule them while they acknowledge my right and my merit is preferable to me than that they should rule me without acknowledging my right and my merit. Therefore I stretched out my hand to you and you pledged allegiance to me.

"O Muslims, among you are Emigrants and Anṣār and those who follow good practice. I have received from you the covenant of your pledge of allegiance and I respond with my agreement through a covenant and agreement (mīthāq) made before Allāh. It was stronger than covenants and agreements made to prophets; (you pledged) that you would support me, listen to my command, obey me, and consult me, that you would fight with me against every tyrant, aggressor or one who deviated, if he deviated. You all gave me that (pledge). I demanded from you all the covenant and promise made before Allāh and (under) the protection of Allāh and His Apostle and you responded to me by (giving me) that. I made Allāh the witness to your (words) and I made some of you witnesses to others. Then I applied the Book of Allāh and the sunna of His Prophet, may Allāh bless Him and His Family, among you. Then surprisingly Mu'āwiya b. Abī Sufyān disputes the succession (khilāfa) with me and denies me the (right to) the Imamate. He claims that he has more right to it than me, an act of boldness against Allāh and His Apostle concerning something which he has no right to and no argument for. None of the Emigrants have pledged allegiance to him for it, nor have the Anṣār and Muslims submitted to him.

"O men of the Emigrants and Anṣār, people who hear my words, have you made obedience to me something required of yourselves, whether you have pledged allegiance to me as subjects, or I have received a promise from you to accept my words. On that day your pledge to me was more certain than the pledge to Abū Bakr and 'Umar. Therefore why did those who have opposed me not revoke (their pledge) to those two until they had departed, while they have revoked (their pledge to me) and have not carried out the instructions which I was entitled to expect them (to obey) and they have not kept to my commands? Do you now know that the pledge of allegiance to me is required of those of you who are present and those of you who are absent? Who do Mu'āwiya and his followers find fault with in the pledge of allegiance to me and why do they not fulfil it since my close relationship (to the Prophet), my priority (as a Muslim), and my being son-in-law (of the Prophet) makes me more entitled to authority than those who came before me. Have you not heard the words of the Apostle of Allāh, may Allāh bless Him and His Family, at Ghadir concerning my authority (wilāya) and my being the one entitled to rule (mawlā)?

"Muslims, fear Allāh and rise to battle against Mu'āwiya, the one who has broken his pledge and the unjust man, and (rise) against his unjust followers. Listen to what I recite to you from the Book of Allāh which was sent down to His Prophet, the man He sent (to you), so that you may understand. By Allāh it is a warning to you, so take advantage of Allāh's warning and hold back from disobedience to Allāh. Allāh warned you through (His warning to others) when He said to His Prophet, may Allāh bless Him and His Family: Have you not considered the leaders of the Banu Isrā'īl after Moses when they said to one of their prophets: Send us a king so that we may fight on the path of Allāh. He replied: Perhaps if fighting was ordained for you, you would not fight. They answered We have no other (idea) than to fight on the path of Allāh and we have been brought out of our houses and our villages. When fighting was ordained for them, they turned their backs except a few of them. Allāh is aware of wrong-doers. Their prophet said to them: Allāh has sent Tālūt to you as a king. They asked: Shall he have (the right of) kingship over us when we are more entitled to kingship than he is? He has not brought any extent of wealth. He said: Allāh has chosen him to be over you and has increased him extensively in knowledge and substance. Allāh gives His kingship to whomsoever He wishes. Allāh is all-embracing, knowing (II 246-7).

"People, in these verses is an example so that you may learn that Allāh has given the succession (khilāfa) and the command after prophets to their progeny. He favoured Tālūt and brought him forward over the people (jamā'a) by His choice of him and by increasing him in Abundance of knowledge and substance. Do you think that Allāh has chosen the Banū Umayya over the Banū Hāshim and has increased Mu'āwiya extensively in knowledge and substance? Therefore, servants of Allāh, fear Allāh and strive on His path before His anger takes hold of you for your disobedience. Allāh said: May those of the Banu Isrā'īl who disbelieved be cursed by the tongue of David and Jesus, son of Mary, because they disobeyed and used to exceed the limit. They used not to forbid each other the hateful things (which) they did; certainly evil was that which they did! (V 77-79) Only the believers who believe in Allāh and His Apostle and then have not doubted and have striven with their wealth and their lives on the path of Allāh, only they are the truthful ones (XLIX 15). O you who believe, shall I show you a trade which will grant you escape from dread punishment. You should believe in Allāh and His Apostle and you should strive with your property and your lives on the path of Allāh. That is better for you if you would (only) realise it. That will bring forgiveness of your sins and cause you to enter gardens beneath which flow rivers and in the gardens of Eden are beautiful houses. That is the great triumph. (LXI 10-12).

"Servants of Allāh, fear Allāh and rise to fight on behalf of your Imam. If I had a group of you only the number of the men (who fought) at Badr, when I ordered them, they would obey me. When I urged them to rise, they would rise with me so that with them I could dispense with many of you and hurry to rise in battle against Mu'āwiya and his followers. For it is a required battle."

*****

Among his speeches, peace be on him, (which he delivered)

when he heard about Mu'āwiya and the Syrians and the harmful words they were saying, (is the following):

"Praise be to Allāh, the Eternal yet the New. However the sinful men have become my enemy, Allāh becomes their enemy. Are you not amazed that this is a great matter. Indeed sinners, not satisfied and turning aside from Islam and its followers, have deceived some of this community and have filled their hearts with the love of discord. They have inclined their passions towards lying and slander. They have prepared for war against us and have embarked on putting out the light of Allāh. Yet Allāh is the one who terminates His light even though the unbelievers may dislike it. O Allāh, they have rejected the truth, so scatter their army, break up their words and destroy them for their sins. May him whom I have befriended not be humiliated and may him whom I fight against not be made strong."

*****

From his words, peace be on him, urging battle at Ṣiffīn, (are those when he said) after praising and glorifying Allāh:

"Servants of Allāh, fear Allāh, lower your glances and your voices, be sparing in your words, make yourselves ready for battle, dispute and combat, and to pave the way and make the place ready, to be friendly and to be generous. Be strong and mention Allāh much. Perhaps you will be successful. Obey Allāh and His Apostle. Do not dispute with one another, for then you will fail and lose your spirit. Be steadfast. Indeed Allāh is with those who are steadfast. O Allāh, inspire them with steadfastness, grant them victory and make the reward for them great."

*****

Another of his speeches, peace be on him, in the same sense (is the following): "Muslims, Allāh has shown you a trade by which He will grant you an escape from dread punishment and which will bring you great good. It is faith in Allāh and His Apostle and striving on His path. He has made the reward for it forgiveness of sin and beautiful houris in the gardens of Eden. Therefore I told you that He loves those who fight on His path in ranks like a tightly-packed building. Therefore bring forward the man clad in armour and keep back the one who loses (his spirit), bite hard on the teeth. This makes swords stronger (to shield) against the head. Twist the edges of lances; this is a matter for the points of spears. Lower your glances; it is a firmer bond of the brave and surer for (men's) hearts. Deaden your voices; for that is the pursuit of failure and (quiet) is more appropriate for dignity. As for your standard, do not incline it and do not desert it. Only put it in the hands of the brave among you. Those who defend honour and are steadfast at the revelation of truth are the defenders who are right in their opinions and make them public. May Allāh have mercy on any man of you who comforts his brother with his own life and does not leave his opponent with his brother so that his own opponent and his brother's opponent gather against (his brother). For by that he will acquire blame and inferiority will come upon him. Do not expose yourselves to the loathing of Allāh and do not flee from death. Allāh, may He be exalted, says: Say: Flight will never benefit you if you flee from death or being killed, then you will only enjoy it for a little (XXXIII 16).

"I swear by Allāh that if you flee from the sword which is at hand, you will not be safe from the sword of the next world. Therefore seek help in steadfastness, prayers, truthfulness of intention. For Allāh, the Exalted, will grant victory after steadfastness (is shown)."

*****

Among his words, peace be on him, (are those) when he passed the standard of the Syrians and the followers of it did not withdraw from the positions (but remained) steadfast to fight the Commander of the Faithful. He said to his followers:

“These men will never withdraw from their positions without a successful attack by which life will be taken (from them) and a blow which will split their heads, chop down their bones and cut off their wrists and hands. (They will not do it) until their brows are beaten down by iron rods and (the blood from) their brows is scattered over chests and their chins. Where are the people of victory? Where are those who seek reward?”

Immediately a group of Muslims rose against them and defeated them.

*****

Among his words, peace be on him, in the same sense (are the following): “These people have not been acting for truth nor have they responded to the words of an equal, until the vanguard attacks, followed by the front line (‘asākir), until phalanxes are hurled against them, followed by the reserves (jalā’ib), until army after army drives through their land, until the cavalry remains in areas of their land with its reins over their river beds and lands, until raids will be made in every direction and their standards will shake in their hands. A true people will come against them. Their steadfastness will only increase the destruction of those of their killed and dead who will be destroyed in the path of Allāh (by those) renewing obedience to Allāh and anxious to meet Allāh. By Allāh, we were with the Prophet, may Allāh bless Him and His Family, when our fathers, our sons, our brothers and our uncles fought together. That has only served to increase us in faith, submission and endurance in face of the tribulations of suffering and (to increase us) in bravery to fight against the enemy and to scorn fighting anyone except equals. One of our men and one of our enemies will assault each other ferociously and contend with each other to take each other's life. Which one of the two will make his opponent drink the cup of death? At one time it could be for us (to do it) to our enemy, at another for our enemy (to do it) to us. Yet when Allāh beholds our endurance and our faith, He will send down the decrees against the enemy and He will send down victory to us. However, by my life, if we were to give an example like the one you have just given, neither would religion be sustained nor Islam strengthened. I swear by Allāh, that you will lose fresh blood (as a result of your inactivity). So remember what I say."

His Words about the Truce and the Revolt of the Khārijites

Among his words, peace be on him, when his followers had returned from the battle at Ṣiffīn after Mu'āwiya had deceived them by raising copies of the Qur'ān and thus they withdrew from the fight (is the following):

"You have committed an action which has pulled down the power from Islam, reduced its strength and bequeathed (it) weakness and humiliation. When you were successful and your enemy was afraid of being destroyed, for the fighting was crushing them and they felt the pain of wounds, they raised copies of the Qur'ān and called you to (accept) something which was only so that they might turn you away from themselves and bring to an end the battle between you and them and that they might cause the suspicion of death to lay in wait for you. It was deception, trickery. What have you done? You have agreed to what they wanted and have given it to men who only asked for it out of deception. I swear by Allāh, I do not consider you have any guidance after (failing to obey) my views nor any resolution (after failing to follow) my purpose."

*****

Among his words, peace be on him, (spoken) after the writing of the document for a truce and arbitration and the dispute about it among the Iraqīs (are those when) he said:

"By Allāh, I did not consent (to do this) and I did not want you to consent. However you refused everything except giving consent. So I consented. Since I have consented, it is not proper to withdraw after giving consent and to change after acceptance. Indeed we would rebel against Allāh by breaking the covenant and by transgressing its text through abrogating its agreement. Therefore fight against whoever abandons the command of Allāh. As for what you have mentioned about al-Ashtar having abandoned my command to put his signature to the document and being opposed to it, he is not such a man and I have no fear of him doing that. I wish there were two men like him among you. Indeed I wish there was a single man like him among you, who could see in your enemy what he sees. Then your burden would be lightened for me. I hope that he will straighten some of your crookedness for me. I forbade you (from doing) what you did and you disobeyed me. Myself and you are as the man of Hawāzin described:

Am I anything with regard to Ghuzzaya?

If she is mistaken, I am mistaken. If Ghuzzaya are right, I am right."

*****

(The following is) among his speeches to the Khārijites when he returned to Kūfa. He was on the outskirts (of Kūfa) before entering it. After praising and glorifying Allāh and calling for blessings on Muḥammad, His Apostle, may Allāh bless Him and His Family, he said:

"O Allāh, this is a position where whoever succeeds in it, will be more entitled to succeed on the Day of Resurrection and whoever is wrong and commits a crime in it will be blind and lose the path in the next world. I commend Allāh to you. You know that when they raised the copies of the Qur'ān, you said: We will answer their call to the Book of Allāh. I told you then: I know these people better than you. They are not followers of religion nor of the Qur'ān. I have been with them and I have known them as children and as men. They were evil children and they are evil men who seek to exploit your right and your belief. The people have only raised these copies of the Qur'ān before you as a deception, as a sign of weakness and as a trick. You rejected my opinion and said: No, rather you accept (this call) from them. I told you: Remember my words to you and your disobedience of me. Then when you refused everything except to make a truce (kitāb). I made the condition on the two arbitrators that they should allow to revive whatever the Qur'ān revives and make obsolete whatever the Qur'ān makes obsolete. None of us can oppose the judgement of anyone who judges according to what is in the Book. However if (the two arbitrators) rejected that, then we would be exempt from their judgement."

One of the Khārijites said: "Tell us, do you regard the arbitration of men concerning blood (which has been shed) as just?"

"We do not judge men," he, peace be on him, answered. "The Qur'ān judges us. This Qur'ān is only lines of writings between two covers. It does not speak. It is only men who speak it."

Then (the Khārijite) said to him: "Tell us about the time-limit you made in what is between you and them."

He answered: "Let the ignorant learn and let the one who knows be confirmed (in his knowledge). Perhaps Allāh will set right the community during this armistice. Go into your city, may Allāh have mercy on you."

They departed to the last man.

His Words concerning the Syrian Raids after the Truce

(The following is) among the words which he spoke, peace be on him, when Mu'āwiya broke the covenant and sent al-Daḥḥāk b. Qays on a raid against the Iraqīs. 'Amr b. 'Abs b. Mas'ūd had met him and al-Daḥḥāk had killed him and some of his men. After praising and glorifying Allāh, he said:

"People of Kūfa, go out to a good man, to your army. Part of it has been struck down. Therefore go out and fight your enemy. Protect your women if you are men who act."

[The narrator reported:]

They rejected him weakly and he perceived weakness and failure in them. Then he said: "By Allāh, I wish I had one man of them for every eight of you. Woe upon you, go out with me. Then withdraw from me, if it seems good to you. By Allāh, I am not unwilling to meet my Lord as a result of my resolution and perception. In that I would have a spirit which is great and a release from your (malicious) whispering, your ill-treatment and your deceit which is like the deceit of wilful brides and nagging women; whenever they sew one side, they tear the other for their husbands."

*****

(Here is) another of his speeches, peace be on him, summoning the people and finding them slow to go to war. (When) he learnt that Busr b. Arṭa'a had gone to Yemen, (he said):

"People, the beginning of your unseemly talk and your refusal was the loss of the men of influence and authority (ra'y) among you. These were men who would meet and speak the truth; they would discuss and follow the just course; they would ask and they would answer. By Allāh, I have summoned a second time and a first, secretly and aloud, at night and by day, in the morning and in the afternoon. Yet my call to you does nothing except increase your flight and (your turning) your backs. Does not warning and a call to guidance bring you benefit?

"Indeed I am one who knows what is of advantage to you and what will straighten your crookedness for me. Yet, by Allāh, I will bring you no (worldly) advantage by the corruption of my soul. Grant me a respite. By Allāh, it is as if you are with a man (i.e. Mu'āwiya) who has come to you, forbidding you and punishing you. Then Allāh will punish him just as He will punish you. Indeed (his actions) are the humiliation of the Muslims and the destruction of religion. Indeed the sons of Abū Sufyān summon (men) to wicked vices and (their call) is answered. I summon you as virtuous and good men and you are deceitful and put me off. This is not the action of pious men."

*****

Another of his speeches, peace be on him, concerning the dilatoriness of those who held back from supporting him, is:

"People, whose bodies are gathered together but whose inclinations are diverse, your words would weaken the firmest of hard-hearted men. Yet your actions would make your doubting enemy full of confidence against you. In your gatherings you say 'such and such' but when the battle comes, you say 'turn aside'. The call of the one who calls you (away) is not strong. The heart of the one who will make you endure uncertainties and weaknesses will not rest. You ask me to delay defending religion. Holding back (from its defence) will not prevent humiliating oppression. Nor will right be achieved except by serious endeavour. What house will you defend after your own house (is destroyed)? With what Imam will you fight after I (am killed)? By Allāh, deluded is the one whom you have deluded. Whoever acquires you, acquires the most deceitful partner. By Allāh, I have come not to believe in your words nor to aspire to your help. May Allāh make a separation between me and you. May He give me in exchange for you those who will be better for me than you. By Allāh. I wish I had for every ten of you, one man from the tribe of Firās b. Ghanam. It would be exchanging dirhams for dīnārs."

*****

In a further speech of his, peace be on him, concerning the same idea, after praising and glorifying Allāh, (he said):

"I can only think that these people - meaning the Syrians - will overcome you." "Why is that, Commander of the Faithful?" they asked.

"I can see their affairs in the ascendancy," he said, "while your fires are dying away. I see them as in earnest while I see you as being weak. I see them as united while I see you as divided among yourselves. I see them obedient to their leader while I see you as disobedient. By Allāh, if they overcome you, you will find them evil masters for you after me. It is as if I was looking at them now. They have become partners of you in your land. They carry off your share of the booty held by the central government to their land. It is as if I was looking at you rustling like lizards without taking your due and without protecting those sacred to Allāh. It is as if I was looking at them killing the righteous men among you and terrorising your reciters of the Qur'ān; they are forbidding you and hindering you; they are bringing other people close to themselves apart from you. If you could see the privation, the selfishness, the blows of the swords and the coming of terror, you would regret and be sorry for your neglect in going to war and you would remember the ease and well-being you had today when the memory will no longer benefit you."

*****

(This is) from his words, peace be on him, when Mu'āwiya b. Abī Sufyān broke the terms of the truce and began to launch attacks against the people of Iraq. He said, after he had praised and glorified Allāh:

"What is (the intention) of Mu'āwiya, may Allāh kill him. He wants me (to involve myself) in a dreadful matter. He wants me to act as he has acted. Then I would have broken my compact and revoked my covenant. He would use that as a proof against me and it would be disgrace against me until the Day of the Resurrection whenever (my name) was mentioned. If it was said to him, 'You began it', he would reply: 'I did not know about (those raids) and I did not order them'. Then some will say, 'He is truthful' and others will say, 'He is lying'. By Allāh, indeed Allāh is the (true) possessor of compassion and great forbearance. Forbearance was shown by many of the first Pharaohs and by those who followed the Pharaohs. If Allāh gives him a respite now, He will never let him escape. He is at the watch-tower looking down on the path he follows. Let him do what seems appropriate to him. We will not break our compact, we will not revoke our covenant. We will not terrorize a man who has submitted, nor one who has made a covenant until the terms of the truce between us are proved to be nothing, if Allāh wishes."

*****

The following is from his speech in another place:

"Praise be to Allāh and peace be on the Apostle of Allāh, may Allāh bless Him and His Family. Indeed the Apostle of Allāh, may Allāh bless Him and his family, was pleased to make me his own brother and he described me as his helper (wazīr). People, I am the very nose of guidance and its eyes. Do not keep yourselves isolated from the path of guidance because of the small numbers of those who come to it. Whoever claims that the one who will kill me is a believer (is wrong). It is time which will kill me. Indeed at some time there is an avenger for all blood that is shed. The avenger of our blood, the judge concerning the rights of himself and the right of those who are kin, of orphans, of the poor, and the traveller, is the one who does not fail to get what he searches for and whom no one who flees will escape. Those who do wrong will be aware of it. By what kind of change shall they be changed (XXVI 227). I swear by Allāh, Who split the seed and created man, you will be seized by the throat, Banū Umayya, on account of it (i.e. dominion) and you will recognize it in the possession of others and in the house of your enemy after (only) a short while. You will be aware of His prophecy after a time."

*****

This is another speech with the same idea as the previous one. (He said:) "People of Kūfa, make your preparations to fight against your enemy, Mu'āwiya and his followers."

"Give us a respite, Commander of the Faithful," they said. "He will leave the land."

He said: "By Allāh, Who split the seed and created man, let these people overcome you. It is not because they have greater right than you but because of their obedience to Mu'āwiya and your disobedience of me. By Allāh, all the nations have come to fear the tyranny of their rulers but I have come to fear the tyranny of my subjects. I have appointed to office men from among you and they have been treacherous and betrayed (me). Some have gathered the booty which they were entrusted with for distribution to the Muslims and carried it off to Mu'āwiya while others took it to their own. Thus they have ignored the Qur'ān and have been bold before the Merciful. (It has come to such a state) that if I entrusted anyone with the handle of a whip, he would betray it. You have made me tired."

Then he raised his hand to heaven and said: "O Allāh, I loathe life amid these people, I am weary of hope. Let my companion (i.e. the angel of death) come home so that I may rest from them and they may rest from me. They will never be successful after me."

*****

This is a speech which he, peace be on him, made on another occasion: "People, I have summoned you to fight against these people and you have not helped. I have asked you to listen and you have not answered. I have given you sincere advice and you have not accepted. You are present and you are like absent people. I have recited to you (Allāh's) wisdom and you have turned aside from it. I have given you eloquent warnings and you have refused them. It is as if you were scared donkeys who had fled from a lion (LXXIV 50-51). I urge you to fight against men of oppression and I do not reach the end of my words before I see you scattering from me like the people of Saba' (after the breaking of the dam) in Yemen. You go back to your own councils, you sit in your circles, you coin maxims, you recite poetry. You know the news yet when you leave, you are asking about poetry, ignoring any other kind of knowledge, careless of any other conduct and distracted from fear, you have forgotten the war, the need to prepare for it. Your hearts become empty of any talk of it. You occupy them with diversion and idle (chatter). It is wonderful, completely wonderful. But it is not for me to feel wonder that people have agreed on the wicked plan and to deprive you of your rights.

"People of Kūfa, you are like the mother of Mujālid: She became pregnant and gave birth. Then her husband died and her widowhood was long. Her inheritance was lost to her. By Him Who split the seed and created man, behind you, who are one-eyed and keep turning away, is the hell of the present life which does not remain and does not leave anything. After it are wolves and lions in various packs. So Banū Umayya will inherit from you. Their number from first to last will not treat you with compassion except for one man. It is a tribulation which Allāh has decreed for the community which is inescapable. They will kill your choice men and enslave the wicked among you. They will take out your treasure and your stores even from within the bridal chamber as a punishment for what you have abandoned of your affairs, the goodness of your own souls and your religion.

"People of Kūfa, I tell you of what will happen before it happens so that you may be on your guard against it and warned of it; whoever (of you) will be warned and consider. Sometimes you say that 'Alī is a liar, just like Quraysh said of their Prophet, may Allāh bless Him and His Family, their master, Muḥammad b. 'Abd Allāh, beloved of Allāh. Woe to you, it is I who am accused of lying. May Allāh be exalted, I was the first to worship Him, to believe in His unity. Or (is it) the Apostle of Allāh, may Allāh bless Him and His Family (who is accused of lying)? I was the first who had faith in him, who believed in him, who helped him. No, by Allāh, they are deceitful words.

You would be better without them. By Him Who split the seed and created man, you will know their news after a time but that will be when your ignorance has brought you to it. Then your knowledge will not benefit you. Disgrace upon you, you mere images, you are not men but dreams of children with the minds of the ladies of the bridal chamber. By Allāh, their bodies are present but their minds are absent from them and their inclinations are diverse. Allāh has not strengthened the support of the one who calls to you (to desert). Nor will the hearts of those who will treat you harshly take rest. There is no joy for anyone who seeks refuge with you. Your words would weaken the firmest of hard-hearted men.

"Yet actions would make your doubting enemy full of confidence against you. Woe upon you, what house will you defend after your own house (is destroyed)? With what Imam will you fight after I (am killed)? By Allāh, deluded is the one whom you have deluded. Whoever acquires you, acquires the most deceitful partner. I have not come to aspire in your help or believe in your words. May Allāh make a separation between me and you. May He give me in exchange for you, those who will be better for me than you. May he give you in exchange for me one who will be worse for you than me. Your Imam obeys Allāh and you disobey him. The Imam of the Syrians disobeys Allāh and they obey him. By Allāh, I wish Mu'āwiya would agree with me to exchange you: it would be exchanging dirhams for dīnārs. He could take ten of you and give me one of them. By Allāh, I wish that I did not know you and that you did not know me. For it is a knowledge that flows with regret. You have wounded my breast with anger, you have brought my affair to nought through your desertion and disobedience so that Quraysh have begun to say: "Alī is a brave man but he has no knowledge of war.' Yet is there anyone among them who has been longer engaged in it than I and are there any of them fiercer in battle than me? I was involved in it when I had not reached twenty and I am still in it now when I am more than sixty. However a man who is not obeyed has no power. By Allāh, I wish that my Lord had taken me from among you to His Paradise. Indeed death is looking down on me. There is nothing preventing the most wicked of (the community) from dyeing (this)" - he put his hand on his head and his beard - "It is a promise which the unlettered Prophet made to me. Whoever makes false statements is lost, whoever is pious and is truthful about the good is saved.

"People of Kūfa, I have summoned you to fight these people at night and during the day, secretly and in public. I have said to you: Attack them before they attack you. Only men who are humiliated are attacked in the ruins of their own home. You rely on one another and desert one another. My words weigh heavily on you. My command is difficult for you. You put it behind you as something to be neglected until attacks have been launched against you and abominations and detestable things appear in your midst which will be with you at night and in the morning. (This is) just as happened to the people of the stories of old (mathalāt) before you, where Allāh gave information about haughty tyrannous despots and those weakened by seducers in His words, the Mighty and High: They slaughter your sons and disgrace your women. In that there is great tribulation from your Lord (XIV 6). By Him who split the seed and created man, what you were promised has happened to you.

"People of Kūfa, I have remonstrated with you by reminding you of the warning of the Qur'ān, yet I have not benefited you. I have punished you with the whip, yet have not corrected your attitude towards me. I have flogged you with the lash, with which the revealed criminal punishments (ḥudūd) are carried out, yet you have not abstained from unlawful things. I know that the only thing suitable for you is the sword but I would not bring about your righteousness at the cost of the destruction of my own soul. However, after me a harder authority will have domination over you. It will not show respect to the old among you, nor be merciful to the children among you. It will not honour the learned among you, nor will it distribute the booty for distribution fairly among you. It will strike you down, humiliate you and kill the wounded among you in battles. It will hinder your path and block you at its door so that it may gorge itself on your strong men, on your weak men. Allāh will only destroy those of you who do wrong. Rarely can one turn one's back on something and then go forward. I think you are in a period (where there is no prophetic help). It is only my duty to give you sincere advice.

"People of Kūfa, I have been tested by two or three among you who are deaf while having ears, who are dumb yet have tongues, who are blind but have eyes, brothers who are not trustworthy at a meeting, brothers who are not reliable in a test. O Allāh! I make them bored and they bore me. I disgust them and they disgust me. O Allāh! Let no commander please them and let them please no commander. Mix their hearts as salt is mixed with water. By Allāh, if I could find an escape from your words and your correspondence, I would use it. I have remonstrated with you for your guidance until life has become distasteful. (Despite) all that you repeat the sneering at my words, fleeing from the truth and deviating to the false. Allāh will not strengthen the religion of those who support (the false). I know that the only thing you do more of for me is to cause me loss. Whenever I order you to fight against your enemy, you lower your heads to the ground and ask me to postpone the defence of the religion which is being nullified. When I say to you in the winter 'give me assistance', you say 'this is (impossible) in such a cold time'. If I say to you in the summer 'give me assistance', you say 'this (is impossible) in such intense heat. Call us when the heat has left us'. All that is fleeing from Heaven since you were unable (to act) because of the heat and the cold, by Allāh, you are more unable because of the heat of sword, much more unable. We belong to Allāh and to Him do we return.

"People of Kūfa, an Arab has come to me to tell me that a man of the tribe of Ghāmid has descended on the people of al-Anbār at night with four thousand men and attacked them as if he was attacking the Byzantines or the Khazars. He killed my governor there, Ḥassān, and with him he killed righteous men of merit, devotion and courage, may Allāh make a home for them in the blessed gardens (of Heaven). Indeed He has declared it to be permitted (for them). I have learnt that a group of Syrians broke in on a Muslim woman and another who was protected by treaty. They tore off her veil and took her scarf from her head, the earrings from her ears, the bracelets from her wrists and legs and upper arms, and the silver-bands and waistwrapper from her legs. She was unable to defend herself except by the repetition of the verse of return to Allāh and by calling out: 'O Muslims'. But no one gave her help. No one gave her assistance. If a believer died in sorrow at this, I would not blame him. On the contrary in my view he would be pious and good. The strangest of all is the gathering of these people in support of their falsehood and your failure to support your truth. You have become a target which is shot at and you do not shoot back. You are attacked and you do not fight back. (The enemy) rebels against Allāh and you are content. May your hands be filled with dust, O men like camels whose masters are absent from them so that as soon as they gather at one side, they begin to split up on the other side."

*****

[Among his speeches complaining of his enemies and defending his rights is the speech reported by al-'Abbās b. 'Abd Allāh al-'Abdī, on the authority of 'Amr b. Shamir on the authority of his narrators, who said:]

We (i.e. the narrators of 'Amr b. Shamir) heard the Commander of the Faithful, peace be on him, say:

"Since Allāh sent Muḥammad, may Allāh bless Him and His Family, I have never seen (a time of) ease. Praise be to Allāh. By Allāh, as a little one I lived in fear. When I was bigger, I fought in battle against the polytheists and made war on the hypocrites until Allāh took His Prophet to Himself. Then tribulations were worse. I have not ceased being careful and cautious. I was afraid that something would happen which would make me rise up. I have seen only good, praise be to Allāh. By Allāh I have not ceased striking with my sword from the time I was a boy until I have become an old man. What gives me endurance for what I am involved in is that all that is for the sake of Allāh and His Apostle. I am hopeful that the Spirit is near at hand. I have seen its threads."

[They reported:]

Only a few days after this speech he, peace be on him, was struck down.

*****

['Abd Allāh b. Bukayr al-Ghamawī reported on the authority of Ḥakīm b. Jubayr, who said: One who was present when 'Alī spoke at al-Raḥaba told us:] Among the things he said was:

"People, you have refused me. I say, by the Lord of the heavens and the earth, my bosom friend promised me: 'The community will betray you after me'."

[Ismā'īl b. Sālīm reported on the authority of Abū Idrīs al-Awdī, who said:]

I (i.e. Abū Idrīs) heard 'Alī, peace be on him, say: "Among the things which the unlettered Prophet, may Allāh bless Him and

His Family, promised me was: 'The community will betray you after me'"

His Words about the Succession and Men's Desertion of him

[Among his words, peace be on him, about the consultative committee (shūrā) (for the election of a successor to 'Umar b. al-Khaṭṭāb) at the house is (the conversation) which is reported by Yaḥyā b. 'Abd al-Ḥamīd al-Ḥimmānī, on the authority of Yaḥyā b. Salama b. Kuḥayl, on the authority of his father, on the authority of Abū Ṣādiq, who said:]

When 'Umar made a consultative committee (to elect a successor) consisting of six, he said: "If two make the pledge to one man (of the six) and two to another (of the six), the people must be with the three (i.e. the two men and their candidate) among whom is 'Abd al-Raḥmān (b. 'Awf) and kill the three who do not include 'Abd al-Raḥmān."

The Commander of the Faithful, peace be on him, came out of the house, leaning on the arm of 'Abd Allāh b. al-'Abbās. He said: "Ibn al-'Abbās, the people have opposed you after your Prophet just as they used to oppose your Prophet, may Allāh bless Him and His Family, during his life. By Allāh, nothing will bring them back to the truth except the sword." "How is that?" Ibn al-'Abbās asked him.

He answered: "Haven't you heard 'Umar's statement: If two make the pledge to one man (of the six) and two to another (of the six), (the people) must be with the three among whom is 'Abd al-Raḥmān and kill the three who do not include 'Abd al-Raḥmān?"

"Yes," replied Ibn al-'Abbās.

"Don't you realise," he went on, "that 'Abd al-Raḥmān is the cousin of Sa'd and 'Uthmān is the brother-in-law of 'Abd al-Raḥmān?" "Yes," he replied.

"'Umar knew," he said, "that Sa'd, 'Abd al-Raḥmān and 'Uthmān would not differ in their view. Therefore whoever among them they make the pledge of allegiance to, will have two of them (as supporters). Then he ordered that those who oppose them should be killed. He does not care if Ṭalḥa is killed as long as he kills me and al-Zubayr is killed. By Allāh if 'Umar lives, I will make known to him his evil attitude toward us which has existed of old and recently. If he dies there will be a day which will bring him and me together and on which will be the Last Judgement."

*****

['Amr b. Sa'īd reported on the authority of Jaysh al-Kinānī, who said:]

When 'Abd al-Raḥmān struck the hand of 'Uthmān as (a token of) his pledge of allegiance to him on the day of (the meeting at) the house, the Commander of the Faithful, peace be on him, said: "Marriage relationship has made and encouraged you (to do) what you have done. By Allāh what you expected from him is what your colleague (i.e.'Umar) expected from his colleague (i.e. Abū Bakr). May Allāh spread among you the perfumes of death."

*****

[A group of traditionists (ahl al-naql) report by a variety of chains of authority (ṭuruq) on the authority of Ibn 'Abbās, who said:]

I (i.e. Ibn 'Abbās) was with the Commander of the Faithful at al-Raḥaba. I mentioned the caliphate and those who had preceded him. He breathed heavily and said:

"By Allāh, Ibn Abī Quḥāfa (i.e. Abū Bakr) took on its clothes although he was aware that my position with regard to it was like the position of the axle of a mill. The stream (of knowledge) flows from me and the birds cannot rise to (the exaltedness of) my position. I allowed myself to let another robe cover me instead of it and I turned aside from it. I began to consider whether I should attempt to attack (when I would be like a man) with a hand cut off or I should endure the blind darkness (of oppression), in which the old man would grow feeble and the young become white-haired, while 'a believer' would toil until he meets his Lord.

"I realised that endurance in this was most appropriate. So I endured while all the time there was a mote in my eye and an obstruction in my throat. I could see my inheritance plundered until the time of his death came to him (i.e. Abū Bakr) and he handed it down to 'Umar. How amazing that, while he used to offer to give it up during his life, he should make a bequest ('aqd) of it after his death! How eagerly the two divided its two udders between them:

How different was my time in its saddle and the time of a man of wickedness, my brother Jābīr.

"By Allāh, he (i.e. Abū Bakr) directed it towards a coarse direction (i.e. 'Umar) whose touch was harsh, who was wounding in his roughness. The man in control of it was like the rider of an obstinate camel. If he pulled its reins, he choked it. If he held its reins loosely, he caused it to go at random so that it stumbled frequently and its excuses were few. In the name of Allāh, the people were afflicted with disorderliness, with refractoriness, with constant changes and with obstruction until death came to him. Yet even then he made it (the decision of) a consultative committee consisting of a group among whom he claimed that I was merely one. O Allāh! O what a consultative committee it was when doubt was stirred up against me through (being put alongside) the leading members among them so that I now come to be regarded (as merely an equal) with these men as my equals. However I descended (like a bird) when they descended and I flew like (a bird) when they flew (acting) out of a patience as a result of the long trial (I had endured) and the passage of time. One man (of the group) inclined (against me) because of his jealousy (i.e. Sa'd b. Abī Waqqāṣ). Another man (i.e. 'Abd al-Raḥmān b. 'Awf) favoured his brother-in-law (i.e. 'Uthmān) for other reasons which I will not mention. Eventually the third person (i.e. 'Uthmān) among these people arose lifting his chest from out of his excrement and his trough. His family (i.e. the Umayyads) rushed to devour the treasury of Allāh like the camel devours spring vegetation until its stomach is satiated by it. His actions brought about his death. The action of the people which shocked was that they (came) as messengers to me - like waves of hyenas - asking me that I should give them my acceptance of the pledge of allegiance. They were crowding in on me so that (my two sons) al-Ḥasan and al-Ḥusayn would have been trampled underfoot and my two shoulders pulled apart. Yet when I undertook the affair (of the Caliphate), a group broke their oath of allegiance, another deviated from the truth and others acted wickedly as if they had never heard Allāh say: That last abode is that which we have made for those who seek nobleness on earth and not corruption. Good health is for those who fear Allāh (XXVIII 83). Rather, by Allāh, they heard these words and they were aware of them but their own world was more attractive to their eyes and its adornments excited wonder in them.

"By Him who split the seed and created man, if it was not for the presence of those present and the necessity of a proof (ḥujja) to man through the existence of such supporters and the fact that Allāh does not give the true possessors of authority it without them being resigned (to it being swallowed) by the over-full bellies of the wrongdoers while the oppressed starve (for their rights) - (if it was not for all that) - I would throw down the reins (of the Caliphate) on to its withers and I would swallow the last with the cup of its beginning. Then in my view, they would find their world scantier than snot from the nose."

A man from the Sawād came before him and handed him a letter. He broke off from his speech.

[Ibn 'Abbās added:]

I have never regretted anything nor felt such distress like the distress I felt at losing the rest of the speech of the Commander of the Faithful, peace be on him. When he had finished reading the letter, I said: "Commander of the Faithful, would you continue your speech from the point which you reached?"

He answered: "In no way, in no way. It was like foam on the camel's mouth (shiqshiqa) as it opens its mouth to bellow and then falls silent."

*****

[Mas'ada b. Ṣadaqa reported: I heard Abū 'Abd Allāh Ja'far b. Muḥammad (al-Ṣādiq), peace be on them, say:]

The Commander of the Faithful, peace be on him, addressed the people at Kūfa. He praised and glorified Allāh. Then he said: "I am the master of the white-haired men and in me is an example of what happened to Job. Allāh will gather my family for me just like He gathered his family for Jacob. That will be when the globe turns around - and you have been told - and it goes astray and is destroyed. Indeed, therefore before that put on the garment of endurance and acknowledge your sins to Allāh. You have cast off your sanctity, you have put out your torches. You entrusted your guidance to those who do not even have control over themselves. You have neither ear nor eye, which is (even) weak. By Allāh, the seeker and the sought are thus. If you had not forsaken your task, abandoned support for the truth which is in your midst, and become weak through the weakening power of the false, one who is not like you would not have taken courage at you, and the one who becomes strong against you would not have become strong and (been able) to destroy your obedience and take it away from those of you who had it. You went astray like the children of Isrā'īl went astray in the time of Moses. I speak truly (when I say): Indeed your being astray will be doubled for you after me through your persecution of my sons; it will double the loss which the children of Isrā'īl suffered. If you have drank and filled yourselves with the illnesses brought about by the authority of the tree cursed in the Qur'ān, you have gathered with the one who calls croakingly (to you) to go astray and have run to answer the false. You have betrayed the one who summons (you) to the truth; you have cut yourselves off from those close to the men who fought (for the Prophet) at Badr and you have joined those of the sons of war who are furthest away (from the Muslims who fought at Badr). Indeed if what they had possessed had melted away, the test for punishment would have been near, the covering would have been revealed and the period would have been brought to an end. Then the threat (of hell) would be near. The stars would have appeared to you from the east and your moon would shine for you like the full moon. Since that is clear, come back to repentance and throw off sin.

"You should be aware that if you are obedient, the rising star of the east will take you along the path of the Apostle of Allāh, may Allāh bless Him and His Family and grant them peace; you would then have treated yourself for deafness and have sought a cure for dumbness; you would have been given sufficient provisions against straying from the path and seeking them (outside it); you would have cast a crushing burden from your necks. Allāh only destroys those who refuse His mercy and forsake His protection: Those who do wrong will be aware of it. By what kind of change shall they be changed? (XXVI 227)."

*****

[Mas'ada b. Ṣadaqa reported: I heard Abū 'Abd Allāh Ja'far b. Muḥammad (al-Ṣādiq), peace be on them, say:]

The Commander of the Faithful, peace be on him, addressed the people at Medina. After praising and glorifying Allāh, he said:

"Allāh, the Exalted, never destroyed tyrants except after showing forbearance and giving a respite. He did not rejoin a broken bone of anyone in (all) the nations except after constraint and testing. People, the problems which you have faced in the times which have passed are a lesson. Not every one who has a heart is gifted with sound judgement. Not every one who has ears can hear. Not everyone who looks through an eye can see. Therefore, servants of Allāh, make your view good concerning (the things) which Allāh makes your concern and look at the ruins of those whom Allāh has destroyed because He knew that they were following the practices of the people of Pharaoh. They were people with gardens, with fantasies, with farms and high position. Those are the ruins of those who were oppressors. Indeed it is everlasting hell which will warn the one who sees it of destruction. (It comes) after well-being, joyfulness and temporary security and happiness. To whoever is steadfast, there is the happy end. The final end of affairs belongs to Allāh. How surprising for people with intelligence! How would they live amid the rolling torrents and how would they gain sustenance without one who was protected a friend and ruler (walī) for His community which thirsts in its journey and which desires guidance? For they do not follow the tracks of a prophet, nor do they copy the practice of a testamentary trustee of authority (waṣī), nor do they believe in supernatural (things), nor do they turn away from sin. How indeed, while they resort to their own minds in ambiguous matters? Each person among them, being the leader of himself, adopts in (these matters) what he considers appropriate without authorities who are able to follow a just path. They will never increase (in anything) except after violence. Some are kind to each other, and believe one another in disagreement to everything which the Apostle, may Allāh bless Him and His Family, bequeathed, and in deserting whatever he carried out on the authority of the Creator of the heavens and the earths, the Aware, the Knowing. They are people from the darkness of caves of shadows, leaders of bewilderment and doubt. Whoever trusts to himself, will sink into errors. This is so for Allāh has guaranteed the end of this path: So that whoever is destroyed will be destroyed with proof (which has been given to him) and whoever lives will live with proof. Indeed Allāh is hearing, aware (VIII 42). What is in greater error than a community which shuns its rulers and turns away from its shepherds. O sorrow, sorrow, the heart is wounded and grief becomes a habit as a result of the actions of our Shī'a after my death despite the nearness of its love and the intertwining of its friendship. How do some of them kill others and how does their friendship turn to hatred? By Allāh, tomorrow (there is) the family caused to deviate from its root, encamped around a branch, given hope of victory from another direction, expecting spirit from a place other than which it will come. Every group among them will cling to a branch by which they will be taken wherever the branch inclines despite the fact that Allāh - and praise be to Him - will gather them like the scattered clouds of spring, will bring them together and make them heaped together like heavy clouds. He will open gates for them to which they will flow, at (the advice of) their advisor, like torrents of rain where no land can resist it, no dam can stop it and the base of a lofty mountain cannot resist its path. Allāh will plant them in the middle of valleys. He will make springs in the land for them. Through them, He will remove the privation of people and He will make available for them the estates of people so that they will take forcibly what had been taken from them forcibly. Through them, He will pull down columns and through them He will break down the casings of bricks at Iram. He will let them enjoy the stones of olives. By Him Who split the seed and created man, what they possess will melt away after they have had power in the land and high position over men just as tar and lead melt in the fire. Perhaps Allāh will gather my Shī'a after scattering them because of the evil day of these men. No man has a right to goodness from Allāh. Rather goodness belongs to Allāh and the matter is all (with Him)."

*****

The historians (naqalat al-āthār) report that a man from the tribe of Asad stood before the Commander of the Faithful, peace be on him and said to him: "Commander of the Faithful, there is wonder among you, Banū Hāshim, how this authority came to be diverted from you. You are the highest in family and in connection and closeness to the Apostle, may Allāh bless Him and His Family, as well as in understanding of the Book."

The Commander of the Faithful, peace be on him, replied: "Son of a worm, you are unstable and the gap is narrow so that you shoot in a way which is not straight. You have protection through your relationship by marriage and therefore the right to ask. You have sought information so know then that it was preference through which the souls of the people were generous while other souls were niggardly with it. Therefore leave off plundering the rooms which are (already) empty. Pay attention to the disasters concerning the affairs of the son of Abū Sufyān (i.e. Mu'āwiya). Time has made me laugh after it had made me weep. There is no deceit which the people despaired of. By Allāh, through my restraint and my dignity they tried to act in a false way with regard to the nature of Allāh. How very far that is from me. They have mixed drink and dwelling between them and me. If the trials of misfortune are taken from us, I would make them responsible for the truth in its purity. If it is otherwise, do not give yourself sorrows for them and do not console sinful people."

Some of his Words of Wisdom and Warning, Peace be on him

May Allāh have mercy on you, take your (eternal) abode from your transitory (life).

Do not rend your veils before One from Whom even your secrets are not concealed.

Take your hearts out of the world before your bodies are taken from it.

For the next life you were created and in the world you are imprisoned.

When a man dies, the angels ask about what he has brought while the people ask about what he has left behind. By Allāh, your fathers brought some of what was for you. Do not leave behind anything at all, for then you will owe it. The world is like a poison which the one who does not recognise it eats.

*****

There is no life without religion and there is no death except through the denial of certain truth.

Drink the sweet water. It will wake you from the slumber of rest. Beware of the pestilential torrid winds which bring destruction.

*****

The world is the abode of truth for those who know it and the place of salvation for those who take provisions from it. It is the place to which the inspiration of Allāh has been sent down and the market place of His friends. So trade and gain the profit of heaven.

*****

Similar words were addressed by him, peace be on him, to a man whom he heard blaming the world without knowing what he ought to say about its (true) meaning:

"The world is the place (dār) of truth for those who believe in it, and a place which is to be wiped out for those who understand it. It is a place which is full of wealth for those who take their provision from it and the place of prostration for the prophets of Allāh and a place to which His inspiration has been sent down. It is the place of prayer for His angels and the market-place of His friends, in which they gain mercy and in which they earn the profit of Heaven. Who is the man who blames it when it has called out (for men) to keep apart from it and it has cried out (for men) to separate from it, when it has announced its own death? Through its own joy it has yearned for joy. Through its own tribulation it has warned against tribulation, bringing fear, giving warning, trying to turn (men) away and terrify them. O you who blame the world and (yet are one) who is seduced into rushing blindly into it, when did it tempt you to kill your fathers as a test and to sleep with your mothers under the earth? How did it weaken your hand and make your arm sick so that a cure is necessary for them, and doctors prescribe for them and medicines are sought for them without your search bringing them any benefit, without your (seeking) intercession bringing them any intercession? The world has made an example of them for you with your killing and your intercourse so that your weeping will not avail you nor will your darlings be of any use to you."

*****

People, take five things from me. For by Allāh if you travelled on a camel for them, you would exhaust it before you found anything like them. No one should hope for anything except from His Lord, nor should one fear (anything) except his sins. The scholar ('ālīm), when asked about something he does not know, should not be ashamed to say that Allāh knows. Steadfastness is of the same rank with faith as the head is to the body. He who has no patience has no faith.

*****

Every statement in which Allāh is not mentioned is a vanity. Every silence in which there is no thought (of Him) is carelessness. Every reflection in which there is no consideration (of Him) is an idle pastime.

*****

One who buys his soul and sets it free is not like the one who sells his soul and imprisons it.

*****

The one who gets to the shade first has been exposed to the sun. The one who gets to water first is thirsty.

*****

Good breeding takes the place of a good family.

*****

The man who is abstemious towards the world increases his renunciation of it whenever it increases its manifestation of itself to him.

*****

Affection is the greatest of traps. Knowledge is the noblest of qualities.

*****

If work is an effort then being concerned with avoiding (it) is an act of corruption.

*****

The man who goes to the extreme in rivalry commits a sin. The man who falls short in it will be subjected to it.

*****

Forgiveness corrupts the wicked to the same extent as it restores the noble.

*****

Whoever loves noble actions avoids crimes.

*****

Men cast their eyes on a man whose thoughts adorn him.

*****

The ultimate generosity is that you should give what you are able.

*****

There is no distance for one who is present and no nearness for one who is separate.

*****

One of the greatest sins of a man is to be unaware of his faults.

*****

The perfection of moderation is a willingness to accept what is sufficient.

*****

Generosity is perfected through the adoption of noble deeds and the payment of debts.

*****

Nobility is revealed through loyalty to brotherhood in hard times and easy times.

*****

If the sinner is displeased, he slanders. If he is content, he lies. If he is covetous, he wounds.

*****

One who is not more concerned with his reason for what is, will more (inevitably) come to his death.

*****

Put up with an error by your friend for the time of an attack by your enemy.

*****

A good confession wipes out the act of committing a wrong.

*****

What money is spent to make you aware of reforming your character is not wasted.

*****

Acting moderately is easier than acting immoderately and restraint is greater in protection than profligacy.

*****

The evilest of provisions for the return (to Allāh) is the committing of a crime against men.

*****

No benefit is wasted if it is received with thanks. No grace remains if it is received ungratefully.

*****

Time is of two kinds: time you have and time you owe. When you have it don't undervalue it and when you owe it, be steadfast.

*****

Often a mighty man is the humblest of creatures and a humble man is the mightiest of creatures.

*****

Whoever is not tested by affairs is deceived and the one who struggles against the truth is brought down.

*****

If the allotted span of life is known, hope is diminished.

*****

Thankfulness is the ornament of sufficiency and steadfastness is the ornament of tribulation.

*****

The value of each person lies in the good he does.

*****

People are the children of their own good actions.

*****

The person is found under his tongue.

*****

Whoever consults those with understanding is guided correctly.

*****

One who is satisfied with little can do without much. Those who cannot do without much have need of wicked men.

*****

Whoever has sound roots has branches which will bear fruit.

*****

Whoever gives hope to man regards him with awe. Whoever is deficient in the knowledge of anything, shames him.

*****

Part of his speech, peace be on him, describing man are his words:

"The most amazing thing in man is his heart. It loves wisdom and its opposite. If hope occurs to it, ambition reduces it. If ambition rouses in it, covetousness destroys it. If despair possesses it, sorrow kills it. If anger occurs to it, rage intensifies it. If it comes near contentment, it forgets to be on guard. If fear takes hold of it, caution (totally) occupies it. If protection is provided for it, heedlessness takes possession of it. If a blessing is renewed for it, (love of) power seizes it. If a tragedy befalls it, violent grief disgraces it. If it acquires wealth, riches make it unjust. If poverty gnaws at it, misfortune (completely) occupies it. If hunger presses upon it, weakness makes it idle. If it has earlier satisfied its stomach to satiety, then every diminution of it is harmful and every increase of it is corrupting."

*****

When Shāhzamān, daughter of Chroesroe was captured, he, peace be on him, asked her: "What did you learn from your father after the Battle of the Elephant?" "I learned from him," she replied, "that he used to say: When Allāh controls a matter, ambitions are brought to nought without Him and when the allotted time comes to an end, death is in view."

"How well your father spoke," he, peace be on him, answered. "Affairs are led towards their destinations until death takes part in their control."

*****

One who followed certain truth and then was struck by doubt, should remain with his certain truth. Indeed certain truth cannot be removed by doubt.

*****

A believer is tired of himself while the people find themselves in comfortable position with regard to him.

*****

The man who is lazy does not love Allāh's truth.

*****

The best kind of worship is steadfastness, silence, and waiting for relief.

*****

Steadfastness is of three types: steadfastness in tragedy, steadfastness against disobedience, and steadfastness in obedience.

*****

Clemency is the helper of the believer. Knowledge is his friend, gentleness his brother, piety his father and steadfastness is the commander of his troops.

*****

Three things (which will earn) the treasures of Heaven are: giving alms secretly, keeping tragedy hidden and keeping sickness hidden.

*****

Feel need for the one whose prisoner you wish to be, dispense with the one whose equal you wish to be and prefer the one whose leader you wish to be.

*****

There is no satisfaction for the licentious, no rest for the envious and no affection for the weary.

*****

He, peace be on him, said to Aḥnaf b. Qays:

"The silent is the brother of the one who gives consent. Whoever is not with us is against us."

*****

Generosity belongs to the nobility of nature but over-generosity is a corruption of creation.

*****

The abandonment of a promise to a friend is the motive for being cut off (from his friendship).

*****

Rumours of anything among the ordinary people are evidence for the beginnings of its existence.

*****

Search out sustenance. It is guaranteed to one who looks for it.

*****

Four kinds of men whose prayer will not be rejected: the prayer of the just Imam for his subjects; the son who is respectful to his father; the father who is respectful to his son; and the oppressed man. Of them Allāh says: By My strength and My majesty, I will support you even after (some) time.

*****

The best kind of wealth is the abandonment of begging. The worst kind of poverty is the clinging to subservience.

*****

Good behaviour lies in protection from destruction. Gentleness is the alleviation of distress.

*****

A man who laughingly acknowledges hissing is better than one who behaves boldly towards Allāh in tears.

*****

If it was not for discussion, the (different) schools of thought would be ignorant.

*****

No tool is more beneficial than intelligence. No enemy is more harmful than ignorance.

*****

One who widens his hopes lessens his effort.

*****

The most grateful of the people is the most satisfied of them. The most ungrateful of them is the most covetous of them.

*****

In such speeches as these wisdom may be gained. We have not included in this chapter of speeches, all of those which have been reported with these ideas from him, lest by that the speeches would become too diffuse and the book become too long. In what we have presented, there is sufficient for those with intelligence.

SOME OF THE MIRACLES OF THE COMMANDER OF THE FAITHFUL

(The following are) some of the signs of Allāh, the Exalted, and His clear proof of the Commander of the Faithful, peace be on him, which indicate his position with regard to Allāh, the Mighty and High, and his special endowment with miracles by which he was set apart from everyone else through the call for obedience to him, to remain steadfast in respecting his authority and closeness to Allāh (wilāya), to recognise his rights and the certainty of His Imamate, and to be aware of his protection (from error), perfection and the demonstration of the proof of him.

The Miracle of his Wisdom while still a Boy

Among these are some qualities which make him equal to two of the prophets, apostles and proofs of Allāh to His creatures and about the authenticity and correctness of which there can be no doubt. Allāh, the Mighty and High, said in mentioning Jesus, son of Mary, the spirit (rūḥ) and word of Allāh, and the prophet and Apostle of Allāh to His creatures, when He mentioned the story of his mother's conceiving and giving birth to him and the miraculous nature of that: She said: How can I have a son when no man has ever touched me and I have not been adulterous. He answered: As it (shall be), for your Lord said: That will be easy for Me and We will make him a sign to the people and a mercy from us. It is a matter which is decreed (XIX 21).

Among the signs of Allāh, the Blessed and Exalted, concerning the Messiah, Jesus, son of Mary, peace be on him, was his speaking in the cradle. By that normal human behaviour was transcended and in it there was great wonder and an illustrious miracle to the minds of men. Among the signs of Allāh concerning the Commander of the Faithful, peace be on him, was the perfection of his intellect, dignity and knowledge of Allāh and His Apostle, His blessing and peace be on Him and His Family, despite his youth and his being in outward form still only a child when the Apostle of Allāh, may Allāh bless Him and His Family, summoned him to believe in him and acknowledge him, and made him responsible for knowing his rights, and recognising his Creator and His unity. (He also) entrusted him with the secrets of His religion, the defence and preservation of it, and the fulfilment of the trust in it. At that time, he, peace be on him, was according to some statements a boy of seven years of age, according to others a boy of nine but according to the majority he was a boy of ten. The perfection of his intellect, peace be on him, (at that age) and the occurrence (in a boy of that age) of the ability to acknowledge Allāh and His Apostle, may Allāh bless Him and His Family, is an illustrious sign from Allāh which transcends normal human behaviour, and thus indicates his position with Him, his special endowment and his being worthy for what he was nurtured for the Imamate of the Muslims, and the proof (of Allāh) to all mankind. In this transcendence of ordinary human behaviour which we have mentioned there is a similarity with Jesus and John the Baptist as we have described. If it was not for the fact that at that (time) he was perfect, complete and (capable of) acknowledging Allāh, the Exalted, the Apostle of Allāh, may Allāh bless Him and His Family, would not have made him responsible to acknowledge his prophethood, nor would he have bound him to believe in himself and to accept his mission, nor would he have summoned him to accept his rights, nor would he have begun his mission with him before every other person except his wife, Khadīja, peace be on her.

Because the Prophet of Allāh, may Allāh bless Him and His Family, entrusted him with his secret which he ordered him to protect and because he set him apart by that from all the other children of his time and endowed him apart from all others as we have mentioned, that indicates that he, peace be on him, was perfect despite his youth, (capable of) acknowledging Allāh, the Exalted and His Prophet, may Allāh bless Him and His Family, before adolescence. This is the meaning of the words of Allāh, the Exalted concerning John the Baptist, peace be on him: We gave him wisdom while still a boy (XIX 12). There is no wisdom dearer than knowledge of Allāh, nor more obvious than the knowledge of the prophethood of the Apostle of Allāh, may Allāh bless Him and His Family, nor more celebrated than the ability of rational deduction, nor more discerning than the understanding of speculation (naẓar) and consideration and the knowledge of the aspects of elucidation, by which one is able to arrive at the realities of the unknown. If the matter is as we have explained it, it confirms that Allāh, the Exalted, caused ordinary human behaviour to be transcended in the case of the Commander of the Faithful, peace be on him, by an illustrious sign which is equivalent to His two prophets whom the Qur'ān speaks of in its great verses as we have explained.

The Miracle of his Military Prowess

Among the signs of Allāh, the Exalted, concerning the Commander of the Faithful, peace be on him, which transcend ordinary human behaviour is that He never endowed anyone else, with regard to fighting in single combat against one's rivals and against heroes, with what is known about him, peace be on him, in terms of the vast amount of (fighting) which he had to engage in during the course of time. Among those who have engaged in warfare there can only be found men to whom it brings disgrace and who acquire wounds and deformities through it except the Commander of the Faithful, peace be on him. Despite the length of time which he fought against his enemies, he acquired no ugly wound nor was anyone able to do him any harm until there occurred what happened at his assassination by Ibn Muljam, may Allāh curse him. This is a marvel by which Allāh set him apart through this sign and endowed him with illustrious knowledge of its meaning. By that He indicated his position with regard to Him and his being characterised by miracles, the favour of which set him apart from all other men.

Among the signs of Allāh, the Exalted, concerning him, peace be on him, is the fact that there is not mentioned a single contestant during the battles whom he met as an opponent, whom he did not overcome at one time and did not overcome at another time. He did not give any of his enemies a wound unless that man died of it immediately or recovered after a time. No rival escaped from him in battle, no one could escape his blow. For that it is appropriate that there was no doubt about his victory over every rival who came against him and his killing of every hero who fought. This is also among the things by which he, peace be on him, was set apart from all other men and by which Allāh caused ordinary human behaviour to be transcended at every time and occasion. It is among the clear indications of his (position).

Among the signs of Allāh, the Exalted, concerning him is the fact that despite the long period in which he was engaged and occupied in warfare and in which he was tested by the bravery of his enemies and their leaders, and by all the efforts which they made to gather against him and to bring about his death through deceit, he never turned his back and fled from one of them, nor did he weaken in his position or show fear to any of his rivals. He never met any opponent in battle without transfixing him at one time or turning aside from him (to another part of the battle) at another time. He would advance against him immediately and attack him at that time. Since his conduct was as we have described, it confirms what we have mentioned about his being set apart by an illustrious sign and a clear miracle transcending ordinary human behaviour by which Allāh indicated his Imamate and revealed the duty to obey him. By that He set him apart from all mankind.

The Miracle of the Survival of his Reputation and his Family despite Suppression and Oppression

Among the signs and indications of him, peace be on him, by which he was set apart from those who opposed him is the clear appearance of his outstanding qualities to both the Shīʿa (khāṣṣa) and the general populace (ʿāmma). (This has been sufficient) to force the people to transmit reports of his merits and his qualities endowed by Allāh and for them to be admitted to even by opponents of the proof that there is in them. It has occurred despite the great number who have attempted to deviate from him and oppose him and the great number of occasions they have been prompted to suppress his merit and deny his rights. (It has occurred when) the (control of the) world has been in possession of his rivals and has been turned aside from his friends (awliyāʾ). (Despite this) his opponents who possess authority over the world and the narrators of the people, have not been able to put out his light and to deny his career (amr). Allāh has caused ordinary human behaviour to be transcended by spreading his merit and revealing his outstanding qualities, by forcing everyone to recognize that and to admit its truth, and to refute the deceitful attempts of his enemies to conceal his outstanding qualities and to deny his rights so that the proof of him may be brought about and the justification of his rights may be revealed. Because the normal view among those who agree to render his career obscure continues to oppose what we have mentioned, and yet it has not been able to bring that about with regard to the Commander of the Faithful, peace be on him, and the normal view has been transcended, that indicates his being apart from the rest of men through the illustriousness of the sign which we have described.

The report is well-known and widespread on the authority of al-Sha'bī that he used to say:

"I (i.e. al-Sha'bī) used to hear the preachers of the Umayyads curse the Commander of the Faithful, 'Alī b. Abī Ṭālib, peace be on him, on their pulpits." He would raise his finger to the sky and (go on): "I used to hear them praising their ancestors on their pulpits as if they could reveal their corpses."

One day al-Walīd b. 'Abd al-Malik said to his sons: "My sons, your duty is to religion. I do not see that religion has built anything which the world has destroyed. I see that the world has built a building which religion has destroyed. I still hear our followers and the members of our family curse 'Alī b. Abī Ṭālib, peace be on him, suppress his merits and urge the people to hate him. Yet that does not bring the people's hearts anything but closeness (to him). They strive to bring the spirits of the people closer to themselves. Yet that does not bring their hearts anything except (to make the people) more distant from them."

The manner of suppressing the merits of the Commander of the Faithful, peace be on him, of the deception practised by the religious scholars and of their spreading of what seemed authentic to a rational being reached the extent that when a man wanted to report a tradition on the authority of the Commander of the Faithful, peace be on him, he was not able to refer to him either by mentioning his name or his family background. Necessity required him to say: "A man from the Companions of the Apostle of Allāh, may Allāh bless Him and His Family, told me." Or he might say: "A man from Quraysh told me." Some used to say: "Abū Zaynab told me."

'Ikrima reported on the authority of 'Ā' isha in her account of the sickness and death of the Apostle of Allāh, may Allāh bless Him and His Family, that she said in a sentence of it: "The Apostle came out, leaning on two men from his House, one of whom was al-Faḍl b. al-'Abbās." When he (i.e. 'Ikrima) reported that on her authority to 'Abd Allāh b. al-'Abbās, the later asked: "Do you know the other man?"

"No," he replied, "she did not name him."

"That was 'Alī b. Abī Ṭālib, peace be on him," he told him. "'Our mother' would not mention any good of him while she could (avoid it)."

The tyrannical governors would flog anyone who mentioned any good of him. Indeed their heads were cut off for doing that and exposed to the people to make them disassociate themselves from him. The normal course (of events) followed this pattern for it to become accepted that no good should be mentioned of him in any way much less his outstanding merits be mentioned, his qualities be reported and proof of his rights be set out. Yet since the appearance of his merits and the spreading of his qualities has taken place as we have mentioned its being widespread both among the Shī'a (khāṣṣa) and the general populace ('āmma), and since the compulsion of both enemy and friend to report it is now established, (this) has transcended the normal course of events as far as he is concerned and the nature of the proof of this idea is explained by the illustrious sign (of Allāh) as we have said before.

Another of the signs of Allāh, the Exalted, concerning him, peace be on him, is that no one has suffered such tribulation with regard to his sons and his offspring as he, peace be on him, suffered with regard to his sons and offspring. The fact is that no terror is known to have encompassed the group of children of any prophet, of any Imam, of the king of any period whether pious or profligate like the terror which encompassed the offspring of the Commander of the Faithful, peace be on him. Nor were any so much subjected to being killed, to being pursued from their houses and lands, and to being terrorised as the offspring and sons of the Commander of the Faithful were subjected to. The different kinds of severity meted out to them did not occur for any other group of people. They were killed by murderous treachery, by treason and by deception. It was done to most of them during their lifetimes as an example. They were tormented by hunger and thirst until their lives were taken by death. This required them to scatter throughout the land and to become separated from their houses, their families and their countries. (It required) their family background to be kept secret from the majority of the people. The fear surrounding them extended to keeping themselves hidden from those who loved them in addition to their enemies. Their flight extended from their lands to the furthest east and west, to places which lacked civilisation and where the majority of the people were without knowledge of them. They avoided bringing such people close to them and mixing with them, out of fear for their own lives and their offsprings' from the tyrants of those times. All of these are the reasons which should bring about the disruption of their organisation, the pulling out of their roots, and the paucity of their numbers. Yet they, despite everything we have described, are the most numerous offspring of any one of the prophets, the righteous men and the friends (of Allāh). Indeed they are more numerous than the offspring of anyone else among the people. They have extended across the lands through their great number and have become more numerous than the offspring of most men. They have done this despite their marriages within their (family circles) to the exclusion of those outside them and by limiting them to those possessing their own genealogies of the nearer members of the relations. In that the normal practice has been transcended as we have explained. It is proof of the illustrious sign concerning the Commander of the Faithful, peace be on him, as we have already described and explained.

This is something about which there can be no doubt. Praise be to Allāh, Lord of the Worlds.

The Prophecies and Inner Knowledge of the Commander of the Faithful

Among the illustrious signs of Allāh concerning him, peace be on him, and the special characteristic by which he has been set apart, the miraculous nature of which is evidence for his Imamate, for the duty to obey him, and for the confirmation of his proof, are the group of arguments by which Allāh, the Exalted, makes known prophets and apostles, peace be on them, and which He gives as signs of their truthfulness. Of these are the widespread reports of him, peace be on him, concerning the unknown and (foretelling) things which will happen before they happen. He never asserted anything of that without his statement agreeing with the report of the event so that in this way his truthfulness was established. This is one of the most illustrious of the miracles of prophets, peace be on them. Will you not look at the words of Allāh, the Exalted, in which He makes manifest Jesus, son of Mary, peace be on him, through illustrious miracles and signs which indicate his prophethood? I will tell you what you will eat and what you will store in your houses (III 49). He, may His name be mighty, made similar miraculous signs for the Apostle of Allāh, may Allāh bless Him and His Family, when he said at the defeat of the Romans' (i.e. Byzantines) horsemen: Alif Lam mim, Rome has been conquered in the lower lands (of its empire) but in a few years after their defeat they will conquer (XXX 1-4). The matter turned out just as Allāh, the Mighty and High, had said. He, may His name be mighty, said of those who took part in the Battle of Badr before the battle (occurred): The groups (of the enemy) will be defeated and they will turn their backs (in flight) (LIV 45). The matter occurred just as Allāh, the Exalted, had said without there being any difference in it. He, the Mighty and High, said: Indeed you will enter the Sacred Mosque in safety, if Allāh wills, with your heads shaved or shortened, without fear (XLVIII 27). The matter took place as Allāh, the Exalted said. He, may He be praised, said: When the help of Allāh comes and victory, you will see the people entering the religion of Allāh in parties (CX 1-2). The event occurred as He, the Exalted, described. He, may He be praised, said, giving information about the inner feelings of the Hypocrites: They say within themselves: If it was not for the fact that Allāh would punish us for what we say (LVIII 8). Thus He gave information about the inner feelings and the secrets which they kept hidden. He, may the mention of Him be extolled, said concerning the story of the Jews: Say: O those who have been guided, if you claim that you are friends of Allāh apart from other people, then you should seek death if you are truthful. Yet they do not seek it in an attempt to escape from (the crimes) which their hands have committed. Indeed Allāh is aware of the wrongdoers (LXII 6-7). The matter happened as Allāh, the Exalted, had said and not one of them dared to seek it. That established (the reliability of the prophet's) reports and by it He made clear his truthfulness. He gave evidence of his prophethood, peace be on him, with similar examples, which, to present in this book, would make it too long.

(The evidence for) this kind (of miracle) by the Commander of the Faithful, peace be on him, is such that it can only be denied through stupidity, ignorance, slander and obstinacy. Can you not see what the reports have made public knowledge, what traditions have been widespread and what everybody hands down about him, peace be on him?

*****

He said before fighting against the three groups after the pledge of allegiance had been made to him: "I have been ordered to fight against those who break their pledges, those who are unjust and those who deviate (from the truth)."

He, peace be on him, fought against them and the matter was just as he had predicted.

He, peace be on him, said to Ṭalḥa and al-Zubayr, when they asked permission to leave to go on the lesser pilgrimage: "By Allāh, you are not going to make the lesser pilgrimage, you are going to Basra."

The matter was as he had said.

He, peace be on him, also said to Ibn 'Abbās when informing him about their asking for permission to go on the lesser pilgrimage: "I have given them permission despite knowing of the treachery they harboured within themselves. I have appealed for the help of Allāh against them. Indeed Allāh, the Exalted, will rebuff their plotting and give me victory against them."

The matter happened as he predicted.

*****

At Dhū Qar, he said while sitting to receive the pledge of allegiance: “Exactly a thousand men will come from the direction of Kufa to pledge themselves to me until death.”

[Ibn ‘Abbās commented:]

I (i.e. Ibn ‘Abbās) was disturbed at that and was afraid that if the number of the people was less or more, the matter would bring failure on us. The anxiety to count them continued to trouble me so that when the first of them came, I began to count them. Their number reached nine hundred and ninety-nine and then the people stopped coming. I said: “We belong to Allāh and to Him we will return. What is the interpretation of what he said!”

As I was thinking that I saw a person coming towards us. He was a man wearing a woollen cloak and he had a sword with him, a shield and (other) weapons. He went up to the Commander of the Faithful, peace be on him, and said: “Stretch out your hand so that I may pledge allegiance to you.”

“On what conditions do you make the pledge of allegiance to me?” the Commander of the Faithful, peace be on him, asked him.

“To hear and to obey and to fight before you until I die or Allāh grants you victory,” he replied.

“What is your name?” he asked.

“Uways,” he answered.

"You are Uways al-Qaranī," he said.

"Yes," he replied.

"Allāh is greater (Allāhu akbar)," he said. "My dear friend, the Apostle of Allāh, may Allāh bless Him and His Family, told me that I would meet a man from his community called Uways al-Qaranī who would be of the party of Allāh and His Apostle, who would die in martyrdom and the number who would gain his intercession was like the number of the tribes of Muḍar and Rabī'a."

[Ibn 'Abbās reported:]

Then, by Allāh, (my anxiety) left me.

*****

Another example of that is what he, peace be on him, said when the Syrians raised copies of the Qur'ān and a group of his followers began to have doubts (about their position) and insisted (that he agree) to making a truce: "Shame on you, this is a deceitful trick. Those people do not really mean (to settle the issue by) the Qur'ān because they are not people (who accept) the Qur'ān. Fear Allāh and carry out your decision to fight against them. If you do not, you will be separated into (different) groups and you will regret it when regret will not bring any advantage."

The matter turned out just as he had predicted. This group of people fell into disbelief after the arbitration (between 'Alī and Mu'āwiya) and they regretted the action which they had previously hastily embarked on and made him accept. They were separated into different groups and destruction came to them soon after.

*****

He, peace be on him, said as he was setting out to fight against the Khārijites: "If it was not for the fact that I am afraid that you would just carry on discussions and abandon (all other) action, I would tell you the decision Allāh has made through the words of His Prophet, peace be on him, concerning those who fight against these people (i.e. against the Khārijites) as a result of seeing them to be misguided. Indeed, among them is a man with a stunted arm who has breasts like the breasts of a woman. They are the wickedest of creatures and the one who fights against them is the closest in relationship to Allāh among His creatures."

The malformation of the man (mukhdaj) had not been known to the people. After the battle, he, peace be on him, caused a search to be made for him among those killed saying: "By Allāh, I have not lied nor have I been lied to."

Eventually (his body) was found among those people and his shirt was torn open, On his shoulder there was a swelling like the breast of a woman, on which were hairs. When the hairs were pulled, his shoulder came forward with it. When they were left, his shoulder went back to its position. When he was found, he said: "Allāh is greater. In this there is a warning for anyone who reflects."

*****

[The historians (aṣḥāb al-sīra) report in their account on the authority of Jundub b. 'Abd Allāh al-Azdī, who said:]
I (i.e. Jundub b. 'Abd Allāh) took part with 'Alī in the battles of the Camel and Ṣiffīn. I never had any doubts about fighting against those who fought him until I took part in the battle of al-Nahrawān (against the Khārijites). Then doubts came to me

about fighting against these people. I said: "It is our reciters of the Qur'ān and our choice men whom we are killing. This matter is dreadful."

In the morning I went for a walk, (taking) some vessels of water with me, until I left the lines (of the army). Then I fixed my spear in the ground, fitted my shield on it and shaded myself from the sun. While I was sitting, the Commander of the Faithful, peace be on him, came along. He said to me: "Brother from (the tribe of) al-Azd, do you have water for ritual purification with you?" "Yes," I answered and I gave him a vessel.

He went aside so that I could not see him. Then he came back after he had purified himself. He sat down in the shade of the spear. Suddenly a horseman appeared asking for him. I said: "Commander of the Faithful, there is a horseman who wants you."

"Make a sign to him (to come here)," he told me.

I made a sign and he came. He said: "Commander of the Faithful, the people have crossed the river."

"No," he retorted, "they have not crossed."

"Yes, by Allāh, they have crossed," (the man) insisted.

"You are lying," he said.

Then another man came. He said: "Commander of the Faithful, the people have crossed."

"No," he replied, "they have not crossed."

"By Allāh," (the man) said, "I did not come to you until I saw the standards and the baggage on that side."

"By Allāh," he declared, "they have not done so. (What you want) is to kill them and shed their blood."

Then he arose and I arose with him. I said to myself: "Praise be to Allāh, who has given me insight into this man and enabled me to recognise his affair. He is one of two men: he is either a thorough-going liar or (one given) evidence (for his authority) by his Lord and a covenant by his Prophet. O Allāh, I give You a solemn undertaking which You can ask me about on the Day of Resurrection. If I find that the people have crossed, I will be the first to fight against him, the first to thrust my spear into his eye. If the people have not crossed, then I will go forth with him and fight alongside him."

We returned to the lines (of the army) and we found that the standards and baggage were as they had been (before).

He took me by the scruff of the neck and pushed me. Then he said: "Brother of (the tribe of) al-Azd, has the matter become clear to you?" "Yes, Commander of the Faithful," I replied.

"Your business is with your enemy," he said.

I killed one man from those people (i.e. the Khārijites) and then I killed another. I and another of them were exchanging blows. I struck him and he struck me. We both fell together. My comrades carried me back. By the time I recovered consciousness, there were none of the people (i.e. the Khārijites) left (there).

This is a famous account which has a wide circulation among the reporters of historical traditions (āthār). In it the man tells of his own solemn undertaking towards the Commander of the Faithful, peace be on him, and (what happened) after that. There is no way that it can be rejected or its truthfulness denied. In it (the Commander of the Faithful) provides information about the unknown, gives clear evidence of his knowledge of the inner conscience (of man) and his knowledge of what is in men's souls. The evidence in it is outstanding which could only be equalled by evidence of a similar nature in terms of the greatness of the miracle and its clear proof.

*****

Of a similar kind are the narrations which have been reported on a wide scale (tawātur) about him, peace be on him, announcing his own death before it took place and giving information about the event and the fact that he would leave the world as a martyr through a blow on the head, the blood from which would colour his beard. The event came to happen exactly as he described.

Among the expressions which the reporters report concerning that are his words, peace be on him: "By Allāh, this will be coloured by this." He put his hand on his head and his beard.

(Similarly) there are his words, peace be on him: "By Allāh, it will colour it from above." He indicated his white hair. "The most wretched of the community will not be prevented from colouring it with blood from above."

(Other) of his words, peace be on him are: "The most wretched (of the community) will not be prevented from colouring it with blood from above."

He, peace be on him, (also) said: "The month of Ramaḍān has come to you. It is the lord of the months and the beginning of the year. In it the mill of authority will change. (Next) year, you will make the pilgrimage in one rank (i.e. there will be no Imam). The sign of that will be that I will not be among you."

His followers began to say that he was announcing his own death. He, peace be on him, was struck down on the night of the 19th of the month of Ramaḍān and he died on the night of the 21st of that month.

On the same (subject) is what trustworthy men report about him, peace be on him. During this month he used to break his fast one night with al-Ḥasan, one night with al-Ḥusayn, peace be on them, and one night with 'Abd Allāh b. Ja'far, may Allāh be pleased with him. He never used to have more than three mouthfuls. One of his two sons, al-Ḥasan and al-Ḥusayn, peace be on them, commented on that. He replied: "My son, Allāh's command (to leave the world) is coming and I am enduring hunger (in preparation for it)."

It was only one night or two later when he was struck down.

[The historians (aṣḥāb al-āthār) also report:]

Ja'd b. Ba'ja, one of the Khārijites, said to the Commander of the Faithful, peace be on him: "Fear Allāh, 'Ali, for you will die."

"By Allāh," said the Commander of the Faithful, peace be on him. "Rather I will be killed by a blow on this which will colour this." He put his hand on his head and his beard. "It is a promise which will be fulfilled. Let anyone who lies despair."

(Similarly) there are his words, peace be on him, on the night at the end of which the wretched man struck him. He had set out for the mosque and the geese screeched in his face. The people drove them away from him but he said: "Leave them, they are wailing at death."

*****

In a similar vein is the account which al-Walīd b. al-Ḥārith and others report on the authority of the men (whom they cite):

When the Commander of the Faithful learnt what Busr b. Arṭa'a had done in Yemen, he said: "O Allāh, Busr has sold his religion for the world, so take his reason away. Do not let there remain to him in his religion anything by which he would merit Your mercy. May Busr survive until his mind becomes disordered."

(Later) Busr used to ask for a sword and a sword of wood would be brought to him. He would strike with it until he became unconscious. When he recovered consciousness, he would say: "The sword, the sword." It would be given to him and he would strike with it. He continued like that until he died.

*****

The report of these words of his is also well-known: "After I (am gone) you will be exposed to my being cursed. For they will curse me. If they give you the opportunity to disassociate yourselves from me, do not do so, for I was born for (the service of) Islam. Whoever is given the opportunity to disassociate himself from me, let him (rather) stretch out his neck (for his head to be cut off). The man who does disassociate himself from me will gain neither this world or the next."

That matter turned out as he, peace be on him, described.

*****

There is another report of his words, peace be on him, with the same implication: "People, I have called you to the truth and you turned your backs away from me. I have flogged you and you have made me tired. After me rulers will rule you. They will not be satisfied with this (attitude) from you so that they will torment you with whips and iron. Whoever torments people in this world will be tormented by Allāh in the next. The sign of that will be that the ruler of Yemen will come against you to settle in your midst. A man called Yūsuf b. 'Umar will seize the tax-collectors and those who collect the taxes of the tax-collectors."

That happened as he, peace be on him, predicted.

*****

Then there is the report which the religious scholars recount: Juwayriyya b. Mishar stood at the gate of the palace. "Where is the Commander of the Faithful?" he asked. "Sleeping." was the reply.

"You who are sleeping wake up," he shouted. "For by Him in Whose hands is my soul, a blow will be struck on your head from which your beard will be coloured with blood, as you have told us before."

The Commander of the Faithful, peace be on him, heard that. He called out:

"Come, Juwayriyya so that I can discuss with you what you are saying."

He came and (the Commander of the Faithful) said to him: "By Him in Whose hands is my soul, you will be pulled before a rough harsh man. He will cut off your hand and your leg. Then you will be crucified below the tree trunk where an unbeliever (has already been crucified)."

Time went by after that until in the days of Mu'āwiya, Ziyād became governor. He cut off his hand and his leg, then he crucified him on the tree trunk where Ibn Muka'bir (was crucified). It was a long trunk and he was under him.

*****

There is in addition this report:

Maytham al-Tammār was a slave of a woman from (the tribe of) Banū Asad. The Commander of the Faithful, peace be on him, bought him from her and then gave him his freedom.

"What is your name?" he asked him.

"Sālim," he replied.

"The Apostle of Allāh, may Allāh bless Him and His Family, told me that the name which your father gave you in Persian was Maytham," he said.

"Allāh and His Apostle are true and you are true, Commander of the Faithful," he said. "By Allāh that is my name."

"Go back to the name by which the Apostle of Allāh referred to you and leave (the name) Sālim," he told him.

He returned to (the name) Maytham and was given the kunya Abū Sālim. On the same day, 'Alī, peace be on him, told him: "After me, you will be seized and crucified and stabbed by a spear. On the third day your nostrils and mouth will flow with blood which will colour your beard. So wait for that colour (to come). You will be crucified on the gate of the house of 'Amr b. Ḥurayth. You will be the tenth one of ten (crucified) men. You will have the shortest timber among them but you will be the nearest of them to the place for washing. Come so that I may show you the palm-tree on (the timber of) whose trunk you will be crucified."

He showed it to him. Maytham used to go there and pray at it.

He used to say: "What a blessed palm-tree you are. I am created for you and you grew up for me."

He continued to frequent it until it was cut down and he knew the place in Kūfa where he would be crucified. He used to meet 'Amr b. Ḥurayth and say to him: "I will be your neighbour, so show neighbourliness to me."

"You want to buy the house of Ibn Mas'ūd or the house of Ibn Ḥakīm," 'Amr used to say, because he did not understand what he meant.

In the year in which he was killed he made a pilgrimage. He visited Umm Salama, may Allāh be pleased with her.

"Who are you?" she asked.

"I am Maytham," he said.

"By Allāh, how often I heard the Apostle of Allāh, may Allāh bless Him and His Family, mention you," she said. "He used to commend you to 'Alī in the middle of the night."

Then he asked her about al-Ḥusayn, peace be on him.

"He is at an estate of his," she said.

"Tell him that I would have liked to greet him and that we will meet before the Lord of the Worlds, if Allāh, the Exalted, wills," he told her.

Umm Salama called for some perfume and she perfumed his beard.

"Soon it will be coloured by blood," she said.

He went to Kūfa and 'Ubayd Allāh b. Ziyād, may Allāh curse him, had him arrested and brought to him. He had been told that that man was one of the closest people to 'Ali, peace be on him.

"For shame, is he not a Persian?" he said.

"Yes," he was told.

"Where is your master?" he asked him.

"He is looking down on every wrongdoer and you are one of the wrongdoers," he answered.

"Despite your foreign accent you say what you mean," he said. "What has your leader told you that I will do to you?"

"He told me that you would crucify me as the tenth one of ten men," he answered. "I will have the shortest timber among them but will be the nearest of them to the place for washing."

"We will oppose him" ('Ubayd Allāh) declared.

"How could you oppose him?" he retorted. "He did nothing but give me information on the authority of the Prophet, may Allāh bless Him and his family, on the authority of Gabriel, peace be on him, on the authority of Allāh, the Exalted. How could you oppose these? I know the place in Kūfa where I will be crucified. I am the first of Allāh's creatures to be bridled in Islam."

He imprisoned him and he imprisoned al-Mukhtār b. Abī 'Ubayda with him. "You will escape," Maytham told him, "and you will rebel to avenge the blood of al-Ḥusayn, peace be on him. Then you will kill this man who is going to kill us."

When ‘Ubayd Allāh called for al-Mukhtār to kill him, a messenger (barīd) arrived with a letter for ‘Ubayd Allāh from Yazīd, ordering him to free (al-Mukhtār). He freed him and ordered Maytham to be crucified.

A man who met (Maytham) said to him: “Would not something satisfy you rather than this, Maytham?”

He smiled and said, pointing to the palm tree: “I was created for it and it has grown for me.”

When he was put on the wood, the people gathered around him at the gate of ‘Amr b. Ḥurayth.

“By Allāh he used to say: I will be your neighbour,” ‘Amr said. After he had been crucified, he ordered a maidservant to sweep under the wood, to sprinkle it with water and to fumigate it.

Maytham began to speak of the virtues of Banū Hāshim and it was reported to Ibn Ziyād: “That slave has insulted you.” “Bridle him,” he ordered.

He was the first of Allāh’s creatures to be bridled in Islam. Maytham, may Allāh have mercy on him, was killed ten days before al-Ḥusayn came to Iraq. On the third day after his crucifixion, he was stabbed with a spear, and He declared the greatness of Allāh. At the end of that day blood flowed from his mouth and his nose. This is one of the group of reports about the unknown which have been preserved concerning the Commander of the Faithful, peace be on him. Its reputation is extensive and the narration of it is widespread among the religious scholars (‘ulamā).

*****

[Another such report has been related by Ibn 'Abbās. It has been reported on the authority of Mujālid, on the authority of al-Sha'bī, on the authority of Ziyād b. al-Naḍr al-Ḥārithī, who said:]

I was with Ziyād when Rushayd al-Hijrī was brought to him. Ziyād said to him: "What did your leader say to you?" - meaning 'Alī, peace be on him – "For we will do that to you."

"You will cut off my hands and my legs and then you will crucify me," he answered.

"By Allāh, I will make his word false," declared Ziyād. "Free him."

When he was about to leave, Ziyād said: "By Allāh, we do not find anything wrong with what his leader told him. Therefore cut off his hands and legs and crucify him"

"Wait a moment," Rushayd said to him, "I still have something (to tell) you which the Commander of the Faithful, peace be on him, told me." "Cut out his tongue," ordered Ziyād.

"Now, by Allāh, is the verification of the words of the Commander of the Faithful, peace be on him," declared Rushayd.

This report has also been handed down by those friendly and those hostile on the authority of men they regard as trustworthy, on the authority of those persons whom we have named. Its content is well known to all the religious scholars. It is one of the group already mentioned of (his) miracles and giving information about the unknown.

*****

[A further account is reported by 'Abd al-Azīz b. Ṣuhayb on the authority of Abū al-'Āliyya, who said: Mazra' b. 'Abd Allāh told me:]

I (i.e. Mazra' b. 'Abd Allāh) heard the Commander of the Faithful, peace be on him, say: "By Allāh, an army will advance so that when it is at al-Baydā' it will be swallowed up."

"You are telling me about the unknown," I said.

"Remember what I tell you," he said. "By Allāh, what the Commander of the Faithful, peace be on him, tells you, will happen. A man will be taken. He will be killed and crucified between the two sides of the walls of the mosque." "You are telling me about the unknown," I said.

"The trustworthy, the one protected by Allāh, 'Alī b. Abī Ṭālib, peace be on him, told me," he replied.

[Abū 'Āliyya reported:]

Friday had not come when Mazra' was seized, killed and crucified between the two sides of the wall.

[(Abū 'Āliyya) said: He used to tell me about a third thing but I have forgotten it.]

*****

Yet a further example is reported by Jarīr on the authority of al-Mughīra, who said:]

When al-Ḥajjāj, may Allāh curse him, became governor, he sought for Kumayl b. Ziyād. The latter fled from him. (al-Ḥajjāj) deprived his people of their allowances ('Aṭā'). When Kumayl saw that, he said: "I am an old man and my life is nearly finished. It is not right for me to deprive my people of their allowances."

So he went and offered his hand to al-Ḥajjāj. When the latter saw him, he said:

"I would have liked to have found a way to get you, myself."

"Don't gnash your teeth at me and don't threaten me," Kumayl replied. "What is left of my life is like mere specks of dust. Therefore give judgement as long as you are a judge. For there is an appointed time to be with Allāh and after death there is the reckoning. The Commander of the Faithful, peace be on him, told me that you would kill me."

"Then that is evidence against yourself," al-Ḥajjāj said to him.

"But the judgement is yours," answered Kumayl.

"Indeed," he retorted, "you were among those who killed 'Uthmān b. 'Affān. Strike off his head."

Then he was executed.

This report is also recorded by the non-Shī'a ('āmma) which they report on the authority of men whom they regard as trustworthy. The Shī'a (khāṣṣa) participate in reporting it. Hence it has been included in this section where we mention miracles, proofs and evidence (concerning him).

*****

There is, in addition, the account recorded by the historians (aṣḥāb al-sīra) on various authorities:
One day al-Ḥajjāj b. Yūsuf al-Thaqafī said: "I would like to strike down one of the followers of Abū Turāb (derogatory name of 'Alī). Through his blood, I would get closer to Allāh."

"We know of no one who was a companion of Abū Turāb for a longer time than Qanbar, his retainer," he was told.

He sent in search of him and he was brought.

"Are you Qanbar?" he asked.

"Yes," he replied

"(Your kunya) is Abū Hamdān?" he asked.

"Yes," he replied

"Is your master 'Alī b. Abī Ṭālib?"

"Allāh is my Master," he replied, "and the Commander of the Faithful 'Alī is the master of my provisions."

"Disassociate yourself from his religion," he ordered him.

"If I disassociate myself from his religion, will you show me another better than it?" he asked.

"I will kill you," he answered. "So choose what sort of death you prefer." "I leave that to you," he responded.

"Why?" he asked.

"Because in whatever way you kill me, you will be killed in the same way," he said. "The Commander of the Faithful, peace be on him, told me that my fate would be to be slaughtered unjustly and without right."

Then he ordered him to be slaughtered.

This is also one of the reports which is established with regard to the Commander of the Faithful, speaking about the unknown. It has been included in the section concerning the compelling miracles and outstanding evidence and the knowledge which Allāh specially endowed to His proof among His prophets, apostles and chosen ones, peace be on them. Therefore it follows on from what has been presented before.

*****

[Of a similar kind is the account reported by al-Ḥasan b. Maḥbūb on the authority of Thābit al-Thumālī, on the authority of Abū Isḥāq al-Sabī'ī, on the authority of Suwayd b. Ghafla, (who said):]

A man came to the Commander of the Faithful, peace be on him. He said: "Commander of the Faithful, I have passed through Wadī al-Qarnī and I saw that Khālid b. 'Arfaṭa had died there. I asked forgiveness for him."

"Nonsense!" declared the Commander of the Faithful. "He has not died and he will not die until he leads an army of error whose standard-bearer will be Ḥabīb b. Ḥimāz."

A man from below the pulpit said: "Commander of the Faithful, I belong to your Shī'a and I am one who loves you."

"Who are you?" he asked.

"I am Ḥabīb b. Ḥimāz," he replied.

"Beware," he said, "you will carry (that standard). Indeed you will carry it and you will enter from this gate." He pointed with his hand to the Gate of al-Fīl.

After the death of the Commander of the Faithful, peace be on him, and al-Ḥasan, peace be on him, after that, and the events concerning al-Ḥusayn and his revolt, Ibn Ziyād sent 'Umar b. Sa'd against al-Ḥusayn, peace be upon him. He put Khālid b. 'Arfaṭa in command of the vanguard and he made Ḥabīb b. Ḥimāz the standard-bearer. He went there until he entered the mosque through the gate of al-Fīl.

This is also a widespread report which the traditionists (ahl al-'ilm) and the narrators of historical reports ('āthār) have not refused to acknowledge. It is widespread among the Kūfans and well known in their circles. Not even two of them have denied it. It belongs to the class of miraculous (knowledge) which we have mentioned.

*****

[Another example is the report of Zakariyyā b. Yaḥyā al-Qaṭṭān, on the authority of Faḍl b. al-Zubayr, on the authority of Abū al-Ḥakam, who said: I heard our shaykhs and our religious scholars say:]

'Alī b. Abī Ṭālib, peace be on him, preached. In his sermon, he said:

"Ask me before you lose me. But, by Allāh, do not ask me about a group who will lead a hundred astray and which will guide a hundred, otherwise I will tell you about the screecher of that group and the driver of it until the day of Resurrection."

A man rose before him and said: "Tell me how many pieces of hair there are on my head and my beard?"

The Commander of the Faithful, peace be on him, said: "By Allāh, my bosom friend, the Apostle of Allāh, may Allāh bless Him and His Family, told me about what you have asked. For every piece of hair on your beard there is an angel who curses you and for every piece of hair on your beard there is a devil who provokes you. In your house there is a worthless (child) who will kill the (grand) son of the Apostle of Allāh. That will be the proof of the truthfulness of what I have told you. If it was not for the fact that it is difficult to prove what you asked about, I would (simply) have informed you of it. However the proof of (my answer to) that (question) lies in the information I have given about your curse and your cursed worthless (child)."

At that time his son was a small boy still crawling. When the (tragic) events in the affair of al-Ḥusayn, peace be on him, occurred, he took part in killing him. So the event occurred as the Commander of the Faithful had described.

*****

[In the same way Ismā'īl b. Ṣabīḥ reported on the authority of Yaḥyā b. al-Musāwir al-'Abdī, on the authority of Ismā'īl b. Ziyād, who said:]

One day 'Alī, peace be on him, said to al-Barā' b. 'Āzib: "Barā', my son al-Ḥusayn, peace be on him, will be killed while you are alive and you will not help him."

After al-Ḥusayn, peace be on him, was killed, al-Barā' b. 'Āzib used to say: "By Allāh, 'Alī b. Abī Ṭālib, peace be on him, spoke the truth about al-Ḥusayn being killed and my not helping him."

He showed (much) grief and regret about that.

This belongs to what we have mentioned about him giving information about the unknown and the prevailing attitudes of men's hearts.

*****

[Another account is reported by 'Uthmān b. 'Īsā al- 'Amirī on the authority of Jābir b. al-Ḥurr, on the authority of Juwayriyya b Mishar al-'Abdī, who said:]

When we set out with the Commander of the Faithful, peace be on him, to Ṣiffīn. We reached the plains of Karbalā'. He stood at the side of the camp and looked right and left. He cried and he said: "By Allāh, this is the place where the camels will kneel for their riders. This is the place of their fate."

"Commander of the Faithful, what is this place?" he was asked.

"This is Karbalā'," he said. "Here people will be killed who will enter heaven without any reckoning (against them)."

Then he went on and the people did not understand the explanation of what he had said until the tragedy of al-Ḥusayn b. 'Alī, peace be on them, and his followers took place on the plain. Then those who had heard his words recognised the truthfulness of what he had told them.

This has been (a summary) of his knowledge of the unknown and his telling what would happen before it happened. It is clearly miraculous in nature and wonderful knowledge as we have mentioned. Reports conveying the same sense are so numerous that their explanation would make the book unduly long. What we have presented is sufficient for our intention.

His Miraculous Strength at Khaybar

Among his wonderful signs is the ability by which Allāh set him apart and the strength which he specially endowed to him, and the transcendence of normal events through miracles.

Of that kind is that which has been handed down in the historical reports and has become well-known through accounts. The religious scholars have agreed on it and both opponents and friends accept it, (namely) the story of Khaybar and of the Commander of the Faithful, peace be on him, removing the gate of the fortress with his own hand, and laying it on the ground with his own hand, while it was of such a weight that (it took) not less than fifty men to carry it.

['Abd Allāh b. Aḥmad b. Ḥanbal has mentioned that in what he reports on the authority of his transmitter. The latter reported: Ismā'īl b. Isḥāq, the qāḍī, told us: Ibrāhīm b. Ḥamza told us: 'Abd al-'Azīz b. Muḥammad told us on the authority of Ḥizām, on the authority of Abū 'Atīq on the authority of Jābir:]

At the battle of Khaybar, the Prophet, may Allāh bless Him and His Family, gave the standard to 'Alī b. Abī Ṭālib, peace be on him. After he had prayed for him, 'Alī, peace be on him, began to rush forward while his comrades were telling him to go slowly. He came to the fortress, and pulled away its gate throwing it to the ground. Then seventy of us gathered around it. It was only as a result of their (combined) effort that they could lift the door.

This is an example of the special strength with which Allāh endowed him. Through it the normal (human) qualities were transcended and it became a miraculous sign as we have said before.

The Miracle of Moving the Rock and the Water under it

Another example is reported by the historians (aṣḥāb al-siyar) and the account of it is widespread among both the non-Shī'a ('āmma) and the Shī'a (khāṣṣa) so that poets have written verses about it, rhetoricians have compiled sermons on it and men of understanding and learning have reported it. (It is) the story of the monk in the area of Karbalā' and the stone. Its reputation (is such) that it does not need the presentation of its chain of authorities (isnād).

[It is that the whole group (of scholars) report.]

When the Commander of the Faithful, peace be on him, headed toward Ṣiffīn, a terrible thirst came on his followers. The water with them had been used up. They began to search for water to right and left but they did not find any trace of it. The Commander of the Faithful, peace be on him, turned off the main road with them and went a little way. A hermitage appeared before them in the middle of the desert. He went with them towards it. When he reached its courtyard, he ordered those (with him) to call for its occupant to come before them. They called him and he came. The Commander of the Faithful, peace be on him, asked him: "Is this residence of yours near water, which will quench the thirst of these people?"

"There is more than six miles between me and water," he answered. "There is no water nearer than that to me. If it was not for the fact that I brought enough water for each month to sustain me, I would be destroyed by thirst."

"Did you hear what the monk said?" the Commander of the Faithful, peace be on him, asked.

"Yes," they answered. "Order us to go to the place which he indicated. Perhaps we will reach water while we still have strength."

"There is no need for you to do that," the Commander of the Faithful, peace be on him, told them. He turned the neck of his mule in the direction of the qibla (i.e. towards Mecca) and he directed them to a place near the hermitage. "Uncover the ground in this place," he ordered them.

A group of them went straight to the place and uncovered it with iron shovels. A great shiny rock appeared. They said: "Commander of the Faithful, here is a great rock on which the shovels are useless."

"This rock is over water," he told them. "If it moves from its position, you will find the water."

They struggled to remove it. All the people gathered together and tried to move it but they could find no way to do that. It was too difficult for them. When he, peace be on him, saw that they had gathered together and striven to remove the rock but it was too difficult for them, he put his leg over his saddle until it reached the ground. Then he rolled up his sleeves. He put his fingers under the side of the rock and he moved it. He removed it with his hand and pushed it many yards away. When it had moved from its position, the white (glitter) of water appeared before them. They hurried to it and drank from it. It was the sweetest, coldest and purest water that they had ever drunk from on their journey.

"Get supplies and quench your thirst," he told them.

They did that. Then he went to the rock and took it with his hand and put it back where it had been. He ordered that its traces be removed with earth. The hermit had been watching from on top of his hermitage. When he realised what had happened, he called out: "People, help me down, help me down."

They helped him to get down. He stood in front of the Commander of the Faithful, peace be on him and said: "Man, are you a prophet sent (by Allāh)?" "No," he replied.

"(Then are you) an angel who is close to Allāh?" he asked.

"No," was the answer.

"Then who are you?" asked (the hermit).

"I am the testamentary trustee of the Apostle of Allāh, Muḥammad b. 'Abd Allāh, the seal of the prophets, may Allāh bless Him and His Family," he replied.

"Stretch out your hand," said the hermit, "so that I may submit to Allāh, the Blessed and Exalted, at your hands."

The Commander of the Faithful, peace be on him, stretched out his hand and told him: "Make the two-fold testimony."

He said: "I testify that there is no God but Allāh alone without any partner. I testify that Muḥammad is His servant and His Apostle. I testify that you are the testamentary trustee of the Apostle of Allāh, the one with most right among the people to authority after him."

The Commander of the Faithful, peace be on him, made him understand the conditions of being a Muslim and then asked him: "What is it that has prompted you to enter Islam after your long residence in this hermitage in opposition to it?"

"I will tell you, Commander of the Faithful," he said. "This hermitage was built to seek out the one who would remove that rock and then water would come from underneath it. Scholars before me died and they did not attain that (knowledge) but Allāh, the Mighty and High, has provided me with it. We find in one of our books and a prose writer of our scholars that in this land there is a spring with a rock over it. No one knows its place except a prophet or the testamentary trustee of a prophet. He must be a friend of Allāh who calls (men) to truth, whose sign is the knowledge of the place of this rock and his ability to remove it. When I saw you do that, I realised what we had been waiting for. The object of desire had been attained. Today I am a Muslim (converted) at your hands, a believer in your right and your servant (mawlā)."

When he heard that, the Commander of the Faithful, peace be on him, wept until his beard became moist with tears. He said: "Praise be to Allāh, by Whom I have not been forgotten. Praise be to Allāh in Whose books I have been mentioned."

Then he summoned the people and told them: "Listen to what your brother Muslim says."

They listened to his words. Then they gave much praise to Allāh and thanks for the blessing which he had bestowed upon them in giving them knowledge of the right of the Commander of the Faithful, peace be on him. Then they went on and the hermit went before him amid a group of his followers until he met the Syrians. The hermit was among a group of those who were martyred there. He, peace be upon him, carried out the prayer over him. He buried him and sought much forgiveness for him. Whenever he was mentioned, ('Alī) would say: "That was my servant (mawlā)."

In this report there are (several) kinds of miracle. One of them is knowledge of the unknown, a second is the strength by which normal human capabilities were transcended, and (another) is the distinction (of him) from other men through the confirmation of the message about him in the first Books of Allāh. This is validated by the words of Allāh, the Exalted: That is their example in the Torah and their example in the

Gospels (XLVIII 29).

Al-Sayyid Ismāʿīl b. Muḥammad al-Ḥimyarī, may Allāh have mercy on him, speaks of the same thing in his glorious golden ode:

During his journey he went by night after the evening prayer to Karbalā' in a procession.

Until he came to one who devoted himself to God on a piece of raised ground. He made his camp on inhospitable land.

O wilderness, it is not (a place) where he meets a living soul other than the wild animals and the balding white haired man (i.e. ʿAlī).

He approaches and cries out at it. (The holy man) looks down as he stands, like the defender (looks down) over his bow from a watchtower.

Is there water which can be attained near the position which you have settled at. He answers: There is nothing to drink,

Except at a distance of six miles and the water I have with me (here) between the sandy hill and the vast desert.

He turns the reins towards the flat ground. He uncovers a smooth rock which shines like golden leaf-paste for camels.

He says: Turn it around. If you turn it around, you will see. You will not see if it is not turned around.

They gang together to remove it. It is impossible for them. It is a difficult impossible task which cannot be performed.

When it had weakened them, he stretched a hand towards it --

when the conqueror comes, it is conquered.

It was as if it was a ball of fallen cotton in a skein, which he pushed in a playground.

He gave them sweet delicious water to drink from under it, which was better than the most delicious, the sweetest.

Then when they had all drunk, he put it back and went away. Its position is left alone. It cannot be approached.

Ibn Maymūn added these words concerning that:

The signs for the monk were a miraculous secret there and he believed in the noble born testamentary trustee of authority (waṣī).

He died a martyr, truthful in his (statement of) support, most noble of monks who have become fearful (of Allāh).

I mean that the son of Fāṭima is the testamentary trustee of authority. Whoever declares (their belief in) his outstanding merit and his (illustrious) actions does not lie.

He is a man both of whose sides are (descended) from Shem, without any father from Hām, nor a father of a father.

He is one who does not flee and in battle only the striking of his sword dyed red (with blood) can be seen.

His Miraculous Victory over the Jinn

Another example is the tradition which has become well-known about the Apostle of Allāh, may Allāh bless Him and His Family, sending him to the valley of the jinn. Gabriel, peace be on him, had told him that groups of them had gathered to plot against him. (The Commander of the Faithful) took the place of the Apostle of Allāh, may Allāh bless Him and His Family, and through Allāh was sufficient for the believers against the plotting (of the jinn). He repelled them from the believers through his strength by which he was set apart from the rest of them.

[Muḥammad b. Abī al-Sirrī al-Tamīmī reported on the authority of Aḥmad b. al-Faraj, on the authority of al-Ḥasan b. Mūsā al-Nahdī, on the authority of his father, on the authority of Wabira b. al-Ḥārith, on the authority of Ibn al-'Abbās, may Allāh have mercy on him, who said:]

When the Prophet, may Allāh bless Him and His Family, set out against the Banū al-Muṣṭaliq, he avoided the road. Night came and he stopped near a rugged valley. Towards the end of the night, Gabriel, peace be on him, came down to tell him that a group of unbelieving jinn had gone into the valley with the intention of plotting against him, peace be on him, and causing harm to his Companions. He called for the Commander of the Faithful, peace be on him, and told him: "Go to this valley, those of the jinn who are enemies of Allāh, who want (to attack) you, will come against you. Repel them with the strength which Allāh, the Mighty and High, has given you. You will be protected by the names of Allāh, the Mighty and High, which He has specially endowed you with knowledge of."

He sent with him a hundred men from different groups among the people. He told them: "Stay with him and obey his orders."

The Commander of the Faithful, peace be on him, set out for the valley. When he was near the side of the valley, he ordered the hundred men who had accompanied him to stand close to the side and not to do anything until he gave them permission. He went forward and stood at the edge of the valley. He sought refuge with Allāh from his enemies and he named Allāh, may His name be magnified. He signalled to the people who had followed him to come closer. They came closer and there was a gap between him and them of the distance of a bow-shot. Then he began to go down into the valley when a hurricane arose, which almost made the people fall on their faces because of its violence. They could not keep their feet on the ground because of terror of opposition and terror of what would come upon them. The Commander of the Faithful, peace be on him shouted: "I am 'Alī b. Abī Ṭālib b. 'Abd al-Muṭṭalib, the testamentary trustee of authority (waṣī) of the Apostle of Allāh, may Allāh bless Him and His Family, and his cousin. Defy (us) is if you want to." Persons in the form of gipsies appeared before the people who seemed to have torches of fire in their hands and they dried up (all) the sides of the valley. The Commander of the Faithful, peace be on him, penetrated deep into the valley, while reciting the Qur'ān and signalling to right and left with his sword. It was not long before the persons became like black smoke. The Commander of the Faithful, peace be on him, magnified Allāh. Then he climbed back the way he had come down. He stood with the people who had accompanied him. The place became yellow as a result of what had happened to it. The Companions of the Apostle of Allāh, may Allāh bless Him and His Family, said to him: "Abū al-Ḥasan ('Alī), we almost died of fear and anxiety for you because of what you met. It was worse than (anything else) that has happened to us."

"When the enemy showed themselves to me," he told them, "and I shouted the names of Allāh, the Exalted, among them, they became smaller and I knew the terror which had come upon them. Therefore I went into the valley without any fear of them. If they had remained in substantial forms, I would have attacked them to the last one. Allāh was sufficient (protection) against their plotting and He was sufficient (help) for the Muslims against their wickedness. The rest of them will go ahead of me to the Apostle of Allāh, may Allāh bless Him and His Family, in order to (confess that they) believe in him."

The Commander of the Faithful, peace be on him, returned with those who had been with him to the Apostle of Allāh, may Allāh bless Him and His Family. He gave him the news. (The Apostle) was delighted with him and prayed for his well-being. Then he said to him: "'Alī, those whom Allāh filled with fear through you have come ahead of you to me. They submitted to Islam and I accepted their submission."

Then he continued the journey with all the Muslims and they passed through the valley in safety and without fear.

*****

The non-Shī'a ('āmma) report that account as well as the the Shī'a (khāṣṣa) and they do not refuse to accept it. However, the Mu'tazila because of their inclination to the beliefs of the Brahmins reject it. In addition to that they deny it because of their understanding of traditional reports. However, they are following the methods of atheism in imputing error to the Qur'ān and the reports which it includes about the jinn, their believing in Allāh and His Apostle and the information about them which Allāh gives in the Qur'ān in the Surat al-Jinn (LXXII) where they say: We heard a wonderful recitation (Qur'ān) which gave guidance to righteousness and we believed in it (LXXII 1-2) to the end of the contents of the sura which gives information about them. Since the opposition of the atheists to that is invalidated by the possibility of minds (conceiving) the existence of jinn and of their being made responsible (for their action) and the proof of this is through the Qur'ān and the glorious wonder in it. In the same way it demonstrates the invalidity of the accusation of the Mu'tazila against the report which we have given, (when they accuse it) of being impossible to be sustained by (human) intellects. Insofar as it is reported by two different chains of authority and by two groups to give evidence for two dissimilar attitudes, that is proof of its validity. There is no substance in its rejection by those who deviate from true justice like the Mu'tazila and the determinists (mujabbara), nor in the denigration of the necessity of using it which we have mentioned, just as there is no substance in the denial by the atheists, and varieties of agnostics, the Jews, the Christians, the Zoroastrians and the Sabians of the validity of the reports of the miracles of the Prophet, may Allāh bless Him and His Family, such as: the splitting of the moon, the bending of the palm trunk, stones speaking in his hand, the camel complaining, wild calves speaking, the tree moving (to him), water coming from his hands at the place for ritual ablution and feeding great crowds of people. (There are indeed no grounds for them) to denigrate the validity, the truthfulness of their narration and the establishment of the proof of them. Indeed their error in rejecting that, even in finding it weak, is much greater than the error of those who deny the miracles of the Commander of the Faithful, peace be on him, and their proof. Since such things are not hidden to people capable of considering them, there is no need for us to explain their arguments in this place. Since the special nature of the Commander of the Faithful, peace be on him, apart from (the rest of) the people has been established by what we have described as his being separate from all others in the knowledge which we have explained, (this) has made clear the statement of his right to precedence over (the rest of) the community with regard to the position of the Imamate and his right to precedence over them in the place of leadership. (It is further confirmed) by what the Wise Words (i.e. the Qur'ān) contain concerning the story of David and Ṭālūt where He, may His name be exalted, says: Their prophet said to them: Allāh has sent Ṭālūt to you as a king. They asked: Shall he have (the right of) kingship over us while we are more entitled to kingship than he is? He has not brought any extent of wealth. He replied: Allāh has chosen him to be over you and increased him extensively in knowledge and substance. Allāh bestows His kingship on whom He wishes. Allāh is (all) embracing, one who knows (II 247). Allāh, the Exalted, gives the proof for Ṭālūt's precedence over the community of his people. (Similarly) He gave him a proof of (being) His friend and the brother of His Prophet in having precedence of the rest of the community through choosing (him to be) over them and adding to him a (great) extent knowledge and substance. That is corroborated by similar things which have corroborated the right of the Commander of the Faithful, peace be on him, through his wonderful miraculous nature, in addition to him being separate from the people through the addition of the great extent of his knowledge and substance. Allāh, may He be praised and exalted, said: The sign of his kingship is that he will bring you the ark in which there is assurance from your Lord and the rest of what the family of Moses and the family of Aaron left, which the angels brought. In that there is a sign for you if you would believe (II 248).

The transcendence of ordinary human behaviour by the Commander of the Faithful, peace be on him, lies in the knowledge which we have recounted and other things similar to the transcendency of ordinary human behaviour by Ṭālūt in bringing the ark. This is clear. May Allāh be the bringer of success.

I still find the ignorant and the obstinate among the anti-Shī'a (nāṣiba) showing surprise at the report of the Commander of the Faithful, peace be on him, meeting the jinn, and keeping their evil away from the Prophet, may Allāh bless him, his family, and his Companions. They laugh at that and attribute the story to such useless nonsense. They diminish such things concerning reports of similar miracles by him, peace be on him, and say these are forgeries by the Shī'a, and those of them who forge have forged them in order to acquire (prestige) and in order to defend desperately (their beliefs). This is exactly what all the atheists (zanādiqa) and the enemies of Islam say about what the Qur'ān mentions with regard to the report of the jinn and their submission to Islam in its words: We heard a wonderful recitation (Qur'ān) which gave guidance to righteousness and we believed in it (LXXII 1-2). (They take a similar attitude) about the report of Ibn Mas'ūd concerning the story of the night of the jinn and him seeing them like gipsies. (They also have the same view) of the miracles of the Apostle of Allāh, may Allāh bless Him and His Family. They show surprise at all of these and laugh when they hear the account of them, dispute their authenticity, mock and talk nonsense in a slanderous way in which they conduct themselves against Islam and its followers, regarding as stupid those who believe in it and support it, accusing the followers of Islam of deficiency and ignorance, and forging false stories. Let the people examine the crime which they have committed against Islam by their hostility to the Commander of the Faithful, peace be on him, and their relying on removing his virtues, noble actions and signs by which they resemble the classes of the atheists (zanādiqa) and unbelievers through their departure from the roads of (true) proofs into the gates of deviation and ignorance. In Allāh do we seek help.

His Sending back the Sun

Among the wonderful signs which Allāh, the Exalted, has brought forth through the hands of the Commander of the Faithful, 'Alī b. Abī Ṭālib, is one, the reports of which have become widespread among the biographers and historians ('ulamā' al-siyar wa al-āthār) and about which the poets have composed verses (namely) when he, peace be on him, sent back the sun (to its earlier position) on two occasions, once during the life of the Prophet and another time after his death.

The account of it being sent back on the first occasion has

been reported by Asmā' daughter of 'Umays, Umm Salama, the wife of the Prophet, may Allāh bless Him and His Family, Jābir b. 'Abd Allāh al-Anṣāri, Abū Sa'īd al-Khudrī and a group of the Companions.

One day the Prophet, may Allāh bless Him and His Family, was in his house and 'Ali, peace be on him, was in front of him when Gabriel, peace be on him, came to him to speak privately to him about Allāh. When inspiration closed in upon him, he used the thigh of the Commander of the Faithful, peace be on him, as a pillow. He did not raise his head from it until the sun had set. Thus he compelled the Commander of the Faithful, peace be on him, (to remain) in that position. So he prayed the afternoon prayer sitting, giving a nod (with his head) for his bowing and prostration. When (the Apostle) awoke from his trance, he said to the Commander of the Faithful: "Have you missed the afternoon prayer?"

"I could not pray it standing because of your position, Apostle of Allāh, and the circumstances of hearing inspiration which I was in," he answered.

"Ask Allāh to send the sun back for you so that you may pray it standing at its proper time just as (it was) when you missed being able to do it," he told him. "Allāh, the Exalted, will answer you because of your obedience to Allāh and to His Apostle."

The Commander of the Faithful, peace be on him, asked Allāh to send back the sun. It was sent back for him so that it came into its position in the sky at the time for the afternoon prayer. The Commander of the Faithful, peace be on him, prayed the afternoon prayer at its proper time. Then it set. [Asmā' reported:] By Allāh we heard it at its setting, screeching like the screech of the saw in wood.

*****

Its being sent back for him after the Prophet, may Allāh bless Him and His Family, was when he wanted to cross the Euphrates at Babylon, many of his followers were occupied in taking their animals and baggage across. He, peace be on him, prayed the afternoon prayer himself with a group who were with him. The people did not finish their crossing and many of them missed the time of the prayer. The people recalled the merit of being together for that (prayer) and they spoke about that. When he heard their talk about it, he asked Allāh to send back the sun so that all his followers might be together to perform the afternoon prayer at its proper time. Allāh, the Exalted, answered him by sending back the sun for him. The horizons became such as they are for the time of the afternoon prayer. When the people had said the final greeting (at the end of the prayer), the sun disappeared and a violent throbbing was heard from it which terrified the people. They became profuse in their glorification of Allāh, in their declarations of His uniqueness, and in seeking forgiveness from him, and in praising Allāh for the favour which he had shown to them.

The reports of that have reached the (distant) horizons and its account is widespread among the people. Concerning that al-Sayyid b. Muḥammad al-Ḥimyarī, may Allāh have mercy on him, recited:

The sun was sent back for him when he missed the time of the afternoon prayer and sunset had drawn near.

So that its light shone (the same as) at its time for the afternoon. Then it fell like a shooting star.

For him it was sent back another time at Babylon. It has not been sent back for any Arab creature,

Only so that his first (view of it) may be mixed with his later (view of it) and so that it being sent back may be an explanation of a wondrous matter.

The Miracle of Speaking to the Fish

Similar to that is (the account) which the historians (ahl al-āthār) report and which has become famous among the Kūfans because of it being widespread among them. Hence the report has spread to other people in other places. The scholars also confirm it. (It is) that the fish talked to him at the Euphrates by Kūfa.

[They report:]

The waters of the Euphrates overflowed and grew so big that the people of Kūfa became anxious about drowning. They resorted to the Commander of the Faithful, peace be on him. He rode out on the mule of the Apostle of Allāh, may Allāh bless Him and His Family, and the people went with him until he reached the banks of the Euphrates. He, peace be on him, dismounted and performed the ritual ablution and prayed alone, by himself, while the people watched him. Then he called on Allāh with prayers which most of them heard. He went towards the Euphrates, leaning on a stick which was in his hand. He struck the surface of the water with it and said: "Abate, with Allāh's permission and His will."

The waters sank so that the fish at the bottom (of the flood) appeared. Many of them greeted him with title of the Commander of the Faithful. However some kinds of fish did not speak. They were eels, a scaleless fish (marmāliq) and mud fish (zumār). The people were amazed at that and they asked for the reason that the ones who spoke spoke and the ones who were silent were silent. He said: "Allāh made those fish which were ritually pure speak to me and he kept those silent towards me which were forbidden, impure and worse."

This is a widespread report, the fame of which is, through its transmission and narration, like the fame of the wolves speaking to the Prophet, the stones praising Allāh in the palm of his hand, the trunk of the tree bending towards him and the feeding of many with little food. Whoever continues to find fault with ('Alī's miracles) is one who can only find the doubts about it in what the denigrators depend upon, in what we have enumerated of the miracles of the Apostle.

The Commander of the Faithful and the Jinn

The historians (ḥamalat al-āthār wa ruwāt al-akhbār) have also reported the story of the snake and the sign and miraculous nature of it which is like the story of the fishes and the abating of the waters of the Euphrates.

[They reported:]

One day the Commander of the Faithful, peace be on him, was making a speech on the pulpit at Kūfa, when a snake appeared at the side of the pulpit and began to climb up until it was near the Commander of the Faithful, peace be on him. The people shook with fear at that and were worried about its purpose and about driving it away from the Commander of the Faithful, peace be on him. He signalled to them to keep away from it. When it reached the raised platform on which the Commander of the Faithful, peace be on him, was standing, he bent down towards the snake and the snake spread itself up towards him so that it could gobble his ear.

The people fell silent and became distraught at that. It made a croaking sound which many of them heard. Then it went down from its position. The Commander of the Faithful moved his lips in a whisper and the snake acted as if it was listening to him. Then it glided away. The ground had swallowed it up. The Commander of the Faithful, peace be on him, went on with his speech and brought it to a close.

When he had finished it and gone down, the people gathered around him, questioning him about the circumstances of the snake and the wonder of it. He told them: "That was not as you had thought. It was only one of the judges of the jinn, whom a case had confused. He came to me to find out from me about it. I informed him about it. He wished me well and departed."

*****

Often the ignorant among the people regard the appearance of jinn in the form of animals which cannot speak as impossible. However, that was well-known by the Arabs, before the mission (of the Prophet) and after it, and reports from people belonging to Islam corroborate it. Nor is it more unlikely than the report which is agreed on by Muslims (ahl al-qibla) of the appearance of the Devil to the people in the assembly building in the form of an old man from Najd, and his agreement with them to deceive the Apostle of Allāh, may Allāh bless Him and His Family, and of his appearing to the polytheists at the Battle of Badr in the form of Sarāqa b. Ja'sham al-Madlijī. He, the Exalted, said: There will be no conqueror of you among the people today. I am one who grants you neighbourly protection (VIII 48). Allāh, the Mighty and High, said: When the two groups looked at each other, he turned on his heels and said: I am innocent of you. I see what you do not see. I fear Allāh. Allāh is violent in His punishment (VIII 48).

All who continue to find fault with the signs which we have mentioned only say about them the same as the atheists and unbelievers among the opponents of religion, say. They find fault with them in the same way as they find fault with the signs of the Prophet in confirmation of his prophethood, and with the validity of the miracles of the Apostle of Allāh, may Allāh bless Him and His Family.

Some other Miracles of the Commander of the Faithful

[Another example is reported by 'Abd al-Qāhir b. 'Abd al-Malik b. 'Atā' al-Ashja'ī on the authority of al-Walīd b. 'Imrān al-Bajalī, on the authority of Jamī' b. 'Umayr, who said:]

'Alī, peace be on him, suspected a man called al-Ghayzār of giving information to Mu'āwiya. He denied that and disputed it. The Commander of the Faithful, peace be on him, said: "Do you swear by Allāh that you have not done so?" "Yes," he answered and he hurried forward and took the oath.

"If you are a liar," the Commander of the Faithful, peace be on him, told him, "Allāh will blind you."

The Friday had not come when he was brought out blind, being led. Allāh had taken away his sight.

*****

[Of the same kind is what is reported by Ismā'īl b. 'Umayr, who said: Mis'ar b. Kidām told me: Ṭalḥa b. 'Umayra told us:]

'Alī, peace be on him, recited the words of the Prophet to the people: To whomsoever I am his master (mawlā), 'Alī is his master. Twelve men from the Anṣār testified to that but Anas b. Mālik was among the people who did not give testimony to it. The Commander of the Faithful, said to him: "Anas."

"At your service," he replied

"What stopped you from testifying?" he asked. "You have heard what they heard."

"Commander of the Faithful," he replied, "I have grown old and I have forgotten."

"O Allāh," the Commander of the Faithful, peace be on him, prayed, "if he is a liar, strike him with leprosy" - [or he said a word for it which is understood by the ordinary people].

[Ṭalḥa reported:]

"I testify before Allāh, I saw a whiteness (of leprosy) between his eyes."

[Similarly Abu Isrā'īl has reported on the authority of al-Ḥakam b. Abī Salmān, the mu'adhdhin, on the authority of Zayd b. Arqam, who said:]

'Alī, peace be on him, recited before the people in the mosque and said: "May Allāh adjure to arise any man who heard the Prophet, may Allāh bless Him and His Family, say: To whomsoever I am his master (mawlā), 'Alī is his master. O Allāh, be a friend to those who befriend him and an enemy to those who are hostile to him."

Twelve men, who fought at Badr, stood up, six on the right and six on the left, and they testified to that.

[Zayd b. Arqam added:]

I was among those who heard that but I kept it hidden. Then Allāh took away my sight.

He used to regret failing to give testimony and he used to seek forgiveness from Allāh.

*****

[Another example is what is reported by 'Alī b. Mushir on the authority of al-A'mash, on the authority of Mūsā b. Ṭarīf, on the authority of 'Abāya and (also it is reported on the authority of) Mūsā b. Ukayl al-Numayrī, on the authority of 'Imrān b. Maytham on the authority of 'Abāya. (It is further reported on the authority of) Mūsā al-Wajīhī, on the authority of al-Minhāl b. 'Umar, and on the authority of 'Abd Allāh b. al-Ḥārith, 'Uthmān b. Sa'īd, and 'Abd Allāh b. Bukayr, on the authority of Ḥakīm b. Jubayr: They (all) said:]

We witnessed 'Alī, the Commander of the Faithful, peace be on him, on the pulpit saying: "I am the servant of Allāh, the brother of the Apostle of Allāh. I have inherited the blessing from the Apostle. I have married the mistress of the women of Heaven. I am the master of the testamentary trustees of authority, and those who are the last trustees of the Prophet. No one except me can claim that without Allāh striking him with evil."

A man from (the tribe of) 'Abs who was sitting in front of the people said: "Who is not good enough to say this. I am the servant of Allāh, the brother of the Apostle of Allāh."

He had not left his place when the Devil caught hold of him and dragged him by his leg to the door of the mosque. His people asked us about him and we said: "Did you know him to be a man of (stupid) risks before this?"

"O Allāh, no," they answered.

[Al-Shaykh al-Mufīd, may Allāh be pleased with him, says:]

The reports about similar things to what we have mentioned are (such) that the book would become too long as a result of them. We have put forward in this book of ours sufficiency in its outline to do without what is similar to them. We ask Allāh for success and we seek help from Him along the path of guidance.

THE CHILDREN OF THE COMMANDER OF THE FAITHFUL

(This is) an account of the children of the Commander of the Faithful, peace be on him, their number and names, and a selection of reports about them.

The Commander of the Faithful, peace be on him, had twenty-seven children, male and female:

1.\ Al-Ḥasan

2.\ Al-Ḥusayn

3.\ Zaynab the elder

4.\ Zaynab the younger, who was given the kunya Umm Kulthūm.

Their mother was Fāṭima, the blessed, mistress of the women of the worlds, daughter of the master of those sent by Allāh and the seal of the prophets, the Prophet Muhammad.

*****

5.\ Muḥammad, who was given the kunya Abū al-Qāsim.

His mother was Khawla, daughter of Ja'far b. Qays al-Ḥanafī.

*****

6.\ 'Umar

7.\ Ruqayya

They were twins. Their mother was Umm Ḥabīb, daughter of Rabī'a.

*****

8.\ Al-'Abbās

9.\ Ja'far

10.\ 'Uthmān

11.\ 'Abd Allāh

(The last four) were martyrs with their brother al-Ḥusayn on the plain of Karbalā'.

Their mother was Umm al-Banīn (Her actual name was Fāṭima, daughter of Ḥizām b. Khālid b. Dārim. Because she had four sons, she was commonly known as Umm al-Banin ("mother of several sons")), daughter of Ḥizām b. Khālid b. Dārim.

*****

12.\ Muḥammad, the younger, who was given the kunya Abū Bakr.

13.\ ‘Ubayd Allāh

Both of these were martyrs with their brother al-Ḥusayn on that plain. Their mother was Layla, daughter of Mas‘ūd al-Dārimī.

*****

14.\ Yaḥyā

His mother was Asmā’, daughter of ‘Umays al-Khath‘amī, may Allāh be pleased with her.

*****

15.\ Umm al-Ḥasan

16.\ Ramla

The mother of these two was Umm Sa‘īd, daughter of ‘Urwa b. Mas‘ūd al-Thaqafī.

*****

17.\ Nafīsa

18.\ Zaynab, the youngest

19.\ Ruqayya, the younger

20.\ Umm Hānī’

21.\ Umm al-Kirām

22.\ Jumāna, who was given the kunya Umm Ja‘far.

23.\ Umāna

24.\ Umm Salama

25.\ Maymūna

26.\ Khadīja

27.\ Fāṭima

These, the blessings of Allāh be on them, had different mothers.

*****

Among the Shīʿa, there are those who mention that Fāṭima, the blessing of Allāh be on her, after the Prophet had a miscarriage with a son, whom the Prophet, may Allāh bless Him and His Family, had (already) named during her pregnancy as Muḥsin. According to this group there were twenty-eight children of the Commander of the Faithful, the blessing and peace of Allāh be on him. Allāh knows and judges best.

Printed in Great Britain
by Amazon

41458632R00212